MY FOOLISHNESS PREVAILS

How I Became the Star of My Own Epic Drama

Mary Ngwebong Ngu

TEACH Services, Inc.
P U B L I S H I N G
www.TEACHServices.com • (800) 367-1844

World rights reserved. This book or any portion thereof may not be copied or reproduced in any form or manner whatever, except as provided by law, without the written permission of the publisher, except by a reviewer who may quote brief passages in a review.

The author assumes full responsibility for the accuracy of all facts and quotations as cited in this book. The opinions expressed in this book are the author's personal views and interpretations, and do not necessarily reflect those of the publisher.

This book is provided with the understanding that the publisher is not engaged in giving spiritual, legal, medical, or other professional advice. If authoritative advice is needed, the reader should seek the counsel of a competent professional.

Copyright © 2021 Mary Ngwebong Ngu
Copyright © 2021 TEACH Services, Inc.
ISBN-13: 978-1-4796-1335-9 (Paperback)
ISBN-13: 978-1-4796-1336-6 (ePub)
Library of Congress Control Number: 2021914972

Photo Credits
Thanks to Jacob Ambe for the picture of my hostel and the CRTV office building. Thanks to Paulette Southall for my Manhattan photo. Thanks to Madi Ezéchiel for the photo of the medal award for Knight of the National Order of Valor. Also thanks to Clément Tjomb for the back cover photo.

Published by

www.TEACHServices.com • (800) 367-1844

Dedication

To my children—
Mekole and Bih, who were determinant in saving
my life by imploring me to flee our home.

Also to my nephews and nieces, the children I took care
of at work, and the children at church, including all others
whose presence comforted me while I was absent from mine.

Table of Contents

Preface . . . . *vii*

Acknowledgements . . . . *viii*

Chapter 1:   A Fatal Blow 12

Chapter 2:   Yaounde University 17

Chapter 3:   Love or Control? 26

Chapter 4:   Out of Whack Dating 31

Chapter 5:   Holiday Romance 35

Chapter 6:   Hellfire Witnessing 43

Chapter 7:   First Love 46

Chapter 8:   Confiding in Mother 52

Chapter 9:   Primary Bliss 56

Chapter 10: Friendly Advice or Envy? 61

Chapter 11: The Nobility of Love 66

Chapter 12: Lovey-dovey Rebuff 71

Chapter 13: Misfortune Stings Love 74

Chapter 14: The Love of Status 81

Chapter 15:	Romance Magic Wanes.	86
Chapter 16:	Love versus Lust	94
Chapter 17:	The Fruit of Love	100
Chapter 18:	A Baby Out of This World	106
Chapter 19:	Starting a Family on Rocky Ground	113
Chapter 20:	Envy Creeps In	121
Chapter 21:	Moth and Rust Attack	130
Chapter 22:	From Delight to Hollowness	136
Chapter 23:	A Stormy Relationship	143
Chapter 24:	The Game of Disloyalty	152
Chapter 25:	Shaming the Home-wrecker	157
Chapter 26:	Discovering Everlasting Love	165
Chapter 27:	Tragedy Junction	172
Chapter 28:	Seeking Truth for Freedom.	178
Chapter 29:	Surviving in the Fiery Furnace	184
Chapter 30:	In Search of the Home of the Privileged	190
Chapter 31:	My Foolishness, My Fortress	202
Chapter 32:	Banishing God's Love.	210
Chapter 33:	Spiritual Warfare	218
Chapter 34:	The Bomb of Wickedness.	224
Chapter 35:	Sisterly Intervention	229
Chapter 36:	Landing in America.	236

Chapter 37: Warmth from My Earthly and Godly Families 246

Chapter 38: Conquering My New World 257

Chapter 39: A Battle Between Heaven and Earth 266

Chapter 40: Embattled Motherhood. 273

Chapter 41: Defending My Worth 280

Chapter 42: Forgiveness and Healing 289

Preface

Many people miss their purpose in life because they bow to fierce criticism and widespread attacks of their "strange" ideas as well as their nonconformist lifestyle choices. What a loss to society! *My Foolishness Prevails* is a true story of how I overcame devastating and life-threatening circumstances in marriage. I wrote it as a means of trying to make sense of the whys and wherefores of the dangerous turns that my life had taken, way beyond my control. Exploring and evaluating past occurrences in my life was quite revealing, and in the long run became therapeutic.

An unknown number of women have lost their lives in marriage, especially through physical violence. I hope that this story would inspire married couples, young people, relationship experts, counsellors, parents, victims of spousal abuse, young believers, community leaders, media personalities, and more. May it help young people as well as potential victims to avoid some of the pitfalls that placed me on a slippery pathway!

The whole narrative, short of the conclusion, was written in the United States of America, and completed in the year 2003.

The names of the main actors have been changed to protect their identity. Those of other characters have been maintained as an expression of gratitude for healing friendship, heroic acts of rescue, kindness, prayers, encouragement, and more.

Akongshee is not the real name of the protagonist. It means "the love of God" in the Ngemba language of Southern Cameroon.

I got the inspiration for "Foolishness" from 1 Corinthians 1:18-31 in the Holy Bible.

Acknowledgements

It is impossible to remember everyone who has contributed to making this story come to life. Nevertheless, I wish to express my gratitude to the following:

To **God**, who saved my life and by the same act gave me the promise of eternal life. The **Holy Spirit** has also guided me throughout the writing process.

I am grateful to my **parents**—my father, **Sylvester Ngu**, who was the ideal husband; my mother, **Justina Bih Fon**, who was fond of waying that "your education is your first husband." I am deeply indebted to my **siblings—Aza, Mafor, Che, Fon, Ngum, Azunda, Fruawah,** and **Chi**—whose constant help is immeasurable, including rescuing me on several occasions.

Thanks to **Mrs. Marcella Brook** and **Mrs. Ivy Darling**, who were my adoptive mothers in New York. By the same token, I thank **Mrs. Elizabeth Essoka** for connecting me to my children while I was far away from them.

I am thankful to my sister-in-law, **Frida**, as well as my brother-in-law **Fidelis Zama Chi** for welcoming me into their home, and the latter for his generous gift that helped me to sign the publishing contract. Similarly, thanks to my brother-in-law, **Aneneba Akufor** for helping me to move forward with the project.

Immense thanks to **Martha Pufong, Pamela Kisob, Josephine Wouagou, Dorothy Ndikum, Frida Dagobert** in Yaounde, and to **Sarah Thomas** and **Stephana Mitchell** in the US for hosting me when I was homeless.

I am grateful to **Marie-Esther Ngobilla** for introducing me to Bible promises, and to **Mary Lamfu** and **Olive Shang**, former CRTV colleagues, for inviting me to the evangelistic meeting where I was baptized.

Immense thanks to **JJ Nvoto Obounou** for random acts of kindness, and for teaching me the basics of administration upon my return home. To **Jolanta Idzik**, psychologist, for establishing my mental health report; **Dr. Julia Buban Ngu** for providing key health contacts; **Professor Andree-Nicola McLaughlin** and **Eric Chinje** for issuing job recommendations; and **Susan Bamuh Apara** for introducing me to her professional network at a critical moment.

I will be forever grateful to **Dr. Nche Zama** for identifying the writer in me, and to **Dr. Ekema Agbaw** for applauding my initial write-ups. Thanks to former Prime Minister **Philemon Yang**, and to **Professor Jikong Stephen Yeriwa**, who gave me grammar books which have enhanced my writing.

Special thanks to **Professor Ephraim Ngwafor** for professional counseling in legal matters, as well as for words of comfort. I am equally grateful to **Dr. Joyce Ashuntangntang** for her mediation efforts during her vacation in Cameroon.

My friends **Veronica N. Asong**, **Dr. Veronica N. Choundong**, **Grace Neneh Tatah**, **Dr. Vivian Yenika**, **Antonia Agbor**, **Priscilla Sale**, and others, who lent their ears when I needed to let out hurting emotions.

I thank you, **Anne Ngu**, **Elizabeth Ngwa**, **Enanga Kebbi**, and the **TENAS**, and **Kenneth Asobo**, and other colleagues of CRTV, Yaounde, for emotional support. To you **Pauline Ako**, and **Côme Didier Ndongo** for facilitating my integration into the Prime Minister's (PM's) Office. To **Mr. Romanus Fomenky**, **Dr. Wakata Bolvine**, **Samson Hyri**, Madi Ezekiel, **Germain-Flore Ngah**, **Benard Ngwa**, **Motto Young**, **Sissako Tamko**, **Fobella Folefack**, and other former colleagues at the PM's office for creating a conducive working environment.

I am grateful to **Professor Jacques Fame Ndongo**, for helping to reinstate me into the administration. Thanks to **Gilbert Tsala Ekani**, **Martin Moukon**, and **Bernadette Foguila**, who created a friendly atmosphere at our job, the "Maison de la Communication."

How could I ever repay you, **Caroline Njokikang**, a compassionate fellow citizen, who spent long extra hours at work tracking the records of my neglected personal business? Thanks also to **Particia Kuwong** and **Barrister Titanji**, my legal counsels.

The warmth with which my first US home church, the **Worthington SDA** congregation, ushered me into their community, immediately dried the tears of my soul, and gave me hope. Likewise, my church family at the **SDA Mamaroneck** church in New York warmly welcomed me to their state.

Thanks to **Frank Merendino, Janet and Bill Magarvie, Charmaine Darling, Joyce Hosei, Rita Rey**, and others of the SDA church of Hartsdale, New York, for their friendship and for Bible studies, both of which healed my heart and soul.

I am forever indebted to you, my spiritual family of the **First Seventh-day Adventist Church** in White Plains, New York, for nurturing me for the longest time abroad, especially through Women's Ministry. My friends, particularly **Neatlin Francis, Patricia Thompson, Ruth Dwyer, Patricia Tomlinson, Priscilla Cyril, Grace Oyekan, Virginia McDonald**, and **Patricia Richburg** for sisterly support. Special thanks to **Arlithea West** for her healing gospel songs, and for showing me how to witness at the Manhattan subway in New York City, a form of therapy.

Unforgettably my numerous SDA church members in Yaounde, from **Eglise du Centre**, Djoungolo, to Philadelphia, and colleagues of IL EST ECRIT Radio, especially **Abraham Bakari**, along with our regular listeners.

Immense thanks to the **International SDA Church** in Brussels, Belgium, for family warmth and for timely financial aid. I'm grateful to **Natalie Corrie-Kordas, Rebecca Andrew-Kong**, and **Laurence Nagy** for the music we made together, and also for the 2nd Coming Choir we founded. Thanks to its members for our outreach performances. **Neneth Templado** prayed with me for a publisher and contributed financially to the publishing of my book. Thanks to **Ruth Owino** for her timely counsels, and to **Jela Montillano** and **Ina Radesey**, my prayer partners for interceding for years for my family. The Teen Sabbath School class as well as Pathfinders helped to revive the joy of my interrupted motherhood. Thanks to **Dr. Violeta Tudor** and her husband, **Sacha Decouttere**, regular guests, who equally helped me financially.

The dedication of **Philip Alongifor, Victorine**, and other members of the **Santa SDA group** gave me the peace of mind to pursue my mission abroad while they persevered in carrying out the gospel commission in our village.

I am grateful to you, **Betty and Emmanuel Bissong**, alongside **Mary and Gerald Eware**, for hosting me upon arrival in Belgium. To **Maureen Kilo** and **Sarra Mouny** for bonding with me to keep our cultural roots intact in several ways. Thank you **Bernadette Essimi, Charlotte Touba**, and **Frédérique Lébé**, former colleagues and friends of the Embassy, for your kindness and moral support.

I thank God for you, **Esong Ekukole**, for the extraordinary moments of our relationship. The tears of confession you poured out in front of our children sealed our forgiveness session.

How can I thank you, **Philippe Vivier**, for your wonderful friendship as well as your kindness in providing a creative space wherein I dotted my i's and crossed my t's? I equally appreciate the warmth of your family, including that of our numerous mutual friends in Fleurus. You and your network have given me an enduring aroma of the oneness of humanity.

Immense thanks to TEACH Services for their professionalism, and particularly my editor, **Rebecca Silver and her team**, for helping me connect some key dots, fill in blanks, and brighten the tapestry of parts of the narrative, among other tasks.

Finally, thanks to **you**, whose significant contribution I have not mentioned here.

CHAPTER 1

A Fatal Blow

At 2 am on Monday, the pain was excruciating, unbearable. It was cutting through my belly like a blunt knife. Each passing second increased the sharpness of the pangs. The discomfort was such that I could not lie, sit, nor stand. It would be impossible for me to reach the breaking of the day alive.

My husband, who had been somewhat aloof during the recent months of my pregnancy, rushed out of bed and looked around, confused. He scanned around and dashed into the living room, running back and forth. The sudden signal of a complication was beyond him.

> *My body was dangling from one end of the couch to another, onto which I was clinging, hoping that the cushion could absorb some of the aches emanating from the center of my being.*

Of course, seven months was too early for the baby to come, but something was seriously wrong. If he waited till morning, he would have to deal with two corpses. He had to rush me to the emergency room. How? No taxis were available at such an hour, except downtown. We did not have a family car. He ran towards the door, opened it quickly, and stepped out into the opaque darkness, but for a faint reflection from a far-off electric pole.

I do not know for how long he was away, but it felt like ages. Then I heard his quick returning footsteps. He was speaking with a man. They both stepped into the house. Meanwhile, I had rolled out of bed and was on my knees. My body was dangling from one end of the couch to another, onto which I was clinging, hoping that the cushion could absorb some of the aches emanating from the center of my being.

With each muscular man holding me by a shoulder, they managed to drag me with halting steps until we reached outside. "Hold her," said the kind, young neighbor, Joseph. My husband, Mesape, glued his chest onto my back, with one hand wrapped around me to stop my sagging body from drooping onto the floor.

Joseph ran to his car that was parked about a hundred meters away and drove it right to the front of the entrance door. Then, he rushed out and flung open both doors of the back seat. I could no longer move a step. So, the two men carried me and managed to lay me on the back seat. They took their seats in front. Mesape turned around and stretched out his left hand which he placed on me. His hand also served as a shock absorber whenever the bumps on the road caused the car to jolt and veer swiftly from side to side.

I was yelling during the twenty-minute ride. As soon as we reached the clinic, Mesape rushed out of the car and pushed open the main gate. Within minutes, three members of staff in white coats rushed out into the yard.

"*Sauve moi, sauve moi*" ("Save me, save me") was my only plea. The next minute could be my last. The nurses placed me on a stretcher and hurried in towards a bed in the spacious hallway.

I was writhing and wailing, aware that if they did not act fast, it would be the end for me. The instructions of the main attendant were strange. The baby, coming? No, I resisted, but they forced me. The pain grew sharper. It was becoming difficult to breathe, as I kept yelling for help.

Finally, I took a deep breath and the baby came out, amid a sharp pain that almost tore me apart. Had my womb become toxic or was the presence of the baby in me fatal? My doctor arrived shortly afterward. I was all ears, but he could not explain why the baby and I could not be together until term. It was a fleeting thought that disappeared when he came back and announced that the baby would not survive. The flush of tears was uncontrollable.

I returned home a few days after like a sparrow whose nest had been torn apart by a tornado, killing all its chicks. My body was still shivering from the excessive shock and mental anguish. The unfortunate outcome was to become a metaphor for my own life. Not only had we lost the baby, but I was on the verge of losing a relationship with a man for whom my heart had fluttered for about a decade.

For weeks, I lay in bed wondering how to deal with the present as well as the unsettling, immediate future. Apart from my two children who from time to time would fall upon my lap and sigh with blinking eyes at our common loss, I was alone in my tragedy. My husband was unconcerned as if I had become pregnant by gulping down a drink.

Mesape was moody, seeming to need more attention to the point of ignoring my suffering. How could the brightness of my day turn into utter darkness so abruptly? From the day I said yes, he had resisted all attempts to set us apart. He was my king, and I was his queen. By what means had an intruder turned a gentle, loving man into a frowning, cold, indifferent, and impatient person? Or did I have to finally admit that good things do not last long as people often say?

I was not the first to face an emotional avalanche crashing in on me, but mine was a complex case. The intruder was a recruit in the same company where my husband and I worked. How could I deal with painful emotions and at the same time pretend that it was okay? Even the millions of our audience would detect from my voice that I was no longer stable. In addition to my pain, I was embarrassed. I had failed. My amour-proper was shattered, and my health was under direct attack. I suffered dizzy spells while perplexed with burning questions plaguing me. Had I made the wrong choice? What had I done wrong to deserve this sudden rejection? Will our relationship ever come back to normal? I had never been the type of girl that threw herself into the arms of men, not even those who expressed interest in me. Was I going to condescend to plead with Mesape to stay with me? Had it not been for the sake of the children, such a thought would never have crossed my mind. And even if I entreated him, would he care enough to reminisce over the exceptional moments we had spent together amid numerous trials? "It is because they are jealous of us," he often cautioned me.

Where did the girl raised in a stable home with affectionate parents go wrong? Was it because we had married out of our respective tribes? Should I have placed cultural affinity over love? Did the handsome, young man who was the talk of the campus love me? Or did he craftily lure an innocent girl into a den? If he loved me why was he turning his back on me? Whose fault was it—mine or his?

Maybe my family-in-law could intervene and call him to order. As for my parents, my mother especially would feel betrayed. The pureness of the love between us, at least from my perspective, had inspired her to the point of obliging her to ignore relatives who complained that Mesape did not yet have a steady income.

As for Mesape's parents, his mother would have preferred a girl from their tribe. However, when they noticed that he was spending all day during his vacation recounting the winsome personality of the one that he would love to marry, they ceded.

I lay in bed and quietly reviewed Mesape's exceptional qualities that were sadly withering away like the leaves of a cypress tree traversing a drought. Over the years he had proven that his love was genuine. We had overcome multiple hardships and criticisms. Unlike other relationships in which financial stress, compounded by the birth of the first baby, had torn couples apart, Mesape became the first man in town to take his baby along, even to his office. He happily babysat our son whenever I was absent. An outstanding life lesson I learned from Mesape was how to forgive someone promptly. Would he soon admit the gravity of the offense he was causing me and our children?

And why now? The timing of the woe (or was it a war?) left me confused. The tough monetary challenges were behind us. Our immediate community had already confirmed us as a model couple. Some of his former classmates had already elected him as their courtship counselor. Wherever we went as guests, our peers and elders treated us with special honor, as if our relationship were made in heaven.

Now that adversity was encroaching like a clock ticking on every shred of beauty we had shared, what should I do? Would the disruption get to the point of separation? If his estrangement went on, how could I raise balanced children in a hostile environment? Yet, for how long would I continue to pretend that all was well between their father and myself? Soon, they would realize for themselves that we had become like branches cut off from the tree. What example would we be setting for them? Even if matters got worse, divorce was unthinkable. It was a slippery, endless lane strewn with spear grass wherein the women who tread within a patriarchal society like ours were as good as walking bare-footed.

I was indeed drowning in the middle of an ocean without rescuers in view. Yet, I could not dwell on separation; it was giving me palpitations.

Indeed, my heart was like a glacier chilling my body, and freezing tears that would have relieved me and cleared my view.

As I continued to revisit the past, a contrary thought that filled me with rage kept lingering. Firstly, both of us had invested too much of ourselves, time, and care into our relationship. Secondly, I could not pinpoint a direct cause of Mesape's disaffection. Neither had he specifically complained about something that needed fixing between us.

Thus, I could not allow him to call it off at his own volition as if I had become a scrap fit for the trash can. I had to find the answer to the overriding question: how did I get into a maze on the pathway of my life? The only way I could stop hurting and try to shield our children from the impending disaster was to seek the liberating truth. I did not know how to proceed, but I had to arm myself with a magnifying glass and retrace my steps to the beginning. I needed to explore the area where I had stumbled. At least, I had to trace the instances wherein I was deaf to the signal of this tortuous outcome that was making me feel like a precious garment damaged beyond repair.

CHAPTER 2

Yaounde University

All of us passengers were students—three girls and one boy in one of those yellow-colored, creaky, standard city taxicabs in the capital, heading to the Ngoa-Ekele neighborhood. The driver, a dark skinned man in a grey tee-shirt, was probably in his forties. Apart from the Makossa tune playing on the radio, there was no conversation going on.

Meanwhile, the car swerved through busy streets, dodging buses, personal vehicles, and taxis, meandering through the narrow, tar-coated strip, divided by a faded line of white paint, with one lane each in opposite directions. Within a quarter of an hour, we alighted at Chateau d'Eau, at the entrance of the campus.

I followed the trail of students on a dusty, windy footpath leading to a long, unpainted, cement block building. It was the Admissions Office. There were hundreds of students on two endless queues, chatting and waiting.

The day was fresh, bright, and sunny at 8:30 am. Students were registering for the new academic year. It took me three hours of waiting in the queue and about half an hour more to go through the tedious process. As soon as I completed the task, I wanted to see the rest of the campus, including the residential area. Two guys caught up with me, and we introduced ourselves. They offered to be my tour guides.

Classes started effectively on Wednesday. I was one of the lucky ones to be granted a room on campus. However, selected students had to wait for a few more days before receiving their keys.

I finally moved into a double room apartment, room #1 in *Batiment* (block) E. The design was for two occupants. In between the two beds was a twin reading table. Wooden wardrobes occupied part of the opposite wall. Above them was space for suitcases. The shower for four users was

18 *My Foolishness Prevails*

My hostel, Batiment E

1st batch of the 3rd Division, Mass Communication Sch. (ESSTIC), Yaounde

in between two adjacent rooms. At the right entrance wall into the room was a black chalkboard sealed to the wall.

My roommate, Angela, whom I was meeting for the first time, smiled as we hugged each other.

"So, we are the winners," I said.

"Without this room, I would not have pursued my studies here," said Angela.

"Same here."

We had won a "lottery," indeed. With off-campus rent being three times higher, and the cost of transportation to school, the cost of attending university would have been prohibitive for both of us. The probability of choosing dozens among the hundreds was slim.

For the first time in my life as an adult, I had to manage my social life without parental supervision. The challenge was tough. My family had sent me to study and obtain a degree within the prescribed length of time of three years. To that end, they were working hard to give me all the support I needed. However, what they had not budgeted for, and neither was I aware of, was the high taxing of my emotions by the heavy traffic of interactions I had to face each day.

Within days, I realized that there was an established campus tradition to entertain fellow students in our rooms. Why? Our rooms were the most affordable meeting spots par excellence, especially on weekends.

Apart from a few former classmates, our room gradually became a venue for a mini students' social club, the highest guests being boys. Usually, six to eight of them took turns visiting while those who stayed longer or arrived later, ended up crowding our double room. We chatted away all evening until close to midnight while drinking soda and beer and munching on popcorn, groundnuts, and biscuits. Regular guests contributed to keeping the bar in good supply.

Beyond light-hearted conversations, each of the regular guests was aiming at something. After the first three weeks, Angela's guests dwindled while mine increased. From the word "go," she categorically refused to entertain any of the guys. Honestly, I enjoyed their company but struggled with their constant pouncing on the door of my heart. My resistance soon became the talk of the campus.

"What is wrong with her?" was to become a frequent complaint by the second month.

Yet, they kept coming and hoping.

It was the tradition to accompany guests on their return trip, often, right to the taxicab station. However, at night, it was okay for girls to stop at the open grass lawn between the *batiments* to make the adieus.

"Akongshee, please, I just want to tell you again that I love you with all of my heart," John pleaded.

"Oh yeah?" I responded with a tone of pretended surprise.

Then, I made some denial noises and began fidgeting with the grass below my feet. Timidity hugged me all over until the sustained nagging plucked my courage.

"But, I already said no."

The truth is, I wanted and needed their company. Regrettably, none wanted to respect my "No Thoroughfare" sign posted on my heart.

Nonetheless, the Hopefuls kept coming. While we strolled out, sometimes close to midnight, between the moonlit hostel apartment buildings, the current one tried to kiss me. First, the boy clutched my cold, trembling hands into his. Then, he proceeded in silence as he moved closer and began lowering his head towards mine.

Meanwhile, I stood still, watching his closing eyes while fighting back a smile.

> *The truth is, I wanted and needed their company. Regrettably, none wanted to respect my "No Thoroughfare" sign posted on my heart.*

The more they came, the more the question became audible.

"Is there something wrong with her?" they wondered.

Of course, I threw the same question back at them.

While the Hopefuls pressed on, the Defeatists sighed and walked away.

"I see you have turned me down for so and so," Tom said, amidst sighs, still wondering why.

The puzzle was challenging to solve, for two reasons. Firstly, there were no campus jobs or opportunities for other social activities like nonprofessional games. Secondly, girls could not perceive the intention of boys who expressed strong feelings for them. So, while some girls suffered rejection after going all the way with boys, the very guys boasted of the number of one-night stands or free offers, which they seized like a hunter pouncing on prey.

A more frequented, open, and an over-crowded meeting place was the off-licenses and bars. They offered fertile "campaigning" spots for the latest wenches, eager to fall. Beer only rendered the making-of-advances playground more accessible. Drinking was like fighting an enemy in your private backyard. You had the advantage, even if you were injured. It was so much more a way of life, the order of the day. A handful of women also "soaked" themselves in beer regularly, whether they had money or not. Male bibbers seized the opportunity to pay, even on credit.

A few times, I stopped over to chat with the thirsty souls from time to time. Nonetheless, I couldn't penetrate the heart of the fun of the bitter, quinine-like concoction, which provoked a face-twisting debut. Of course, I knew they were after the high than the mere taste of it. It took just a glass to blur my vision and weaken my knees almost instantly.

As for the hard drinkers, they knew, who among them, could gulp up to ten 33-ounce bottles before 10 pm. Exceptionally, one genius of a professor crept onto the benches close to midnight, to support sponges, offering drinks to whoever asked for more, and carried on until the wee hours of the morning.

Come the weekends, the random banter and debates went on till the early morning hours. Occasionally, neighbors woke up to discover one or two drunk victims, fishing their way in the nearby gutter, amidst the flavor of their expectoration.

At the other end of "hell" was the more significant number of students. For fear of failing their exams, they never sat on the benches at the drinking spots. To them, the university was like purgatory, requiring a total sacrifice to gain access into the haven of the celebration of success. Thus, close to the end of the semester, a lot of students stayed up all night studying. Some steeped their feet into cold water while sipping black coffee. It was a popular recipe for effective cramming, especially days or hours before the upcoming examinations.

Between the two groups made of boozers and bookworms, was their shared pursuit of women. Call it an epidemic of sex addiction if you wish. It was undeniably more prestigious to display one's manhood than send peers wondering if impotence was lurking around their professed virility.

Indeed, one of my classmates became a target of ridicule. His crime? He denounced sex. Bell was very friendly but would not violate a woman's virtue.

"Cold guy," complained the women who sexually harassed the tall, handsome, fair-skinned, well-bred young man.

Other guys, especially his friends, sympathized with the women. They chimed in, in the singsong teasing. Eventually, the two forces ganged up against him, until he began to think that something was wrong with him.

Finally, they set him up with a very experienced girl. Bell became initiated. From then on, he kept up the pace. Soon his "concerned" friends started hailing him. They even commented that his effeminate physique was looking more masculine. Bell had earned his ticket into the club.

It was disappointing to watch a defeated Bell, smiling wryly at the applause of classmates. Why would friends drag their comrade onto a slippery pathway and then allow him to fall? I was indignant. Instead, they beat their chests, jeered at me, and celebrated their victory at persuading him to honor the rite of passage into manhood.

On the other hand, virgins were ashamed to divulge their lack of experience to seasoned mates. "What are you waiting for?" asked those with the knowhow. Otherwise, the treacherous sea divers would lash out, "You are lying."

Yet, it was considered a man's good fortune to stumble on any young woman, with "swimming skills," yet "undamped."

In as much as I tried to uphold the Berlin wall against them, sometimes I was obliged to pause for a split second to reconsider my rationale for saying no. How come the perks of intimate dating enchanted mates? At the same time, I saw only broken hearts, abused bodies, and threatened lives? How could I deny that I was not a pessimist?

Friends continued to brush off my village-spun folly without second thoughts. While they labeled me as naive and fearful, I pitied them.

What good was my realization? From time to time, I suffered from a deep sense of loneliness. My solitude became worse because I felt hunted and misunderstood. Their complaints, gossip, and mockery hunted me as if I was a rat, which had strayed into cats' kingdom.

"Why is she like that?" some of my girlfriends wondered aloud.

On the other hand, I pitied my girlfriends for taking up responsibilities that they could ill afford. Once they said yes to the boys, they felt obliged to wait on their boyfriends in their rooms. It took me a long while to finally figure out that theirs was, indeed, a packaged deal, prescribed by tradition.

Despite that awareness, I clung onto my version of things. Either we help each other succeed, or give me a break. And woe betide any guy who caught me in the tedium of cooking. I quickly invited him to join me to prepare the meal.

"Please, can you sort vegetables or peel yams?" I asked Tom, who came visiting with his friend, Daniel, Saturday morning.

"Okay," he said and looked at me like a child, wondering if his "mother" was for real.

I guided him into the bathroom and pointed to the sink. He washed his hands and returned to his seat. Then he pulled up his shirt sleeve and started smiling at his friend. My eyes stayed on him as he picked up the yam and the knife.

It was an awkward sight. Tom's thumb and fingers were at the very tip of the handle. I stood up and placed myself at his right side and made a demonstration. He stretched out his long, stiff fingers and gave it a good grip.

Meanwhile, Daniel helped in picking the greens.

Tom was working hard but chopping off chunks of the yams.

"Is it okay, Akongshee?" he asked.

I nodded, yes. Daniel glanced at me, and we both laughed.

It was time for the tomatoes and onion. Tom asked for the onion. Before he got halfway, he started squinting his eyes. I couldn't help laughing. Yet, he refused to give up. He kept rubbing his eyes with the back of his left hand and making sounds. Tears began rolling down his cheeks as the onion bled.

That Saturday morning, a busy household chore day on campus, a girl in my block stepped through my door but quickly stepped back.

"What an odd sight!" she exclaimed.

"Hi Miriam," I said.

She was not interested in my greetings.

"I would never allow a man in my kitchen," she grunted, banged my door, and walked out.

I dropped my stuff in the bowl and followed her into the long corridor. My room was at the entrance.

"How can you degrade a man like that"? She asked in a loud voice.

Two neighbors opened their doors, and she started explaining the terrible sight she had viewed in my room. The first neighbor twisted her face angrily.

"Akongshee, you're queer," Miriam said, looking at me in disgust.

"Queer? how?" I wondered aloud.

"What do you want to show? You think they would like you more?" she went on, standing with arms akimbo, and frowning.

As I walked back to my room, I started thinking of my mother and my brothers. She never discriminated between her boys and girls in her request for help with household chores. Each took their turn to clean, wash, and cook. Indeed, Tse's okro soup was more delicious than any

I had ever tasted. As for Munga, he was a *ndjamandjama* (huckleberry leaves) expert. If anyone received an invitation to enjoy his stewed vegetables, accompanied by the famous hot cornmeal (*fufu corn*), they had to watch out for lurking gluttony.

My woes had only just begun on campus, as the story spread around. Some female students, who used to enjoy my company, began shunning me. They thought that I was very strange. And their grudges didn't stop with the cooking stories and boys. They also argued that, after taking the guys on culinary torture, I still behaved as if I considered myself on "too high a plane" to accept their friendship.

"But we are friends," I insisted.

"You know what I mean," howled Miriam and Judith.

"I could bet we are better friends than what you have with your guys."

"She doesn't get it," said Judith, somewhat disgusted.

While girls complained, I wondered who authorized them to choose who I should be seeing and how I should manage the relationship.

Barely a few weeks after the chef-crowning incident in my room, three women decided "to put some sense into my head." They came to my place without an invitation.

"Akongshee," they called out, smiling and supporting their hands at their waists. "We've come to have a little talk with you," they announced.

I looked up, wondering what was up.

"This boyfriend issue," the first girl hinted and stared at me.

"What do you want?" the second probed.

I looked at them blankly and didn't know what to say.

"Which kind of man are you looking for?" the third asked. They all planted their feet firmly and shook their heads as if examining me in a wrestling arena for where to land the next punch. I smiled with the fresh air of self-assurance, which they saw as naiveté.

"I'm not interested in boyfriends," I snapped back and felt my pressure rising. My summoned self-confidence must have piqued their curiosity.

"Why?" they insisted in chorus.

"I don't need a boyfriend," I said.

Their sudden silence announced an integrated mental evaluation, in process.

"I've not yet met my kind?" I said, stammering.

As if by remote control, two of them jammed their heads together and laughed. Meanwhile, the third yelled at me in rage.

"You will make your own man," she said, while her forefinger pointed at me.

"I guess so," I said. "The beautiful ones are not yet born," I added. Ayi Amah Kwei's book title came in handy.

They laughed in chorus.

"Excuse me, Oxford Madame," the first announced.

They took the time to scan me from head to toe. Silence took over for a while. Then the dating goddesses took off without a further word.

I knew that my operational diction had turned them off, too. Once, my name went around the block, just for explaining that my pressing iron was "disintegrated" rather than simply "broken."

However, the three dating goddesses or whatever their titles, left me busy combing my soul for sickness or some kind of imbalance. Wasn't it becoming chronic? I wondered. The same reprimand in secondary school, high school, and now at the university. For how much longer was I going to hold men at arm's length?

Paradoxically, I benefited more from the company of guys than many of my girlfriends, or so I consoled myself. On weekdays, I sought out intelligent guys in a chosen subject, and we did homework together. Meanwhile, a lot of the girls with boyfriends spent more time pining over their affairs than finding sleep in the night.

What did I care about what they thought about me? Had they no clue how many of their trustworthy guys had made advances to me? If they knew, those of them who were quick at labeling me would applaud me, if only for refusing to snatch their guys.

In an uncanny turn of events, a girl on my block, who seemingly couldn't tell who the right guy was, waited patiently until one of her friends started dating a boy. Quickly, she would go to work overnight, collecting facts about him, which she used as a bait. Surprisingly, she succeeded, case after case, like a hound, snatching a bone from a chihuahua.

She just did it again, and girls were chatting about it. However, they would not allow me to comment, reiterating that I have to wait until I enter the dating zone.

CHAPTER 3

Love or Control?

Ndikum was a handsome hunk of a man, with a heart-warming smile, fond of cracking witty jokes. I first met him way back in my elementary school days. He had the chance to spend a few vacations with his grandfather in Santa. During that time, he often visited with my parents, who knew his parents.

The instant bonding between him and my dad caught my attention. He fidgeted with my father's bow and arrow with a familiarity that ranked him with my brothers. I was impressed.

Our meeting at the university, many years afterward, was utterly a pleasant surprise. Besides, Ndikum was doing exceedingly well in the faculty of Law and Economics, where other students seemed to be passing a prison term. More so, I admired his fluency in both English and French.

"My Akong, is this you?" he spoke with widely-opened eyes during our first meeting on campus.

"What shall I say for the *beau* (handsome) guy you are today, Ndi?" I beamed.

"This is my wife," he announced to my girlfriend with a seductive smile, written all over his face.

"Oh Ndikum, please, *laisse moi tranquil*" (leave me alone) I responded as I leaned on my girlfriend's shoulder. His searching eyes were piercing.

"Leave you alone, Akongshee? And go to where else?" he asked, shaking his head and wiping his mouth with his right hand.

I burst out laughing, a little embarrassed. I relished Ndikum's idiosyncratic teases. He had a real knack to keep an exciting conversation, like okro soup, slipping down the throat.

Indeed, Ndikum and I often indulged in weaving a blend of English, French, and *Ngemba*, our local language.

I wasn't in the marriage mode yet, but it was easy to tell that Ndikum would be any parent's choice for a son-in-law. I thought that he and I could make a superb couple.

However, I began having misgivings, even about maintaining a casual friendship with him. Each time I visited him in his off-campus studio apartment, he insisted that I stay longer, whether I wanted to or not.

One day, I was on the point of leaving after two failed "attempts." He lurched to his feet and thrust forward his chest towards me, like in a boxing ring.

"Please, I have to leave now," I insisted, heading for the door.

He blocked the entrance with his stretched out, sturdy arms. I tried to force my way, to no avail.

"So, what do you want?" I asked, dropping my bag on the chair, really upset.

"I don't want you to leave now," he insisted.

"So what? Just sit here and watch you?" I complained and frowned.

"I will tell you when to leave," he said, sounding rather like a teacher, addressing a stubborn student.

I pulled the seat and sat down without speaking. After about ten minutes, I stood up and picked up my bag again.

Ndikum stood up too and grabbed my arms, but I resisted. He pulled me back to the couch. I fell onto it with my face. Then he pulled my arms behind my back and tried to twist one over the other. The more I pleaded, the more he squeezed them. I started crying gently, then loudly as the pain increased. Yet he refused to let go. I yelled at the top of my voice, fearing that he would break my arms.

When he finally let go, the pain was excruciating. I dashed through the door, protesting.

Half-way on my journey, he followed and caught up with me at the footpath, which allowed only a single file, by the hillside, invaded by the broad leaves of luxuriant green *cocoyams* (a tuber) and long corn ears on both sides.

Quickly, he forged his way through the plants and charged at me, face to face. I struggled to push him off my path. Instead of letting go, he kept pleading that I return with him. He persisted while twisting my arms. A fight erupted. Barely two inches was the leg space that I risked rolling over the hill, just beyond our toes. Yet, he wouldn't give up, not until other pedestrians stepped onto the pathway.

That evening, I scrubbed the mud off my sandals, hoping to banish every trace of him from my immediate surroundings. I promised myself, never again, to venture into Ndikum's net. He had buried his good qualities in that brown earth, where we quarreled and wrestled.

The clinging mud from my sandals fell off in lumps while I cursed the day I met him. I swung one leg in the air several times to get rid of any trace of dirt. I could have sworn that our story ended there.

Nevertheless, several months after that incident, I met Ndikum at the wedding of my friend in Akum village. He happened to be the only single adult male I knew. He invited me to dance. He came for a second and yet another.

"This will be my last," I whispered to him as the music blasted.

He looked at me and frowned.

"Why?" he asked, sounding rather authoritative.

"I'm simply worn out," I explained.

"Can we meet tomorrow then?" he requested.

"No. My parents are expecting me, and I plan to leave early," I said.

"Akong, you know you are my girl. But you seem to enjoy giving me a tough time," he said while pointing his right forefinger at me.

"Ndikum, I think you'd make a wonderful husband, but," I said, shaking my head from side to side.

He looked at me, anew, and smiled.

"But I can't understand why you enjoy giving me such a tough time," I went on, throwing my hands in the air.

We both laughed, and he tapped my shoulders.

Then he began pleading again. But my head swung from side to side disapprovingly. Pleading and nagging ensued.

"No," I said with emphasis.

Yet, he invited me to another dance, but I declined the offer. I picked up my handbag. His eyes penetrated my whole being with aggression.

I moved out to the balcony for want of space. The fresh air was massaging my tense muscles.

Within minutes, he pursued me and started what sounded like an amicable conversation. I joined in.

Why doesn't he stop asking for a dance? I wondered. His nagging was wearing me out. He stared at me, then tried to pull me into the hall, but

I stood my ground. He held onto my hand. I was too tired to fight. Before I knew what was going on, he gripped my necklace and dragged it. It shattered. Bits of it fell to the ground, irretrievably.

I stared at Ndikum, right into his eyes, without saying a word. Then he started apologizing. I just moved away.

I was desperate to leave, but I needed a companion. Unfortunately, I didn't know anyone else apart from him and the bride. The way home to the bride's mother's house was an unfamiliar footpath. The darkness of that night was opaque. There was no sign that the party was going to end soon. I stood there, homesick and stranded.

Just as I was on the point of tears, Ndikum came out. I turned my back and began leaving immediately. He followed me into the darkness. The road was not only dark but hilly and winding. I had passed there only once during the daylight hours.

Soon, Ndikum became my companion and navigator on call, especially when he began renewing his apology.

"Akong, I care deeply for you. I want you to know that," he said.

"Yes, I believe you, Ndikum," I responded lazily.

"I promise that I will never again try to impose on you," he said, sounding calm.

"Oh, yeah? I thought that you've already shown me who you truly are."

"Akong, please, understand. I feel so close to you. That's why I always find it hard to let you go."

Whether his declaration was worth a pinch of salt or trickle of venom, I was more interested in getting home safely than adding firewood to his fire. His companionship as an efficient navigator, strong enough to protect me against sudden danger, was more than I could have asked.

Ndikum held my right hand when we got to the hilly part of the road. Then he stopped without warning, turned around to me, and requested a kiss.

"Here and now?" I asked, stressing every syllable.

"What's wrong with you?" he yelled.

"You mean wrong with you or with me?"

He sighed and took a deep breath, remaining silent for a while. The night was black and quiet, but for his deep breathing.

"Ndikum, this can't be the place or time," I began pleading when he pulled me closer to himself.

He did not utter a word.

"I mean, it can come later."

He resumed pleading.

Then he started coming close to my face. My head turned away. He let go of my hand and pushed me unexpectedly.

Instantly, I started rolling down the hill. There was no need to cry for help. Both sides of the road were acres of luxuriant corn farm. I was moaning and rolling down.

Thank goodness! A rock arrested my crash and rolling over; my fingers grabbed it. I pressed hard and picked up myself. One of my shoes was almost off, but I was grateful to have both of them still. My hands stretched forward, like guide sticks for the blind.

I began navigating my way through the engulfing darkness. I heard Ndikum calling after me.

However, it was my turn to be deaf. My feet covered more ground as I tried to rush. The part of the way seemed to be level ground. I started running and cutting my way through the darkness as well as through intruding corn leaves.

Finally, I reached the highway. Faint rays of light, shining from nearby homes, reduced my anxiety. I was grateful. I slowed down and tried to catch my breath, even though I was still trembling from fear. I walked briskly, without looking back until I traced my way back to my friend's home.

CHAPTER 4

Out of Whack Dating

Mofor was thin and of average height, warm and gentle. We first met each other at university. He was a postgraduate student, who carried an air of self-confidence about him that distinguished him in the crowd. Mofor was so self-conscious that he made stylish gestures as he spoke. My roommate and I fondly referred to him as Darcy, our local version of Jane Austen's hero in *Pride and Prejudice*.

He was not a top student, but he always succeeded in staying above water, something like the last of the best. Neither was he rich, though no one could describe him as a poor guy. Even so, his bare-faced romantic fervor made him more attractive. Our shared smiles and his regular compliments quickly broke the ice between us. I began learning to like him. His first invitation for a room visit was quite welcome, though I didn't rush it.

Finally, on Saturday, I sat in his cozy room, in one of the prestigious off-campus apartment buildings. He served me citron soda and some cookies. There was a strategically displayed photo of him and a woman sitting on his lap, on the dresser facing me. I turned away and wondered if he intended that as a challenge or what. If I had to sit on a guy's lap like that, it must be that we are already engaged, I thought to myself.

He soon took his place by me in the armchair.

"Thank you so much for coming. I feel special." His face radiated with joy; his bright eyes said it all.

"Well, I had to, right? And I'm glad to be here."

"Finally," he said, smiling. "You don't know how long I've longed for your visit, Akong."

"I'm delighted for the opportunity to discover the man from inside, the real Darcy," I emphasized.

We both laughed heartily.

"Would you be my Jane, then?" he asked, looking at me tenderly.

I just smiled. Consuming shyness began scribbling traces of condensing heat on my nose.

"Well, if and only if you are the original Darcy."

"How do you mean that?" he asked, leaning towards me.

"Parting with your pride," I suggested, in a low tone.

He laughed and fell back in his chair.

It had been almost an hour and getting close to 8 pm; I stood up and announced my departure. Mofor looked at me inquiringly, and somewhat surprised. He moved closer and held my hand. Instead, I froze, my face fixing at the door. He understood and went back in for the key. I stepped out and waited for him.

Since that day, Mofor began visiting me often. We had already exchanged photos, I recalled, seizing my portrait from him, the one in which I barely had on a *wrapper* (a free piece of cloth that women wrap around their body) over my breasts. That was the only one he wanted, however, I did not want to commit so quickly.

Nevertheless, the following month, I stopped by, on the eve of his exams, to wish him success. However, when it was time to go, he wouldn't hear of it. He was visibly upset.

"So, what's wrong in coming to wish you good luck?" I asked.

"I appreciate it, but I love you, Akongshee," he whispered.

"But you don't have to kiss me," I said, looking straight towards the floor.

"Why are you so difficult?" he stressed each syllable.

"Difficult?" I asked, raising my voice. "On the contrary, I'm trying to make things easier for both of us," I went on.

He stared into my eyes without a word.

"I must go," I said, heading towards the door.

He graciously offered to accompany me part of the way.

It was dark, but for rays of light escaping from the nearby rooms of the tall campus apartment buildings. On the way, he suddenly stopped at the lawn between the hostels, to renew his request. I shook my head and turned away.

Suddenly, he caught my arm and tried to force a kiss on me. We started fighting. The fistfight went on until my arms were hurting. So, I began pleading for mercy. He would not let go.

Was he more eager to hurt me than to snatch a kiss? I began wondering. I threatened to yell. Then he gave up. The violent shaking exasperated me; my breathing was loud. Mofor looked unruffled while I panted.

I regretted having visited him that evening. How ungrateful! I reasoned. Or was I inconsiderate in my rebuff? I didn't think so. However, I was sorry for having disappointed him. The lesson was clear—no more visits to his apartment.

Every good story ends with a conclusion. The fight with Mofor finally crushed my hopes of ever having a meaningful relationship with someone close to home. He was indeed the last of the best. Just a handful of guys from my village were at university then. Despite their complaints, I was more determined to uphold friendship above intimate dating. Couldn't they see how much I cherished their company? I wondered. Nevertheless, I wanted to continue to take advantage of the courtesies I had already extended to a wide range of guys. Homework and research were top on my list.

Increasing social battles gave vent to regrets, sighs, and disappointments. It didn't seem like my kind of a world, though I still retained full occupancy rights. So, what then?

I began noticing a difference between francophones and anglophones. Were the former more mature? That would be too lenient. They were more nonchalant while anglophones were more prudent. I needed to think and take the time to not fall victim to my naiveté. However, I gathered from personal observation that anglophones tended to gang up, to pursue women, and later compared notes while francophones single-handedly managed their affairs.

There was a woman in my block whose boyfriend arrived each morning with freshly baked bread. They held hands and crossed the campus, while other students watched from their windows. He was fond of calling her *Chérie* (Sweetheart) all over the place as if they were married. Eventually, she got pregnant. I don't know if they were married or had any such plans, but they just stuck together inseparably.

I equally realized that francophone women tended to marry their boyfriends while anglophone women chose older partners. Indeed, disappointed anglophone graduates described their run-away girlfriends as selfish and insensitive.

Why blame them for making smart moves? Dumping long-term girlfriends for younger women was also a rampant practice. And what to make of the recurrent abuse suffered by heart-broken women, ready to either fall prey, for fear of becoming old mates, or resorting to charms.

In most cases, anglophone men waited to acquire the necessary wealth before getting married. Yet, who could hold time responsible for changes in the equation of propositions? Family members had their say too in the final decision, promises at stake or not.

At a basic level, francophones seemed to place infatuation above love. They tended to treat sex as commonly as a jolly good morning to a stranger. Rightly or wrongly, they gave the impression of pursuing a woman for her skirt. Therefore, she was sure to make a fool of herself if she resisted his proposition upon their first encounter.

Despite those general tendencies, I was fully aware that individual preferences counted more than cultural norms.

The analysis had not yet crystallized in my mind, when I found myself on the verge of savoring the difference.

CHAPTER 5

Holiday Romance

Douala was eager to show off her most handsome and eligible bachelors, upfront and close, like the imposing billboards lifted on her busy street corners.

It was my first long vacation there as a university student. My elder sister, Mafor, had won a holiday job for me at her company, the headquarters of the National Produce Marketing Board, for the commercialization of so-called cash crops.

On Monday morning, I hopped behind her on her motor scooter, on our way to work. That solved a major transportation problem. Ndokoti, where we lived, was a new neighborhood, located at the opposite end of the city to Bonanjo, the administrative headquarters of Douala. Daily rides would have been too costly, even by the urban transport bus, *Sotuc (Société des Transports urbains du Cameroun)*.

The distance of about 20 kilometers was quite a mess on rainy days. It was a severe struggle; I had to grip the driver's waist or shoulder with one hand and the umbrella with the other.

Of course, Mafor was an excellent driver of her brand-new, red motor scooter. Yet, her best effort was no guarantee of dodging all the potholes of slush. Rushing cars splashed on us, after pushing us right to the curb. Then the random boos and jeers of *Bambe* boys (truck loaders) were demoralizing.

At the office, the officer in charge of interns assigned me to the public relations department, thanks to my relative fluency in both English and French. More than seventy percent of the employees spoke French.

My immediate boss was Pierre; he was a tall, extra-fit hunk of a man. His light brown skin seemed tanned by the gentleness of the early morning sun. His smile spread over his handsome face, like fresh *Hausa* butter on a hot piece of toasted *cocoyams*, directly fetched out from grandma's oven of hot ash.

"Hello, *Mademoiselle*," Pierre spoke up first, with a warm smile.

I moved two steps forward and shook his hand. He pointed to the side table, loaded with piles of files. My spot was ready, waiting for me to get to work.

He requested that I place my handbag on top of the counter and make myself at home. Then, he invited me to his table. I pulled the dark leather chair, facing him, and sat down. The training was in process.

Working for a substantial financial reward was truly consoling. As far as I was concerned, it was a tiny little symbol of my parent's day-to-day sweating on the coffee farm, finally trickling down to me. My earnings, after three months of vacation, was sufficient to cover most of my basic needs at the university for the following term.

While I celebrated my momentary victory, temptation silently and steadily reared its head, right in my face. Or was it the kind of sun that steals its way through a gray, dull day, for a split second?

"*Bon, Dieu! Comme elle est belle!*" (Oh, God! How pretty she looks!) Pierre started remarking within my first days at work.

I smiled and thanked him. Soon, it began dawning on me that it was a little more than mere compliments.

Sometimes, when I opened the door, he instantly stopped in the middle of his work, and held his breath, until I finally settled in my seat.

"What good fortune is mine," he said one day.

"What are you talking about?" I asked innocently.

My question seemed to have triggered the fullness of whatever was possessing him. He dropped his pen on the table and stared at me, right through my being, without a word.

"*Tu es mignone* (you are cute), Akongshee," he said, finally.

I smiled again, hoping to use my displayed innocence to deflate his targeting provocation.

"And you don't seem to realize how pretty you are," he added.

At first, I enjoyed every inch of his praise, but each day concocted a more potent dose of it, rendering me dizzy.

What was I to do? I thought to myself. What if Pierre kept on like that? It was already turning into pleasure gone beyond the limits of comfort. And I was ill-equipped to handle the mounting pressure, being young, naive, and the underling. I tried to think of a way out, but nothing was forthcoming.

There was no doubt that no other openings existed in the different departments, judging from the whispered scramble among workers to get their children and relatives selected.

Mafor was neither a director nor a sub-director. Yes, she was an executive secretary, but she had no powers, personal or official, to help transfer me to another office. At least, I wasn't aware of it.

On the contrary, she often complained of frustration suffered by her immediate boss because his suggestions were ignored in some significant issues, even though he was the number two of the corporation. His immediate boss, *Monsieur, le Directeur General* (Mr. General Manager), was francophone. That said it all.

So, I reasoned that if I complained, I might instead jeopardize my job.

"Jacques, I have found my wife," Pierre announced, one day, to his friend, who stopped by the office.

"Who is she? Jacques asked, with a light in his eyes.

"*Tu es aveugle ou quoi*? (Are you blind or what?) Just look at her," Pierre said, turning around towards me.

Jacques took one step backward and stood by Pierre while the two of them admired the object of Pierre's constant gaze.

Pierre chose that moment to request that I take a file to the seventh floor. I stood up and headed towards the door.

"Just watch her walk, Jacques," Pierre requested. "Isn't she gorgeous?" he asked. "*Meme le movement!*" (even her gait). He exclaimed and clapped his hands.

I couldn't help laughing at their dramatized admiration of my humble self. I rushed out, almost jamming the door, in an attempt to stop them from devouring me with their eyes.

Pierre was just exaggerating, I thought to myself as I walked away. Otherwise, he was setting a trap for me, I concluded. So, I began wondering how far this would go. How was I going to be in his face, each day, ride side by side with him in the car during official duty, and find enough strength to resist him? And let's not forget he was a man who simply glowed in his attractive physical fitness.

Each day, I made up my mind that no matter how much he tried, I had to stand my ground. I buried my head into my papers, amidst glances at the Apollo, sitting next to me, wishing I would just fall into his arms. Pierre was well educated, as far as I could see. He had specialized in marketing and advertising. He was meaningfully employed and doing a good job, though he was relatively new in the organization. Pierre could be my opportunity to walk away from drudgery and poverty. Darting images continually crossed my mind.

Nonetheless, somehow, I couldn't come to the point of visualizing myself as his bride. It seemed so farfetched.

"You need to come over and see my fiancée," Pierre was speaking with someone on the telephone. My eyes rolled from one end of the wall to the other, as I tried to escape his broad smile, targeting my face.

Before the day ended, I knew with whom Pierre had been conversing. Therese was the executive secretary for the director-general; she walked through the door with a broad smile, displaying her seductive gap tooth. Sophistication was all over her. Her thoroughly stretched hair was styled to perfection, with tiny loops of loose strands, caressing her forehead. She was wearing a lace suit of *booboo* top and knee-length wrapper, both trimmed with carefully selected pastels. She glowed.

Therese gave me a warm handshake and turned around to Pierre and nodded in approval. Then, with her back gently bent over in dignity, she opened her outstretched right hand, and smoothly swept the air in front of her, as if ushering in Pierre into a world that his desire had taken him captive.

"*Belle, belle, belle, n'est-ce pas?*" (Pretty, pretty, pretty, right?) Pierre asked her. "I'm falling," he added.

"I don't blame you, *beau gars comme toi*," (handsome man like you are) Therese responded. "*Tu as du goût*," (you have good taste) she said while glancing at me, rather thoughtfully.

Though Therese was also an executive secretary like Mafor, she certainly had a lot more influence.

For a split second, I tried again to visualize myself as Pierre's girlfriend and maybe fiancée. Who else was better than him?

If I thought that Pierre was joking, he was not backing out, at least, not yet. To my surprise, he started telling other friends and relatives about his "fiancée". I heard him announcing it in another telephone conversation.

"So, Akongshee, what else can I do to show you that I love you?" he asked during one of our brief outings to another office, downtown. We were at a café, sipping a quick soda to cool down our bodies, baking from the Douala heat.

I looked at his beautiful taut body, glowing in the expression of good health and a handsome measure of wealth. My eyes quickly turned away from his constant regard.

For the first time, it occurred to me that, after all, it was more than mere infatuation. So, for once, I decided to give it a serious thought.

Even so, there was an obstacle beyond the personal level. Pierre was from a tribe that was known to produce aggressive men and women. Oh no, I thought to myself, a little scared. Weird tales existed about the people from a tribe near his own; a man demonstrated his love to his wife by beating her occasionally.

Nevertheless, a contradicting thought reminded me that Pierre was well educated, polished, and exposed to the gentle treatment of women. After all, wasn't France the birthplace of romance? I recalled one evening, on campus, when Guy, whose family lived in France, curtseyed to me, as soon as I opened my door. He had come to borrow my English notes. I ushered him in and thought to myself, what more would he do if I were his girlfriend?

I kept rationalizing, especially since my romantic horizon stretched out beyond the limits of one continent. Not to mention that my tribesmen had failed to treasure my love.

When Pierre extended another invitation, his last-resort proposal, I promised to honor it.

In two weeks, his brother, who works with Cameroon Airlines, was going to return with packages of specially selected French cheese. Both of us were going to savor it at his home, after work.

However, I gave him my condition quickly and clearly. Therese had to be part of the company.

Pierre looked at me, smiled, and shook his head from left to right. He was visibly surprised by my request. He didn't seem to appreciate it, though he accepted it.

"What kind of a woman are you?" he asked after a long pause.

"What do you mean?" I asked.

"You don't trust me, Akongshee?" he worried aloud.

"Not really," I responded.

"So, what is the matter?"

"I believe that I would be more comfortable if someone else came with us," I said timidly.

It was barely two days to the cheese savoring party, scheduled for Pierre's residence, in the upscale neighborhood of Bonamoussadi.

He reminded me of our appointment. I confirmed it, without asking Mafor's permission. What I did not know was that Therese, who was on an official mission, was still abroad.

During the early afternoon, Pierre hinted that it might turn out to be a party for two. Goosebumps began coming over me. Why only two? Therese had not yet returned from Quebec.

My head dropped on the file in front of me. Oh, no. I conjured up the worst scenario. There was no way I could stand a fight with Pierre, and in his house, for that matter.

However, I couldn't muster up enough courage to tell him that it was either my condition or nothing. I had already turned down more than half a dozen invitations. It was becoming clear that I was antisocial. My reputation was at stake. Besides, it was going to be challenging to manage my little space, having to face an angry Pierre.

Wednesday afternoon, a day before our rendezvous, he announced that Therese had called from Quebec. She was going to return only the following week. On hearing the news, I lifted my palms to my face, closed my eyes, and shook my head from left to right.

Meanwhile, Pierre fell back in his seat. He stared at me angrily. That moment, I felt like running out and not coming back there.

However, the choice to leave was not mine. I still had a month to go. I knew that Pierre was very disappointed.

Nevertheless, there was something of a relief to Therese's delay. Not only would Mafor have refused my request for permission, but she would have denounced my naiveté in taking such a risk. I knew it.

I started walking in the office as if I was afraid to step on a baby's toes. I said very little, except in response to his expressed requests. Yet, I saw the longing in his whole face.

"She has rejected me," he said to Jacques, who stopped by the office, two days later.

"Why?" Jacques asked while turning around towards me.

"I don't know why she is afraid of me," Pierre explained, with a wrinkle on his face.

I listened to them, my head bent over the table.

One week after the foiled cheese party, Pierre invited me to the movies. I said yes, without hesitation. This time around, I was ready to go, even if it was just to prove that I was not a coward.

Besides, after the movies, I could take a taxicab home, if Pierre gave me a reason to think otherwise about him.

The following morning, he asked if I was still willing to go to the movies. I said, "Yes." Even so, I kept wondering if my sister would let me go.

In the final analysis, a movie was no big deal, especially for a twenty-year-old. So, I began gauging the appropriate moment to inform my sister of our planned outing.

Thursday evening after dinner, the eve of the outing, I cleared my throat and spoke up, finally.

"No, no, no," Mafor yelled out, stressing every sound while pounding her hand on the table.

I was so disgusted, not only by her refusal but by the way she said it. She was certain that Pierre only wanted to take advantage of me, but why not talk with him instead of presuming his intentions? I left the table suddenly and escaped into my room, with tears filling my eyes.

What was I going to tell Pierre? That I was such a coward or that he was a lion, waiting to devour me in a movie theatre? That thought worried me right into my sleep.

I got to the office the following morning, with a sullen look. Pierre had never seen me like that.

"What's wrong, Akongshee?"

"I'm so sorry I can't go to the movies," I said.

"But it's just the movies," he stressed.

"I know," I said, with a deficient tone.

"So, what happened this time around?"

"We have an important family event this evening," I tried to explain my way out of the deal.

"So, can we go tomorrow or next week?" he asked.

"No, my sister won't let me," I said with a sigh.

"*Ah bon?*" (Really?) he exclaimed and paused for a while as if attempting to pinpoint the reason behind it.

My eyes just kept blinking. Eventually, I mustered up some courage and dragged myself towards the tall, extensive glass window, overlooking the busy, jammed streets, nine floors below where I was standing.

Pedestrians and cars were competing for space. I envied shoppers, exercising their freedom, to go and come at will.

Maybe my sister was right, but it took me quite a while to get over what I considered a misuse of her authority. I would never know if Pierre was an opportunity worth exploring or not.

Mafor sensed my displeasure. Several months after that incident, Mom was advising her on the need to shield me from falling prey to deception. Mafor quickly responded, that had it not been for her quick intervention, a proud guy, newly recruited, would have misled me. She said that he was bragging, giving the impression that he steered enough power to influence important decisions.

I had no clue as to what she was alluding. Neither was I interested.

A lump was trying to block my throat, even as she spoke. It was needless to argue with my sister, whom I believed had only acted out of concern for my wellbeing. I resolved it in my heart.

Years after, as I looked back, I wondered why Pierre preferred me over all those pretty, sophisticated, and accomplished women, some of whom studied in France, too.

Was he genuine in his intentions? I wonder.

It was too late to find out.

CHAPTER 6

Hellfire Witnessing

Curiosity was my middle name at Yaounde University. Anyone could spot me at the Amphitheater 700, watching plays or movies, and attending conferences. Not one scheduled event did I miss. I even nosed into other faculties; I sat in a chemistry class and later considered switching to law and economics. Friends invited me to francophone parties. I was so driven that on Friday evening, I even defied illness and attended the Moot Court of the Year, directed by Doctors Anyangwe and Ngwafor, and staged by student lawyers. Midway into the presentation, I was obliged to leave when dizziness overwhelmed my weakening body. I almost crawled back to my room, as I was limping to catch the next wall and rolled myself on it.

The only exception to my inquisitiveness was the evangelistic campaigns organized by the Born Again. They were a relatively new group of a Pentecostal-type church, mushrooming on campus, and on fire to recruit new members. Poking their tracts into the faces of students turned me off. Their frumpy looks did not impress me, either. Stripping themselves of color and style and concealing their hair with scarves was certainly not my idea of fashion.

Condemning fornication or the drinking of intoxicating alcoholic beverages should have piqued my interest, but it didn't. Maybe that brand of holiness was not for me. So, I dismissed them outright without a second thought.

However, one day curiosity got the better of me. I yielded to the persistent harassment of a Born Again proselytizer. He came to my room to share "the Good News."

"If you are not born again, you will go to hell," he warned, picking up one tract from his pile. "You must confess your sins and repent," he went on. I listened to him while trying to make sense of it all. I thought he was right. However, why threaten and condemn in every breath? Was God that merciless? I was getting weary.

"Else, you will die and burn in hellfire," he said while standing up and spreading out his hands. "All this alcohol and fornication on campus is the work of the devil," he went on and on.

I continued listening, out of sheer politeness. Meanwhile, I was thinking to myself, *"You fun hater, what do you know about having a good time?"* I hoped he would soon realize his folly. Yet he kept on.

Finally, I asked him to rate me on the salvation ladder. He stared at me for a while and smiled. "It's unlikely for you ever to make it into heaven," he said, with a stern look while nodding with pity.

> *I listened to him while trying to make sense of it all. I thought he was right. However, why threaten and condemn in every breath? Was God that merciless? I was getting weary.*

"What? Who are you to pass judgment on me?"

"Didn't I tell you that you are a sinner?" he retorted, frowning. "Hear how you are barking at me."

"Get out of my room. Nonsense," I ordered.

He stood there staring at me. So, I sprang up to my feet and showed him the door.

He picked up his books and headed out. I accompanied him with warnings as he raced down the stairs.

"Never step foot at my door again," I shouted at the top of my voice.

I don't remember ever screaming like that at any adult.

My roommate, Angela, arrived while I was still shouting. She stood at the door and X-rayed me from head to toe.

"Mami, I didn't know there was a hidden lion in you," she said as she dropped her books and files on her bed.

"These Born Agains think they know all," I said, still trying to catch my breath.

"Well, if it took one of them for you to finally realize that not any *Sango* (young man) should walk through that door...." she said but suddenly stopped and closed her mouth with her right palm while smiling at me.

I looked at her but didn't utter a word.

"Sorry, I'm just joking," she said, rather timidly.

No one could disregard the personal warning messages from the Born Agains. Even if the heaven that they preached seemed abstract, a good number of girls quietly suffered after indulging in intimate relations with the boys. Specific periods of the months brought a lot of anxiety.

Yet, who was able to lift and maintain a boundary line between male and female? Some young women happily yielded to the advances of the young men, while others used the means at their disposal to win the attention of the opposite sex. Some girls used contraceptives, without any regard to the health risks spelled out on the labels, including migraine headaches, high blood pressure, and cancer. While a few succeeded in finding genuine love, a lot more became victims; boys jilted them after shagging.

The reality was that promiscuity was prevalent. What could have served as a deterrent?

Angela chose to keep a safe distance from boys. Of course, I knew that she was barely coping with the endless knocks on our door, especially given that she often dismissed her admirers with a single sentence.

"My father didn't send me to the university to look for boyfriends."

"Does she have to be so serious and cold," the guys would complain while retreating.

Usually, we spotted the young men through the window from the east wing as they arrived. "Akongshee, let me run before they get here," she announced, quickly jumping to her feet and gathering her books.

There were indeed a lot of visitors. Those living off-campus seized every opportunity to call on us.

"Oh no, I need to speak with him," I said, upon recognizing one of my guy friends.

"You would have to go and entertain him outside," Angela snapped.

Overall, I agreed with Angela though sometimes she sounded like my mother or big sister. Otherwise, she was jealous. I dared to imagine.

CHAPTER 7

First Love

At the beginning of my third and final year, I moved out of the campus hostels into a new room with a new roommate at an apartment building. Most of the students on the block were older, mature, and married, to my relief.

Indeed, a year of peace, mainly given to exploring more academic avenues, was beckoning. No boy was trying to capture my heart. Just before returning from my extraordinary summer vacation spent in Canada—my first ever travel abroad—I dismissed the most recent young man who had made advances to me before my travel abroad.

He was Cho, a postgraduate student; the mature-looking young man had a fair complexion. He looked composed and reserved. He walked with his body slightly bent forward as if he felt intimidated by his average height. His cautious steps gave him the distinct gait of a man looking older than his real age. Anyone could guess that he would develop wrinkles before reaching elderly maturity. Frankly, I would not have accepted his invitation for friendship, much less considered him as a future partner. In the end, I decided to let go just because he hailed from my village.

I received a beautiful letter from him while I was abroad. Since there was a postal strike going on in my host city, I dropped a postcard to him during my stay in another town, promising that I would write him a more elaborate letter. Days before my vacation abroad ended, Cho wrote a harsh message to me; he reprimanded me for exposing our relationship in an open postcard. He ended up warning me, in strict terms, never to repeat such an irresponsible act. My response was immediate—good riddance.

During my return trip, all I did was reminisce over my vacation to Calgary, Toronto, and Regina, under the aegis of the Canadian Crossroads International Cultural Exchange Program. It had been inspiring. Looking back, I recalled the day when the sociology professor asked us to write an essay. Only two in a class of eighty students won the contest. Each of us won a free air ticket to travel to Canada, with food, lodging, and transportation included.

The highlights were still fresh in my mind, especially the promising contacts made during the most exciting vacation ever. Motivation to perform to my optimum was bubbling inside me and targeting my upcoming bachelor's degree.

However, one particular guy began taking a keener interest in me. Mesape was handsome, slim, fair in complexion, and of average height. He looked calm, friendly, and gentle. His charming smile always lingered. He wasn't one of those gentlemen in western suits. However, he had a definite taste for quality. His designer shirts and well-knotted ties set him apart.

He usually stepped out of the crowd to greet me whenever we met on campus. Nothing more, I mistakenly thought.

More importantly, his gentleness and patience had distinguished him from the dozens who paraded through my former campus room. Even then, his love remained unrequited for one whole year. During that period, he kept coming to my room, on brief stopovers, to deliver my mail. He came, knocked, gave me my letter, and then rushed away.

The first few times were okay. However, when he kept coming, week after week, my roommate started launching enquiring glances at me.

"Akongshee, it's that guy again," Angela, my former roommate, used to say, raising her eyebrows while passing a letter to me.

Meanwhile, a handful of girls were competing for his love. Each made dinner and invited him over, often with a lot of persuasion. Indeed, his former school mates in high school believed that they had an advantage over others. I didn't even feature on their list of potentials and I knew it.

Destiny or design, Mesape was one of my first guests in my new room. Incidentally, he was one of the students admiring my Canadian shopping bag in front of the library, just the day before.

His close friend, James, accompanied him. My new roommate, Beri, and I, along with the two of them, had an animated conversation. Their visit was short. His unspoken mission left us surmising, as Beri, who was his former high school mate, teased me and giggled. She had a point. I couldn't erase the image of his eyes pursuing me all over.

Two weeks afterward, someone called out greetings to me from the second floor of Batiment A while I was crossing the campus.

I looked up and saw Mesape smiling.

"Hi! I'm fine. How are you doing?"

"Pretty good." I responded.

"Please, can you stop over some time?"

I stopped, hesitated, and paused.

"One of these days, maybe?" he urged on.

I was undecided. My mind wanted to say no while my heart was indecisive. It felt like I was standing on ants but couldn't move. Meanwhile, an odd feeling was pressing hard. I didn't want to look like a coward or be unfriendly.

"You promised me, you remember?" he urged.

"Yes, okay," I responded with a nod.

The three days ahead of our promised meeting were filled with indecision on my part. Of course, I had Friday and Saturday to change my mind. Yet, I often felt bound by my promises, in addition to curiosity, tugging at my soul.

Sunday was "D-Day" for us. As evening approached, my heart started beating faster. Uncertain, I found myself between two loyalties. I desired Mesape, seemingly unable to detach myself from the aura of his affection capturing me.

However, intimacy was not an option for me. Yet, could I escape? I had no clue. I was aware of his track record, which was an everyday talk on campus. Former school mates recounted how he and his former girlfriend "reigned" in high school. That story always made me wonder why he hadn't, so far, realized that he and I were centuries apart—the last thing I wanted was being swept off my feet. Neither was I the type to go out of my way to impress a man.

Two long days of emotional labor failed to yield a precise answer. My misgivings had not subsided. Yet it felt like I had come to the point of no return.

Finally, I stood up from my bed, stretched myself, and took a long, deep breath. Okay, I was going to visit Mesape, just for the fun of it, and hopefully not make any promise to commit myself.

Better still, I might be lucky enough to return with a good reason to back out. I preferred a pure friendship.

The yellow taxicab drove me from Obili, the outskirts of the campus. I alighted and picked my way up the stairs with trembling legs to the third floor. My wristwatch flashed in my eyes as my right fingers tapped lightly on room three-zero-six-A.

He ushered me in with a broad smile. I smiled back, struggling to hide my nervousness. He led me to the seat by his study. Then he proceeded to introduce me to his cousin and her fiancé, an architect.

The two lovers were sitting on his bed. What a relief! I thought. Even so, it took me up to ten minutes or so to begin to relax and warm up. My head nodded, and I just concurred as they spoke. It was certainly more comfortable to sit back and admire the love birds than engaging in conversation. After all, what was I to say? Wasn't it enough that love was glowing on their faces?

How ironic that I had promised myself not to fall in love, yet the moment, place, and time, were all bowing to romance! It was almost like, "See what you are missing." The *beau* kept his eyes fixed on his *belle*. His tender smile fused into her cheerfulness and radiated on her face with joy, blending with delicate blushes. She was shy; me, too. I twitched about in a quiet struggle to sit snugly into my seat. My eyes were darting left and right, hardly knowing where to settle, while my heart prayed for an occasion to interject or even to merely laugh.

> *How ironic that I had promised myself not to fall in love, yet the moment, place, and time, were all bowing to romance! It was almost like, "See what you are missing."*

However, I managed to steal glimpses of my host from time to time. Why was it so difficult to control my shivering bones? I kept worrying.

Thank goodness, Mesape passed me his photo album. He proceeded to make introductions and handed me more photos for my enjoyment.

There was one picture taken by the beach that caught my attention. It instantly plunged me into a reverie. My mind wandered into an imaginary love haven—a garden with a countless variety of flowers, a blending of sweet fragrances. What's more I saw a stream canopied by trees with branches filtering the gentle rays of the sunshine. Add to it a soothing warmth emanating from the photograph. Hark! The sound of chirping birds. Delicate pastels. Kindest thoughts. Nothing to worry about, ever.

I lifted my eyes from the photo album and picked up a biscuit from the tray in front of me. Then I fell back on my chair and stole glances at Mesape's room. It was decidedly the right environment for romance. His drapes were custom-made instead of the maroon khaki material, hanging on each window, provided by the university. His polyester blend was more than double the standard length, almost touching the floor. The delicate pastel with green on a yellow background was gentle to the eyes.

Even his bed was remarkable. Sparkling white bedsheets pulled out, folded in straight and taut as if there was a piece of plank underneath.

The room tour went on; my eyes looked to the left and upwards. His closet was also well organized. The smell of the room was pleasing and soothing.

Instinctively, I began scrutinizing the album. In the family photo, Mesape's bright babyface, chubby jaws, and higher-quality suit, contrasted with the casual, unkempt looks of his siblings; he seemed like the most cherished child.

With head bent over, my right forefinger pointed him out. As if he was reading my mind, he began explaining that his mother cherished him so much because she had waited too long for his arrival. After the first child was born, his father traveled abroad for a few years. When he was finally born, all she did was spoil him.

Suddenly, the brightness of the room dimmed; the golden sunshine was disappearing on the horizon. I looked at my watch, but we were in the middle of the conversation. After a little while, I picked up my handbag.

Mesape accompanied me to the taxi stop. He opened the door of the cab and closed it. The driver took off; I turned back and looked. Our eyes met, he smiled and waved.

The ride was less than thirty minutes, with stops here and there, for other passengers. I stepped out of the taxicab and felt a little dizzy. I had not even taken any beer at all!

However, a sense of personal accomplishment filled my evening. Should I accept a close relationship with Mesape or not? I was not sure. Indecision was my dream at night, my food, and my drink the following day.

Should I accept another invitation? I wondered. But why not? Mesape was different from all others. After all, how many guys deliver mail all year long, without pay? And what a fine gentleman! So, I concluded that if he wasn't going to be my Mr. Right, then he must be Mr. Best.

He quickly followed up with two visits during my absence. My legs trembled as my heart tried to digest his words. Hot and cold sweat beat my forehead at the same time. Rising and falling emotions left me dazed most of the time. It was like lying on a surgeon's table and wondering, even then, if that was the right move or not.

We soon met during the eve of our two-week break. I was nervous, even in the company of my roommate. I couldn't believe my shyness.

Mesape held my hands and looked into my eyes. All I could do was smile and blink.

CHAPTER 8

Confiding in Mother

It was a summer vacation filled with unsettling thoughts. Contrary feelings rivaled for domination of my heart the entire time. I kept to myself, struggling to deal with the haunting questions: should I pursue the expected date or not? Should I tell my mother or not?

Not yet, I decided. There was nothing essential to announce, or so I reasoned. Why bother Mother about someone who was not even a prospective suitor? Mesape was just an ordinary campus date.

However, by the end of the week, I was dying to spill out all the pent-up emotions. Missing Mesape was beginning to seem like I was falling ill, where there was no doctor. From behind the banana tree, where I was sneaking to console myself in silence, I looked up in the sky. Was there any solace in the surrounding atmosphere? I asked myself. The gentle wind, chirping birds, and the rumbling of the river near our farm were all present. The expansive countryside with undulating green hills merging into the horizon filled my sight. It was a heaven-made background for the crisp afternoon sun.

Despite the enchanting surrounding, the need to let out the burning feelings was pressing. I felt compelled to talk to Mama. Yet, I had second thoughts. She was going to be very disappointed. Mesape's parents lived some hundreds of miles away, which was a whole day of traveling, and too costly a trip for her to make just to get to meet them. Besides, neither Mesape nor his family members could speak my mother's language. What a deprivation for a woman who relished heart-to-heart conversations with her family and relatives.

I knew better than anyone else that Mother always longed for in-laws "to increase her family." She wished for new brothers and sisters, having

My parents

lost her older brother about a decade ago. Her younger half-brother lived in far-off Douala. He was not that attached to her, though she pined for him daily. Besides, neither Mesape nor I were anywhere close to starting a family. I couldn't suggest to Mom either that I was on the verge of dating, desiring to sleep with a man out of wedlock. How could I ever explain myself to her? My mind and heart split between two opposing worlds. Family expectations and the immoral state of affairs on campus were strange bedfellows. Mama was a total stranger to my university world. Period.

Nevertheless, the high probability of marrying a foreigner someday still plagued me. I wanted a tête-à-tête with her. I needed to begin applying for her carte blanche. Who knows?

"Ouhouwouh," I called out tenderly. "What if, one day, I get married to a white man?" I asked.

I had to keep the stakes high; if Mama would accept a white man, she would be willing to embrace Mesape.

I hoped that the sonorous appellation of endearment, which I had used, would calm her down, thereby diminishing the scandal occasioned by my proposal.

"Will you give me your blessings?" I pressed further.

She instantly stopped the tilling process, now sure that I was for real. Then she dropped her handheld hoe—or it fell out of her hands.

Shock? Dismay? Disappointment? She began looking at me, straight into my eyes.

"Is this what you are planning to do, my daughter?" she said as she took in a deep breath.

Mama had a very effective way of wearing her worries on her face. I could tell from her light complexion that she was blushing.

"Mama, please, don't get so worked up over nothing. I'm just inquiring. Isn't it okay?" I asked, a little impatient.

"Well, if you want my direct answer, it is no," she said, tightening her lips firmly.

I laughed loudly with a high-pitch. The sound scared the birds; they flapped their wings and flew away. Mama looked up and back at me. The white of her eyes was turning slightly pink.

"Can you tell me why you won't let me marry a white man?" I probed with a frown.

"Don't you want to have children of your own?" she asked, looking at me while shaking her head and sighing.

> "Can you tell me why you won't let me marry a white man?"

"Why not?" I asked.

"Because a lot of white couples don't have children," she insisted with a rising voice.

"And even when they do, it is usually an only child, miserable like an orphan," she insisted.

Then she dropped her hoe again and supported her waist with both hands.

"That's not true, Mama. But even so, what's wrong with one child?" I teased.

"Akongshee," she called out loud as if she was waking me from slumber.

"My daughter, do you believe God is selfish enough to put only one child in a woman's womb?" she asked, picking every word. "Some women roast their wombs, you know," she nodded. "You have left me speechless." Then she proceeded to clap her hands. The moist, dark, brown soil fell off in lumps.

The growing concern in her voice was evident. She stared at me as if she was about to lose the child she had always cherished as the perfect clone of her mother of blessed memory.

"But Mama, some white couples have a lot of children,"

I insisted while staring into her face. "Indeed, we read about this couple in my American Literature class who had sixteen children," I added.

She opened her eyes and mouth wide for a while.

"You mean this is real, my daughter?"

I nodded in approval.

It was the best family news she ever heard. Mama would bow to any woman who has more than her nine children.

"Yes, sixteen is wonderful. But why do you want to go so far away from us?"

"Do you remember the plane that flew above us this morning?"

"Yes," she nodded.

"It takes the same time to arrive from America like a bus from Bamenda to Yaounde," I explained.

Her eyes began glowing with delight. But her grievance was not yet over.

"But when you live so far away, how often shall we spend time together?" she worried.

"As often as necessary, Mama," I tried to reassure her.

"My daughter, where will you have all that money to fly across the mighty waters of this world?"

"Well, Mom, I don't think I will marry a poor man. We will come here. Or you can visit us," I said.

"My daughter, what can I say?" she asked while lifting both hands and looking into the blue sky. "May God lead your steps and grant your desires." Mama's blessing was soothing; my eyes closed while I took a deep breath. Then I raised my hands and threw my head backward, letting the sun caress my face.

My limbs were ready to move, and I thought maybe I could drink some water ten ridges away to get them worked out. So, I walked briskly.

The surging feelings had extra room in which to rise and fall, with Mesape at the center of my thoughts. I knew then that I was going to be able to survive the protracted hours of fantasizing over the upcoming meeting between us.

CHAPTER 9

Primary Bliss

Finally, my vacation was over; it was the day of my return to university. I woke up from bed with my heart beating faster, and it kept up the pace until when I got to the bus station.

Thank goodness, I did not recognize any of the thirteen other passengers on the public transportation bus, embarking for the eight-hour ride. So, I gladly isolated myself to a corner, where my thoughts imprisoned me. A mental video of all the times with Mesape paraded through my mind, anxiety building up like a fire inside me at the anticipation of our meeting. Yet, I was gladly basking in it.

We were already at the rest stop—I hadn't realized, not until I heard the driver honking the car repeatedly, for passengers. My lunch remained wrapped up while the smell of food hit me. I turned the lunch pack around a few times again. At the same time, thoughts of him were consuming me. They soared way up into the clouds of unrestricted emotions. Nothing stood in the way of my longing for the one that had set my heart racing. I feared that my heart might explode. For four long hours, I kept turning over four pages of my novel, back and forth. None of the loud discussions piqued my interest. I was as good as dumb.

No passenger interfered either, to my joy. My eyes were dying to see the one who might as well become my perfect knight.

We got to Yaounde by 7 pm. I took a taxicab to my friend's house, where I spent the night. The university was still to re-assign our rooms.

Meanwhile, Mesape was on my mind as I went to bed. I got up longing to see him. My appetite was gone. Eating bread for breakfast was like chewing on logs of wood.

Finally, the early afternoon brought good tidings. Mesape succeeded in finding Tina's house. I bubbled with joy upon seeing him. We had the whole day to ourselves; it was like preparing for classes the next day from a mountain peak of exhilarating moments.

After greetings were over, I accompanied him to the off-license bar next door. We bought two beers and one orange and citron soda each.

The sun was burning hot outside though a big cypress tree sheltered Tina's house, extending its branches over the front part of her room. The three of us settled inside the room-parlor-kitchen apartment. Mesape took the study chair while Tina and I sat on her bed. Our conversation was lighthearted and desultory. We exchanged vacation anecdotes and discussed academics and campus life. We kept coming back on our predicament as anglophones, the English-speaking minority in a French-styled university. The less than five percent passes in both science and law faculties rendered our future bleak. We came from a background where passing was the norm, not the exception.

The culture shock was demeaning.

While we contemplated our common destiny, I was peeling some burning-hot *cocoyams*. Tina was pounding them in the mortar, anchored between her feet. That was our *achu* (traditional dish) dinner. An hour had gone by without our notice.

Mesape and I were closely watching Tina, who was exercising her expertise. She made sure that not a piece of cocoyam escaped the grinding of her pestle. She rubbed it against the bottom and edges of the mortar while pounding.

As for me, I finished my job. My fingers and palms were still pinkish from the heat. Tina continued pounding the crushed *cocoyams* from one end to the other. *Achu* experts know that the dish must be free of lumps, as smooth as butter.

Meanwhile, Mesape sipped his beer while steering the conversation. We laughed and concurred.

Tina lifted the pestle, and I scooped some *achu*. My fingers rubbed the warm paste, feeling for lumps. Indeed, not even one had escaped her pounding. I nodded. She picked up some more between the tip of her thumb and forefinger. She nodded, too. Yet, she took the smooth white mass on two more tours in the sturdy mortar. Mesape looked on and raised his hand to me. I gave him a high five.

Tina got up and searched for three plates. She scooped some *achu* into each one. Then she wrapped the excess into pre-heated plantain leaves.

It was time to compose the golden *achu* sauce. That was yet another test of expertise. As often demonstrated in a chemistry lab, the spices had to blend, to a smooth consistency, with the palm oil and *kangwa*. Mesape's first-ever *achu* meal had to be a real hit.

Achu is one of the staples of the grass field people, from where Tina and I hailed.

What was already second nature to us, turned Mesape into a child. His primary task was to bore the central hole with evenness all around it. He picked up his filled white plate and started rubbing the paste with a spoon, like smearing paint evenly on a surface. A mass got stuck onto the spoon. He stopped and watched Tina. Then he tried to turn it around in one circle to smooth out the edges. His hand was too stiff for the maneuver, which defines the technique as well as the art of eating. When the second attempt failed, he stopped, looked at me, and pleaded with his eyes.

I smiled and stretched out my hand. Quickly, I rubbed Mesape's share of the paste around the center of the sky-blue plate with the wooden spoon and bore an even hole in the middle. Then Tina poured the golden-colored sauce in the center along with pieces of meat and *garden eggs* (eggplant). Next, she took the pot of stewed *ndjamandjama* (hockle berry leaves) and mushroom and arranged some around the circular mound.

A well-arranged *achu* looks like a soccer stadium, the inner for the soup and meat, and the outer space for accompaniments. Like playing soccer, experts eat around the circle, keeping it even with each scoop until it thins away, and the soup flows towards the edges of the plate. It comes with longterm practice. Ever since I learned the art as a child, the technique has never changed.

Mesape watched the demonstration. My curved forefinger neatly picked up a piece of the pounded *cocoyams* by rubbing the tip along the thick circle. Dipping into the sauce turned the white puree into golden yellow instantly. Quickly, my finger raced into my mouth, where my tongue and lips gripped my forefinger. Finally, I smacked my lips, a farewell kiss. Hurray, *achu* made its way down the stomach.

Mesape opened his eyes in amazement. My finger swirled around for inspection.

"*Tchueiy!*" he exclaimed.

All three of us laughed heartily.

It was Mesape's turn. He dipped his forefinger into the golden sauce and took it out. However, his finger got stuck into his mouth. Tina smiled and nodded.

Over to Tina. She stretched her finger around her circular mound of *achu*. We all joined in the game and began playing together.

"Pick up your meat and vegetables as you eat," Tina advised Mesape.

In other words, he needed to alternate the scoops with the accompaniments.

The speed of eating increased; one scoop followed another non-stop. Midway, Tina and I struggled to look away from his direction. Mesape soon caught our conspiring eyes and burst out laughing just when the two of us were choking with laughter.

"You are doing a good job," Tina said as she nodded to Mesape.

"For a first attempt, I give you seven out of ten," I added.

From time to time, I kept a discreet and naughty watch on him from the corner of my eye. It was easy to detect his major hurdle. His plate kept spinning around in sudden circles as he struggled to even out the rough edges of the circular mass. Also, he licked his fingers several times instead of just once per scoop. Also, Mesape had a chunk in his plate while we had eaten ours already.

Tina poured more sauce into our empty plates. We kept dipping, finger after finger, to give Mesape enough time to finish.

"You guys are experts," he said, wiping the sweat from his nose with his left hand.

"To us, this is child's play," Tina explained while pulling her handkerchief from her pocket.

Her face was sweating. Like most people, she enjoyed her *achu,* especially with hot pepper.

"What will you do if you come to the village?" I took over. "*Achu* is served with *egusi* pudding (pumpkin seed pudding), steamed *atisong* (like asparagus), and roasted *ngoorh* (variety of termites), especially during a *born-house* (birth celebration) taking place during the harvesting season," I explained.

Tina quickly rushed her hand to her mouth and licked the sauce escaping between her fingers. Her stretched out tongue made a loud *todd*!

"*Mamamiee!*" Mesape exclaimed.

Our fun day was over. At 6 pm, I set out to accompany Mesape to the nearest taxi stop in the Obili neighborhood. We walked the one hundred meter distance, taking short steps and stopping from time to time. My heart was beating faster, which surprised me. Mesape took my hand in his, and a warm current flowed to mine.

"Akong, I've waited for a long while for this opportunity," he began speaking rather formally. "I almost thought you didn't like me," he went on.

We stopped on the spot without warning. Then he paused and began looking at me, right into my eyes. Soon, he started scanning me, from my hair to my face, as if trying to discover me anew.

My only response was giggling.

"Now I feel like the luckiest man on earth," he said, still staring right into my face.

Our eyes met and spoke. We both smiled at the same time.

"Akong, there's something exceptional about you," he went on.

"Really?" I asked.

Then I looked up into the sky and rolled my eyes, wondering what that might be.

"Oh, yes," he emphasized.

> *"Akong, I've waited for a long while for this opportunity," he began speaking rather formally. "I almost thought you didn't like me."*

Then he rubbed my hands a little while I remained silent like a contented baby.

"I felt so close to you when I saw your portrait last month at the *Fac*," he said, his eyes penetrating mine. "Indeed, I almost seized it from the photographer," he continued.

"I know that photo," I confirmed.

"Yes, it is fabulous," he went on. "You are a pretty woman," he said.

"Thank you," I smiled and began smashing the grass underneath my shoes.

"You needed to see how that photo was going from hand to hand. Students were just staring at it, my!" he exclaimed.

He stopped and shook his head from side to side several times, enchanted by the mesmerizing aura of our face-to-face meeting.

"When I saw that photo, something in me said you'd be mine someday," he added.

I listened intently, cherishing every word. Time and space should have been arrested just for the two of us. However, the sun began setting.

Besides, he had to go. He squeezed my hands into his, looked into my eyes, and moved his lips. I looked back and breathed deeply, in and out.

He crossed the road to enter the waiting taxicab. My eyes followed him until he closed the door and waved goodbye. His smile enveloped me in a feeling of warmth and tenderness.

CHAPTER 10

Friendly Advice or Envy?

Mixed feelings clustered in my mind as I walked back to Tina's house. I was missing Mesape already, though one question was nagging me. Was a glamor boy like him, accustomed to ostentatious girls, a good match for me? A little tear played around my eyelid, and yet, I was smiling.

Nevertheless, Mesape was fast becoming both my cherished subject of discussion and object of constant high regard, even while absent. My brewing thoughts were interrupted as soon as I got back with my hostess. She was looking rather indifferent and then frowning. Suddenly, she turned her back to me.

Adverse reaction or new development? What had happened? I wondered. What could be juicier than Cupid's arrow flying towards me? I, one of the few in class without a boyfriend, falling in love? Wasn't this her opportunity to broadcast it? Yet, she wasn't budging.

"Is that the type of man you want to marry?" she bellowed out.

For a while, I was not sure that she was talking to me. But her inquiring look convinced me.

"What's wrong with him?" I asked.

I was more defensive than curious.

She raised her head and dropped it like a monitor lizard. "Well, do you really want to know?" she asked sternly.

"What's the matter?" I asked again.

A little anxiety was building up inside me. Was there something rather terrible about Mesape, which I didn't know? Already I felt like I had a stake in everything that concerned him.

"Can't you see he is nowhere close to marriage? Can't you see?" Tina sounded like my grandmother.

I felt goose pimples invading my naked arms.

"But he's just a friend. Did I tell you I was going to get married now?" I said with a hard frown.

"Well, I see. Some of you like boys who just fool around," she said, rather curtly.

I was hurt, shocked, and embarrassed at the same time. I wanted to shout, time out, no more chapters about Mesape! Instead, I started thinking everything over to myself. I knew Tina was more experienced than I. Indeed, she had fooled around and almost lost her opportunity to pursue her education.

She was juggling the obligations of school and raising her one-year-old son. I often observed her and wondered whether she had a secret supply of energy. For two years, she walked some two miles a day, to and from the faculty, while it took me barely five minutes from my room. She was one of those students who stepped into class each morning, panting and sweating.

Nevertheless, her question was unsettling. My mind was still grappling for answers. Instead, more questions were coming up. Was she that concerned? Or was she jealous? I wondered. After all, Mesape was every woman's dream man. Even other guys held him in high regard. So what was so wrong?

"I mean, do you want someone from the coastal area?" she interrupted my thoughts.

"What's wrong with that?" I asked in anger.

Why put so much energy into attempting to discourage me? What prompted her to try to steal my joy? The more I tried to reason with her mentally, the more the facts and reality of her world became evident to me.

Tina was a typical young woman of Akum village. My mother grew up there. The people, young and old, were simply obsessed with their hometown. They would marry only someone of their tribe. Sons and daughters living in the cities or abroad routinely returned to the hamlet for all their weddings. Better an ugly or average fellow villager than a prince or princess from abroad.

Incidentally, the village, mushrooming with mansions, here and there, was fondly called Small London.

Even though I understood Tina's position, I did not admire her dutiful waiting on her fiancé, either. Asongwe was just a student like us, and one with a poor academic record. He was one of those student mentors, unfortunately, on the verge of *burning his mandat (exclusion upon failure)* in the faculty of laws. If he failed the promotion exam for the second time, that was it for him. However, he had used his rich experience to write and pass the competitive examination into the highly reputed professional School of Magistracy and Administration. That gave him a financial edge over Tina and myself. He was earning about four times our stipend. With one foot in the faculty and another in professional school, his career balance was stable and sure.

While Tina considered herself lucky to have a viable fiancé, I pitied her for glaring sycophancy. She reminded me of those fawning women who were more eager to grab a fiancé than earn their degree.

Her opinion about Mesape was ruining my evening. The thought of spending another night in her apartment stirred up mental anguish in me. A cold wave numbed my legs. I regretted not having a choice.

Finally, I put out the lights and climbed into bed, arms wrapped around me. My body was like a deflated football abandoned in a muddy playfield, on a cold rainy night. My mind kept stirring her interjections, to the point of exploding.

Yet, how could I disagree when she was voicing a widespread concern? Who hadn't heard statements like "I can't allow my child to marry a coastal person." Or, "what will I do with *Nyongo?*" The dreaded society, whose members sacrifice humans for financial gain, was terrifying.

Meanwhile, coastal people dismissed grass fielders by calling them "Graffy" for primitive—a tongue-twisting, derogatory appellation for the grass field. The fact is that decades ago, colonial masters made their initial entry into the coastal region through the Atlantic ocean, long before modern lifestyles penetrated the hinterlands of the grassland.

Grass field people responded by mocking lazy parents of the coast who live in huts, yet encourage their daughters to dress like celebrities just to win wealthy suitors. Some desperate young women even spoke with the affected speech of *Been-tos* (those who have traveled abroad, especially to the west).

Despite the ongoing social, verbal war, inter-provincial marriages prevailed, though grass field diehards vowed to stop their sons from seeking coastal women.

As much as they tried, coastal women were considered gourmet cooks. Indeed, a popular joke ran thus: if a visiting grass field guy tasted a dish of *eru* or *ekwang*, he would forget the way back to his birthplace.

Grass fielders retorted that coastal women were resorting to the use of charms.

Those thoughts cluttered my mind for hours. The pain of her rejection was choking me. I twitched about and turned around in bed, for more space to breathe free, longing for someone more sympathetic.

Thank goodness it was morning and Monday. My shower was over in minutes. Before noon, I had moved into my room at *École Normale*.

My roommate, Beri, and I began exchanging vacation stories while unpacking our bags. Most of all, we talked about Mesape.

Beri was resourceful, especially since she and Mesape had been classmates in high school. She reassured me that he was a gentleman despite the steamy details of his talk-of-the-school affair with a former girlfriend, who was then pursuing her studies abroad and betrothed to someone there.

Incidentally, Mesape came calling later in the evening. We were all excited. Laughter charged our light-hearted conversation.

It was time for Mesape to leave. I accompanied him to the taxi stop by the main gate of the school. Darkness was enveloping the daylight, and pushing away the escaping sun into think clouds on the horizon. We strolled side by side in the quiet atmosphere, opened like a blank page, waiting for us to transcribe our wishes. Suddenly, we stopped spontaneously, to witness the passage of our solo, dim past, ushering in shimmering stars casting their light into the shadows of our uncharted presence and future.

The sound of silence took over. We started staring into each other's eyes. A captivating presence, like a large coat, seemed to close in on us.

"Akong, I feel like the happiest man on earth," he whispered while breathing deeply.

"Oh yeah?" I said, giggling with a smile.

"I'm lucky to be standing this close to you," he went on.

I looked into the road and was distracted by the light of an oncoming car.

"I love you, Akong," he spoke softly.

"I love you, too," I responded with a shaking voice.

There was a little silence again, providing space for his longing heartbeat to harmonize with mine. He clutched my hands into his and moved his face towards mine. I closed my eyes and paused. His lips were warm.

We waited for a short while as if granting our hearts space and time to cheer each other. Mesape held onto my hands and massaged them while

I mellowed into the moment. He tilted his head forward and began rubbing his forehead onto mine, softly like cotton. We paused in sync with the englobing stillness. Mesape pressed my hands into his again and whispered goodnight.

I stood there, somewhat immobile. My eyes followed Mesape's disappearing silhouette as he crossed the dimly-lit street, opened the taxicab door, shut it, and shouted, "Bye-bye."

Quick steps led me back to my room. That night, I remained steeped in my thoughts. For the first time in my long fight against dating, I realized that I was more willing to proceed than to back out. I could not explain. Was I experimenting, or had Mesape's gallantry bewitched me? Whatever the case, I wanted to give our budding romance a chance.

It was time, indeed, for Vela and company to sign me up as their most recent club member. I imagined them laughing and giving me a high five, yet, wondering why it took me five long years to join. I couldn't help smiling.

The following morning, it dawned on me that I was at the very doorstep of the vicious cycle of rising and falling emotions. Unsettling anxiety was lurking in the corner of my mind.

Our very first kiss, the night before, permeated every activity, like breathing itself.

For better, for worse, I turned to Beri for counsel. Her emotional support was timely.

CHAPTER 11

The Nobility of Love

Beri's boyfriend visited us in our room for the first time. Gradually, the four of us started going out and doing stuff together. Everything seemed to work out pretty okay.

Later, during National Youth Day, a holiday, we invited our boyfriends over to our room for lunch. Our main dish was *eru* and *fufu*, a famous Bayangui (name of a tribe) dish. It was a buffet given that we had the whole afternoon to ourselves. After meals, we spent the rest of the evening savoring drinks offered by Mesape.

Approaching darkness soon announced parting time. Mesape and Alemji showered us with appreciating hugs. We accompanied them to the taxi stop.

On our way back, Beri and I decided to stroll around the campus. The light evening breeze was refreshing. We walked by the green lawn and pausing by the hibiscus and rose flowers for half an hour.

Then we rushed back to our room. Homework was beckoning. As soon as the door clicked behind us, we headed for our separate spaces.

Suddenly, Beri came over to my side, frowning. What was the matter? Was it the smell of the *eru* and beer flavor that was leaving a bitter aftertaste in her mouth? I wondered.

None of the above. Instead, Beri began complaining that her boyfriend was stingy. I imagined that it was just a fleeting observation, but when she sat down and grimaced while stressing it, I realized that she was hurting. She went as far as threatening to break up with him. "Just how could Alemji walk in here empty-handed?" Beri wondered aloud to me.

"But we never asked them to bring anything. So why blame Alemji?" I asked.

"It's unfair, a disgrace, and a mark of selfishness," she insisted, turning her head from side to side.

"Beri, but this is just an isolated occurrence."

"Oh yeah? Even then, how can a student party at another student's without contributing an iota?" she asked with emphasis. Then she paused and stared at me.

"And he says he's my boyfriend?" she wondered and sighed.

"Oh well, I'm sure he will do better in the future," I said.

"*Ashia* (too bad) for him. There will be no next time. I've had enough of this," she said while raising her voice.

"But he's such a cute guy," I said with a smile.

"Akong, you know looks don't say all," she answered rather calmly.

Beri spent the rest of the evening comparing Mesape and Alemji. I listened, most of the time, but added that I couldn't conclude that Mesape was any better. She quickly retorted, announcing that I was in for a treat.

Indeed, my treat did come, almost on the heels of her prediction, two days after. Mesape and I had not seen each other the whole day. I was not particularly worried. So, I went to bed that night, hoping all was well with him.

"Akong, wake up. Akong, wake up," Beri called.

I was dreaming when I heard Beri calling and shaking my arm repeatedly.

I tried to open my eyes, but the overhead light was too bright. My right palm rushed for my eyes while I shivered with fear. What was the matter? I looked at her enquiringly. Instead of speaking, she did a little demonstration. As if acting on stage, she paraded from one end of the room to another, while clapping and calling Mesape's name.

"What's going on?" I pleaded.

"Akong, don't tell me you have a real Romeo for a boyfriend," she said, staring at me in wonder.

"What made you say that?" I asked.

She just kept staring at me, wearing all of her amazement on her face.

Then she sat on my bed and recounted the story. Mesape had come visiting, close to midnight. Beri ushered him in. Then she returned to her side, climbed into her bed, and immersed herself in a novel.

When she didn't hear a sound or movement for a good while, she began wondering if something was amiss. Since she couldn't see beyond the wooden twin shelf separating our beds, she dared to tiptoe to observe for herself. There was Mesape, bending over and staring into my closed eyes. She quickly escaped to her side, without a word. She waited for about ten more minutes, all ears. There was nothing to hear until when Mesape tiptoed towards her section and whispered goodnight.

Beri paused and picked up the red rose flower which Mesape had left at my bedside and stared at it. Then she began singing Mesape's praises, highlighting his classic romance story. Indeed, we talked some more about it the following morning at breakfast and on our way to class. It was like a sweet melody which she was singing, over and over again.

As soon as we returned from class, she came over to my side and sniffed the rose again. I seized the opportunity to spice up our best-seller event, having met Mesape on campus that morning.

> *Beri paused and picked up the red rose flower which Mesape had left at my bedside.*

"Mesape told me that he had come purposely 'to tuck his baby into bed.' That's why he did not wake me up," I explained.

"Akongshee, that guy's love is genuine. He is one in a thousand, a knight."

Beri's gaze went beyond me to horizons that could only be captured by her imagination. She rolled her eyeballs from the wall to the ceiling.

I stood there, playing the silent companion, while she got lost in her thoughts. As far as I was concerned, Beri was turning Mesape into a hero too soon; he had not yet proven his mettle. We had numerous topics on class discussions to dwell on. Besides, I didn't want her to aggravate the situation with her boyfriend further.

Before I proposed a break, she stepped forward and pulled my study chair and sat down.

"Akong," she said, looking grave. "The truth is, Alemji can't do anything like that," she went on, sighing.

I was weary already with the drawn-out story. Yet, Beri was still holding onto it.

"Well, even if he doesn't," I said, shrugging, "I don't think that makes him any less worthy than Mesape."

"You mean that *villageois* (primitive person)? He's cold and distant." She parted her lips as she spoke and began pacing back and forth.

"But why don't you give him a second chance?" I suggested. "I'm sure he's still trying to look for ways to please you."

"Oh, I don't think he will ever get it," she said, shaking her head. "Most of the time when I visit him," she said while bending her head, "I leave more upset than before I arrived."

Beri stopped talking; she was thinking deeply.

"I hope you know that you are a timid person. That could inhibit him," I dared to propose while looking away from her.

"But is he not the man? I don't see you do anything special, and yet Mesape is just doing whatever he can to capture your heart."

She stood still and fixed on me for a while. "Do you ask Mesape for specific favors?" It sounded like she was crosschecking me.

I kept silent.

"Alemji is such a handsome guy," I said, regrettably.

"Who cares if he is fairer than a star? Some cold, ignorant, primitive thing!" she quickly retorted. Then her tongue gave a "touc!" sound in utter rejection.

I was losing the argument. Beri stood up and swung her right hand, from left to right, like lightening slashing a frail branch. "It's over," she announced.

The pulse of her renewed conviction cracked her voice. Her face looked grave and bitter; she tightened her lips. Then without a word, she stood up and walked away in quick steps.

After a moment of silence, she began soliloquizing, complaining about the timorous nature of a significant number of boys, who dared not express any affection towards their girlfriends in public. Her voice was rising higher in torrents of regrets and grievances. I listened without further comment.

The following day brought another pleasant surprise and propelled Mesape to the podium. It was a warm Wednesday morning. I was chatting with fellow students while we waited in the hallway to enter the class for the first lecture of the day. A francophone student walked up towards us. He had a package in his hand. The crowd of English majors lifted their eyebrows, wondering for whom the francophone was searching.

To my greatest surprise, he called my name and placed the package in my hand. It was a carefully sealed flowery wrapped parcel. Before I had even looked up to say thank you, the guy was already wiggling his way through the crowd.

So, I went to work immediately. Quickly, I handed my file to the guy next to me. Then I opened the package. My hands were trembling.

Meanwhile, a student behind me was raising his heels to peep.

A note fell out of the outer layer of the wrapping paper; It was Mesape's handwriting. I stepped to the corner, facing the wall.

"*Akong, please accept this from me. I know your break today is too short to rush to your room and back. Have a nice day! Love and Bon Appetit! Mesape.*"

There and then I opened the snack dish. The smell of freshly made omelet and fried plantains hit my nose, including orange, two slices of bread, and candy. I closed my lunch with a hearty smile.

When I lifted my head, several pairs of eyes were staring at me with renewed interest. Others took a deep breath and clicked their fingers together. "Some of us are not in this world," said Steve, who was standing next to me.

I just burst out laughing.

Despite the "out-of-this-world" occurrences happening between us, Mesape and I soon had our first argument. I invited him to my relatives, living at the other end of the city. He was willing to go.

However, we disagreed over the means of transportation. Mesape would not take the public transport bus, *Sotuc*; he had never ridden on it before. Of course, I understood why. They were often overcrowded and sometimes dirty.

Finally, we came to a compromise. We waited for two more hours for the off-peak period.

Welcome to the bittersweet taste of relationships. Mesape stepped into the bus like a recruit into a war zone. I fell back in my seat and scrutinized his changing face, struggling to adjust to the reality of hard times. Growing up in the village, I used to walk an average of one mile per day, going to the farm, and running other errands. During those moments, the determination and acquiescing spirit of my struggling parents always motivated me.

"Those who aim at the top of the mountain must brace themselves for the sudden shocks of environmental hazards," I thought to myself.

CHAPTER 12

Lovey-dovey Rebuff

The golden, setting sun was piercing through Mesape's pastel drapes; his face glowed in the reflection. Our heads were bending over the stool between us. The warm *sawyer* (steak) and *dodo* (fried ripe plantains) kept saliva flowing.

Suddenly, there was a knock on the door. We exchanged glances. Mesape picked up a napkin and rushed towards the door. Instead of letting the person in, he stood at the door that was ajar. After a few minutes of exchanges, he exited, pulling the door behind him gently until it clicked.

I had no idea who it was; maybe it was his next-door neighbor or a friend, I thought. It did not matter to me. I kept nibbling at the mouth-watering *sawyer* stick, wishing he would return quickly.

Ten minutes, real or imaginary, were gone. The hot pepper sprinkled over the tiny pieces of beef on a stick, was burning my jaws. I couldn't wait to go on eating.

He opened the door and slammed it behind him. Then he sighed and shook his head in disapproval.

"What's going on?"

"Don't worry about it. It's one of those girls."

"Which girl?"

"Eposi," he said.

"Oh, yeah?"

"Can you imagine her coming to ask me to accompany her to the movies?"

"Really?" I asked, my voice pitching higher.

He picked up his *sawyer*, bit into the small piece, then into the larger one. His jaws bulged from left to right, more from anger than from the spicy hot pepper or the piquant flavor of onion.

"So, when are you going?"

"Me? When did that start? A woman dresses in a lavish evening gown and comes to my door as if we had an appointment?"

"You mean she's jamming into your schedule just like that?"

"You don't know them," he said, frowning and shaking his head again.

"I don't get it. Why would a girl do that?" I pressed on while putting my quarter-finished stick on the plate.

He went into his closet and brought out a bottle of Martini. He opened it and poured some of it into my glass of orange soda, and then served himself. I grabbed my drink and took a long sip. My lips smacked.

"Poor girl. What do you want her to do? You are the reigning guy, right?" I teased him.

"Oh yeah? Let them leave me alone," he said, frowning. "You know what I did?" he asked.

I stared at him while shaking my head. He tried to drill the tip of his forefinger into his head. The typical dramatic way of saying, "Are you crazy?"

"I told her I wasn't interested. But since she kept insisting," Mesape explained. "I asked if she knew who was in my room."

Beri and I soon realized that our friendship was a bulwark against the multiple shocks we were experiencing.

"You said that?"

"Of course, I know she is enraged, but she asked for it," he said with widened eyes as his head moved forward.

I picked up the next stick from the plate and twisted it around.

Eposi and Mesape were classmates in high school. She was one of the *Batiment G* gang working overnight to snatch him from me.

Beri only heard about the nabbing attempt after we visited the main campus over the weekend. Eposi and two other girls met us in the corridor of *Batiment G*. We stopped. All three of them turned their backs to me in antipathy. The girl, who was wearing red trousers, turned around and scanned me, from head to toe, with a twisted face, contorted lips, and awkwardly-opened eyes at a forty-five-degree angle. I had to walk away quickly.

"My dear Akong, what did you do to those women?" Beri asked after she joined me later.

"I didn't do anything wrong."

"Then why were they behaving like that?"

"Antagonism contorts the body." I went ahead and related the story of Eposi's foiled "gate-crashing" into Mesape's space.

Beri made some disclosures about the girls, two of whom were her former high school mates; they were reassuring. Besides, at that particular moment, her presence served as a buffer against sudden assaults from women with uncouth behavior.

Beri and I soon realized that our friendship was a bulwark against the multiple shocks we were experiencing.

CHAPTER 13

Misfortune Stings Love

It promised to be an exceptional vacation. I was going to get a chance to meet Mesape's parents, for the first time, at their family home, in Victoria. I was anxious. The excitement of being in love now demanded the mastering of recurring spasms of fear.

Gladly, I took some comfort in the fact that I grew up in Victoria, having completed the last three years of elementary school there. Though my elder sister had moved to Douala, it still seemed like returning home.

Finally, I alighted from the taxicab between the Newtown market and the Atlantic Ocean that Saturday, late in the morning. I had barely walked a few meters and stopped a lady to ask for directions to Mesape's family house.

Meanwhile, Mesape, who had been waiting nearby, spotted me in my pink suit. He ran to me and hugged me. Then, his right hand caught mine in his moist, shivering palm. He held onto me until we got home.

His mother and two sisters were sitting in the yard with an elderly neighbor. The latter couldn't hold her peace. She shouted out loud upon seeing us, arriving hand in hand. A handful of neighbors came out of their homes and stole glances. Others peeped through their windows to behold Mesape's woman, the one who had become his "dream come true."

The glow on Mesape was awesome to behold. He guided me, and we went into the living room, where I met his father. The brown skinned, tall man, stood up and smiled broadly. Mesape's family seemed very easy going; they were warm and welcoming. Within minutes, I felt at home.

He served me a drink and brought along a family album. He pointed to members of his family, which was just as big as mine—nine children. His older brother was away at university abroad.

His mother, a plump woman with fair skin and an inviting smile, invited us to the kitchen to get some lunch. The main dish was fresh fried fish, tomato stew, and steamed plantains.

When we sat at the veranda chatting and enjoying the gentle sea breeze, an older woman, supporting her weight on her walking stick, wobbled towards us from the third house away.

"Is this the young lady?" she asked. She stretched out her right hand to me while staring at me with fascination in her eyes. "Ever since he arrived on vacation, all that he's been talking about is you."

On Sunday afternoon, Mesape took me out for a mini-tour of his area of town, the places I never had the opportunity to visit during my childhood days. We also stopped over at the home of two of his friends during our long promenade.

On our way back, almost as an afterthought, he decided to call on another friend. It was Ebenye, who was living with her parents in the neighborhood of the Victoria General Hospital.

> *"Ever since he arrived on vacation, all that he's been talking about is you."*

We sat at the veranda of the hilly abode and shared some sodas while enjoying the sea breeze caressing our faces. There was nothing exceptional about our conversation. We just looked through photo albums, amidst a light chatter on the goings-on in the town.

In less than an hour, we emptied our glasses, and Mesape signaled to me. I picked up my bag; he announced our departure. We stood up and bid Ebenye farewell.

I followed him down the stairs. He held my hand as we crossed the street to wait for a taxicab. On our way home, Mesape explained that Ebenye's parents were friends of his parents while the young woman, whom I was formally meeting for the first time, used to be his classmate in high school. What provocation to take me to the family home of a woman who had gone out of her way to demonstrate her interest in him! I thought to myself. Or was it a man's way of making a public statement loud and clear?

I returned to Douala on Monday to finish the rest of my vacation at my sister's. Looking back, I felt a sense of satisfaction, spurring me on, as far as our friendship was concerned. I was grateful for the excellent time spent at Mesape's, though I was missing him by the minute.

Finally, I packed my bags and left Douala. It was refreshing to return to Yaounde, having been tired and worn out with household chores.

On Saturday morning, I got up early to clean my room before Mesape arrived. Our shopping rendezvous was in an hour. I finished in time and got dressed.

It was time and past, yet he didn't show up. Anxiety began building up inside. What was taking him so long? I wondered. Mesape had never before been an hour late, without finding some way to let me know of his whereabouts. What was the problem? My mind examined every possible reason without leads.

My eyes glanced at my watch for the twentieth time. "Forget it," I mumbled to myself as I bent down and began taking off my shoes. Then my heart throbbed at a knock on the door. I rushed for the handle and swung open the door; the broad smile on Mesape's face relieved me. However, he was sighing at the same time. We hugged each other. My eyes searched his face for an explanation of the long delay.

"I'm sorry," he said. "Let's go," he pleaded.

He locked the door, and we hurried to the taxi stop, his hand clutching mine.

As soon as we took our seats, he started explaining. It was a long, unusual story about Ebenye, his high school classmate, who visited him that morning. He told me that she came without warning. According to Mesape, she was on a mission to rekindle the flames of what he referred to as their one-night stand in high school. I should have made it clear right then that I would not continue to put up with shouting matches between him and other women. Evidently, Mesape had won my heart and my trust, but I should have nipped external control in the bud.

He went on. Their interaction quickly turned into a fight because he refused to yield to her requests. So, she started yelling. He asked her to leave. She wouldn't hear of it. Ebenye threatened to stay put until he responded favorably.

When Mesape asked her to behave herself, she got into a rage.

"Do you want to say that Akong is better than me?" she asked, still yelling at him.

"No question about that," Mesape emphasized.

"That *Graffi* girl? What are you bluffing about?" Ebenye went on.

"*Graffi* or not, that is none of your business. And what's wrong in being born in the grassland, anyway?"

Ebenye just went on complaining like a buzzing bee.

"Please, get out of my room right now," Mesape ordered her out while showing her the door.

"I'm not leaving. You are trying to treat me as if we were not good friends. What did I do to you?" Ebenye was complaining and crying.

Mesape tried to pull her out, but she planted herself into the seat instead. She stretched her hands and clung onto the edge of the study. A fistfight immediately ensued. They struggled. She started screaming, yelling, and calling Mesape names.

Mesape tried to calm her down. No luck. So, he dashed out of his room, threatening to lock the door behind him. Ebenye remained unmoved. He insisted to no avail. He soon gave up and locked her inside. He stood out for a while. Soon, her yelling invaded the corridor. The noise started reaching neighboring rooms. So, he quickly opened the door. A panting Ebenye glowered at him disapprovingly and rushed out while lashing more insults at him. I thought Ebenye was pitiful. Yet, I felt secure both in Mesape's love for me and my high sense of self-esteem.

I listened and wondered why a woman would choose to risk her honor. What kind of a relationship would that be, anyway? Maybe persuasion could cause the milk of tender feelings to ooze out of a man's heart, though I had no clue how.

Nevertheless, a more pressing issue was at hand. It was the announcement of the end-of-year examination. The mere mention of it usually provoked within me palpitations and the loss of appetite. A whole week of recurring anxiety reduced students to prisoners, treading the campus with unsteady steps, as if afraid of stepping on land mines. That period also marked the reign of shabby outfits. Many students looked like village mourners.

Meanwhile, a committed group of students spent those dreaded days sipping bottle after bottle of beer at the nearby beer parlors or bars.

The publishing of results on the faculty bulletin board bore a note of finality. It was like a blasting gun shut, which sparked off the lamentation of village mourners.

Unfortunately, failures always outnumbered passes. It darkened the clouds over the campus like fumes from Dane guns, cloaking the sunshine.

A handful of students had an idea of what to expect. Without hints from professors, students could not predict the outcome with certainty. Surprises always abounded.

By 8 am on Thursday, students living far away from campus began rushing in from all directions and crowding around the notice boards. I left my room at 10 am and marched alongside my classmates. Most of the female population were either dressed in *kabbas* (long, loose traditional gown) or their three-piece *wrapper* (a three-yard piece of cloth wrapped around the waist). Both of the outfits were prominent in the village during a *crydie* (grieving session). They protected women, stopping them from exposing their bodies, in case they fell to the ground, and rolled themselves while weeping.

There was no standing space between the classrooms and offices. It was like the doorway into a tight prison cell. Some students were courageous enough to keep up a conversation while the majority maintained silence, as if in respect of the dead in a burial ground.

At 11:30, a door clicked open. All eyes moved to the right. A clerk from Professor Mbassi Manga's office came out with a white sheet of paper in his hand. Boom! My heartbeat lashed out.

The massive body of students swayed to one side, some stepping on others, to make way for him. He opened the glass-protected notice board. Then he turned around the paper. All eyes followed his hand movements. He pressed the edges with pins, turned the key, and waded his way back through the crowd.

There was no need for me to risk the twisting of my neck. A handful of us women stepped back. Exclamations met wailings, shouts, and jubilation. A few chanted a dirge while taking a freefall on the spot. Hefty guys picked up the weeping girls and moved them a few meters out of the way.

My heart was beating uncontrollably while my eyes began brimming with tears. The pushing increased as more students joined the crowds. Finally, I was standing behind a guy who seemed to have glued his face onto the board. My neck stretched out like a giraffe's. A mixed feeling of cold and warmth flushed over my veins. My name was on the list, far away from the red line. Three of us, standing next to each other, shouted out, "yeah, yeah, yeah" in a chorus, as our feet stamped the floor.

Then my eyes quickly moved to the far end of the board in search of Mesape's class list. One, two, three sweeps of my eyes, from the first to the last.

Alas, he didn't make it. My stomach started churning. A cold wave stabbed me, right into the depths of my soul.

I started fighting my way out of the crowds of students. A friend, who passed, caught my hand in the air and dragged me towards her in dancing steps. We moved away from the notice board and stood close by the rose flower beds. She was still hugging me and skipping. I was thankful, but tears crowded my eyes. She quickly understood.

We sat down on the grass lawn and searched all over for Mesape. Where was he? I decided to go to his room.

My feet plodded the narrow grassy footpath like massive logs of wet wood. A feeling of loneliness overtook me.

He opened the door; our eyes met, and I noticed that his natural glow was gone. Instead, he was wearing an apology on his face. His swollen eyes caused tears to well up in mine. I wanted to console him, but where were the words? My file just dropped on his bed. He walked towards me and threw his head on my shoulder.

"Akong, I've let you down," he cried.

We exchanged glances while tears rolled down his face. We both cried. For the first time in our relationship, we did not know what to do. It felt like we had lost someone close to us. I sat by him, lost for words, while he was trembling. Our bodies collapsed onto his bed. We just laid across it, our feet hanging down.

> *We exchanged glances while tears rolled down his face. We both cried. For the first time in our relationship, we did not know what to do.*

We remained silent for a long while. Then Mesape turned around, interrupting the silence, to congratulate me. I looked at him and did not respond.

When I returned to my room that evening, an overwhelming feeling of guilt permeated every thought. I felt responsible for Mesape failure, at least, to a certain extent. For days, the pain of our loss haunted me. My sleep was disturbed. My appetite was gone. Mesape's failure was a blow to our love. It was not normal for a woman to be in a relationship with a man of a lower class, whether academic, professional, or financial. Everyone was waiting for me to dump him.

Mesape visited me two days afterward. I suggested that we separate for a while. He needed to pick up the pieces of his life without my interference, I explained. Instead, his eyes pleaded. He pulled me to himself and just held on.

"Akong, this is all my fault. It has nothing to do with you," he tried to explain.

"You think so?"

Anxiety cut through my stomach when he announced that his older brother was due to arrive from abroad, on a short visit. My feet didn't touch Mesape's room for a whole week. I had no plans to go back there, and I didn't, not until his brother wrote and canceled his trip.

It was time to find ways to cope with Mesape's loss. My smile was returning.

However, a silent battle was developing around us. Some of my classmates asked if I was going to continue my friendship with Mesape. Their very looks convicted me. I began feeling indignant when the question persisted. I knew where they were coming from; I was offbeat. They were reminding me politely that it was not proper for a woman to date her academic junior.

More than at any other time in my campus life, it felt like I was either born in the wrong era or into a graceless culture. Shame on them, I thought to myself.

CHAPTER 14

The Love of Status

After the long vacation, Mesape and I maintained our love affair, as if nothing had happened. Beri was taken aback by my unrelenting pursuit of the relationship with Mesape. On Tuesday afternoon, she confronted me after she overheard my fight with a student. He had been openly teasing and mocking me, right in class.

"Akongshee, what do you intend to do, to continue with him?" asked Beri.

"What kind of question is that?" I retorted while frowning.

She turned away without a word but came right back.

"You are a very courageous woman," said Beri, tightening her lips. "I honestly cannot have anything to do with a student in a lower class. I don't care who he is," she emphasized her words, raised her right forefinger, and shook it from side to side.

"Beri, wasn't Mesape my friend, long before the publishing of examination results?" I asked, looking straight into her eyes.

"I know, but now the reality is not the same," Beri said with a grave look.

"Well, too bad," I responded.

I was about to turn my back away and carry on with my own business when she looked at me, anew, and paused.

"Akongshee, I can't do like you," she began. "But I truly admire your daring," she added, shaking her head.

Then she tightened her lips and looked away.

Gradually, the derogatory remarks indirectly aimed at Mesape reduced. Maybe my friends and classmates were adjusting to my stance already, or so I thought. I was wrong.

Mesape and I had the most humiliating attack in a face-to-face confrontation. He was my guest for our class graduation party. Ostensibly, nothing was out of order because each student was allowed to bring a friend or companion.

We arrived on time at our American professor's home in Cité Verte. Dr. Hegarty and his wife were kind enough to let us use their home. His living room and the veranda were big enough to accommodate thirty-something of us.

As soon as any student stepped through the door, for the first time, they exclaimed. His collection of dozens of wooden skulls, hanging on the beige walls of the living room, was weird. It became an instant topic of discussion.

Guests began taking their seats. Faces glowed with excitement, reflecting the variety of colors in the room. The mood for partying was very evident. The laughing, chatting, exclamations, and the clicking of fingers set the stage.

Close by the inner window was an inviting buffet supper, prepared mostly by female students. There were also cartons of a variety of beers and sodas.

We all knew the procedure. Eating and then dancing. There was no set time to quit. Nonetheless, we all agreed not to abuse our professor's kindness and leniency.

The chitchat was going on, here and there. We served ourselves and took the time to eat. The *ekwang*, *fufu*, *koki*, chicken, fish, *jollof rice*, and plantains were all a delight. Our host's American wife was also having a great time discovering some of the traditional dishes. We were thankful for that.

While some students were putting away the used plates, the rest quietly sipped their drinks while waiting to hit the floor. Mesape and I were sitting in two separate groups. I heard him respond to a guy and saw them click their fingers. I was happy for him. Almost immediately, Ndifor, who was sitting at the next table, ordered Mesape to shut up. Mesape turned around and began frowning enquiringly.

"What's wrong with you?" Mesape asked.

Ndifor moved towards Mesape and searched him all over with haunting, mean eyes.

"Can't you see everything is wrong with you?" Ndifor said, throwing his right hand forward as if inviting him for a fight after the manner of elementary school boys.

Mesape raised his eyebrows in amazement. Then Ndifor went on raving.

"To begin with," Ndifor said, opening his eyes and stretching out his neck, "these are not your classmates. You are not qualified to take part in this conversation," he said, moving his head like a monitor lizard.

"What's the matter, Ndifor?" I asked.

I couldn't take it any longer.

"Tell that your boyfriend to get out of here. Let him go look for women at his level," Ndifor yelled. He was standing up and pointing his forefinger at Mesape.

"You hold on, Ndifor, that's none of your business," I shouted, trembling with anger.

"*Ashia* for you. If you insist on keeping him, I'm sorry he can't rub shoulders with his seniors," Ndifor insisted.

He fell back into his seat and started canvassing for support around him. Fellow students looked more confused than willing to follow suit.

Finally, a neutral voice intervened. It was the oldest member of the class, Annie, whose bizarre outfit and affected voice had won her the nickname "Miss Havisham," as in Charles Dickens' *Great Expectations*. She stood up and challenged Ndifor.

"Just why don't you leave them alone, Ndifor?" she spoke up aloud.

Everyone turned around and listened.

"This gentleman has done nothing to you. I don't see why you should confront him as if it's a personal issue," she went on.

Everyone was quiet and listening to her.

"Behave yourself and let's have some peace here," Miss Havisham spoke with authority. She stood up, adjusting her glasses onto her nose and waiting for calm to return. Ndifor was still visibly upset; he was grumbling.

Miss Havisham raised her voice again when matters got worse. Ndifor and Mesape were now pointing fingers at one another. A fistfight was in the making. My efforts to calm down Ndifor were in vain. Miss Havisham moved and planted herself between the two men.

Mesape and I exchanged resigning looks with sighs. We realized that we were in the wrong place. So, we gathered our stuff to leave, resisting Miss Havisham's pleas to stay, though we were grateful for her intervention.

As we rode in the taxicab, I quietly considered the issue within myself. Ndifor was my tribe's man. Yet, his manner of showing how much he cared for me was unwarranted. I didn't expect anything close to that from him. After all, we only met in class and occasional tribe meetings. Why interfere in my business? I couldn't figure out why.

Finally, a tough academic year came to a successful end. I graduated as an English major, among the top third of the forty students in my class.

That same week, I moved to Douala to live with my sister. Where else to begin haunting for a job but the economic capital?

The change of atmosphere and the break from criticism was refreshing.

As for Mesape, he had a full year to go. His class was due to travel to France, to complete course work within the Bilingual Degree Program.

Four months after he left, I was still mailing in job applications. There was no response yet from the ministries and corporations.

Meanwhile, he kept writing. Each week I received mail from France. His romantic scripts kept me on an emotional high. We exchanged letters, postcards, and photos. He wrote to my sister, too. A bold move, I thought.

Suddenly, I began losing the fun of it all. My enthusiasm in our relationship was waning. I couldn't explain why. The more life became dull, the more our friendship seemed to be intruding. I needed a break, but my dilemma was how to tell him. The time did not seem right. Yet I didn't want to go on pretending.

My opportunity finally came. He was preparing to return home. So, he wrote and requested my shoe and dress size. My response was unfriendly. "Why are you so concerned about me when your brothers and sisters need everything you can afford?" I wrote back.

Mesape was shocked. He pleaded for forgiveness. He was ready to toe the line, he promised. Good and okay, I concurred.

Yet, I was in no mood for passion. Even the desire to write was gone. Two weeks slipped by without my response. It was the third week.

He wrote again, recounting how he had lost his appetite. He had sleepless nights. He was the most unhappy of his mates. He would fail his exams if I jilted him, even though his performance so far was among the best.

Those words brought tears to my eyes. Everything was looking gray and cold despite the burning heat in Douala. It just seemed as if the fire between us was gone. I certainly didn't want to feel responsible for his failure again. So, that same day, I sat up late in my room, way beyond midnight.

"I'm so sorry that my letter affected you so negatively. The last thing I would do is hurt you. I just don't want you to go out of your way for me. Please, don't let anything bother you, okay? I love you," I wrote.

I kept up with the regular correspondence for a couple more months, until he returned.

CHAPTER 15

Romance Magic Wanes

It was break time on a dull morning in March. Dozens of recruits were chatting in front of the Ministry of Information and Culture, in Yaounde.

Suddenly, I turned around and saw Mesape. How did he know I was there? I thought to myself as I looked around for clues. His smile was so broad that a vein formed on his glowing forehead. He forged his way through a group of friends in the circle and pulled me away.

Our meeting was slightly awkward. I met Mesape's overflowing excitement with a casual greeting. He pulled me to himself for a friendly hug, held my hands, moved my body from side to side, and placed his tender hands on my hair. I barely smiled back. I wanted to show some affection, but I was unable. I couldn't explain my lack of steam.

Within the first weeks of his return, a story began filling the gossip mill of my former faculty mates. They said that while in France, Mesape had an affair with one of his classmates, Lucy. That was not news to me. He had related the bits and pieces to me, explaining why and how he became directly involved with Lucy. According to him, he risked his safety to rescue her. It was close to midnight when she made distress calls at the students' residence. She got herself entangled in a misadventure involving a pimp, who happened to be her host. No student, except Mesape, offered to help. He took the midnight train across the city to rescue her.

A week after I first heard the story, Lucy herself visited me, with the express mission to dispel the rumors. The truth is, both of them were more eager to convince me than I wanted to hear the details, repeated to me, time and again. Yes, I believed in Mesape. He had, so far, proven to be a faithful friend. However, that was not the issue then. I just wanted to be free, to be left alone.

As far as I was concerned, our respective goals were going their separate ways. I was planning to eventually quit my job as a reporter for national radio to further my studies abroad.

Meanwhile, Mesape was still searching for a job. He was planning to settle down as soon as he got one. He had no plans for further education. He had never shown any interest in that direction. So, I didn't expect him to encourage me, though the prospects were high. At that time, my brother, Munga, was studying in the US.

So, I proposed a temporary separation. Mesape wouldn't hear of it. And that complicated the matter.

Therefore, while he was clinging onto me, I was instead seeking ways to limit my involvement with him. It was not easy to go our separate ways because we had more free time, compared to the university days. Mesape frequented my office at the Central Provincial Station in Yaounde. The radio house was about a ten-minute walk away from where he was living- in with one of his friends, Nguti. He could visit at his leisure, from Monday to Friday. The truth is, he had too much time on his hands.

Besides, he was having a hard time at Nguti's, having turned down his parent's invitation to return home until he landed a job. What holder of a bachelor's degree paraded the streets of a small town like Victoria, in search of a job?

There seemed to be no other way out other than for me to continue to stand by Mesape. And why shouldn't I? Mesape was a very kind and caring person. Not once did he ever visit me without a candy, a fruit, or a flower, even if he had to spend the last franc.

My understanding of the situation, notwithstanding, I still felt a need to draw the line between material backup and his emotional needs. I spent sleepless nights brainstorming.

Finally, I decided to stop visiting him, though he kept calling at my job. Besides, I started spending longer hours at the British council and the American Cultural Center, downtown, after work. Even then, I often returned home and found his notes, waiting for me. With time, I began ignoring them.

There was a strong need to be by myself alone. I needed to spread out the map of my life, so far, over every inch of my private space, stretching out every dim spot, for an all-round X-ray. I needed to pinpoint the disjointed places and tarry at those beckoning areas until I invented the method to stitch them back together. I needed to figure out where I had lost the thread, beginning at my tender years, when my mother used to counsel me at the farm or in the kitchen in Santa. And of course, do something about it! I wanted to start over with a clean slate, on higher ground.

By the third week, I was just about breathing free of the relationship when Nguti came calling. The unusual timing, on Saturday morning, set my heart beating faster. He looked grave, too. I couldn't wait for the preliminary greetings to be over.

"Akongshee, I've decided to intervene because things are getting out of hand," he began.

I tried to steady myself from shivering while searching his face for the undesired details. He cleared his throat several times and looked up and down. "What is the matter?" I dared to ask, moving my head forward, as if to discern the answer from his sparkling, white shirt.

"You need to see Mesape for yourself. He is in deep pain, and has not eaten or drunk anything for days," he explained.

"Why? What's going on?" I probed further.

"Can't you guess why? What else can I say? He needs you," he said.

> "Can't you guess why? What else can I say? He needs you," he said.

"Me? Why can't you help him?" I asked, stressing every word and pointing at him. My voice was rising in anger. Nguti took a step backward, a little surprised.

"I'm at a loss. I've tried everything, but Mesape is not responding," Nguti insisted.

"If you didn't succeed, why should I?" I asked.

"Akong, I've tried, but he would not talk to me. He's in bed, helpless," he explained.

Meanwhile, I just listened.

"I just thought I should let you know since it's urgent," he went on.

"I hate this. What am I supposed to do?" I said, frowning.

I was tired of going against my own will. I wanted to opt-out of the relationship.

Nguti must have read my reluctance. There was a silence while I bit my fingers. He stretched out his hand and tore the leaf of the fresh corn in the garden by us.

"Akongshee," he called with a serious tone.

I began looking straight into his face.

"Let me say this," he began. "If anything goes wrong with Mesape, you would be held responsible," he warned.

"Me responsible? Can't I just do what I've chosen to do?" I shouted.

"Akongshee, you don't know," he began pleading. "He cries for you all day long," he went on. "He doesn't want to see anyone else but you," he ended his plea with a mischievous smile.

My battle was not with Nguti; he was just a messenger. He had done his job very well. I saw the relief on his face. He waved me farewell and turned his back.

My eyes followed him as he climbed the hill leading to the street. How could I be responsible for this? I thought. Yet, it seemed like an emergency. My heart was throbbing against my chest. There and then, I determined to rescue my friend.

Firstly, I adjusted my plans for the day as I rushed back to my studio apartment. Quickly, my hands fished into my cane food closet. Bundles, tins, and containers landed on the table, one after another. It was easier and quicker to prepare *fufu-corn, okro soup,* and *ndjamandjama* than go grocery shopping.

In an hour, everything was ready. I dashed into my room and put on the most relaxed dress. It was my brown flowery dress with a matching belt. My brown pair of sandals were a perfect match. I grabbed the basket and rushed for the street to hire a taxicab. It was not the day for a bus ride, even though his house was far away, and close to Nlongkak.

Mesape was in bed, looking like a patient in the intensive care unit. However, his broad smile was reassuring. The joy and appreciation on his face warmed my heart. He got out of bed and sat up, facing me. We hugged. He held onto me while I stared at the food basket on the table, to my right.

I finally extracted myself from his firm grip and started setting the mini table by his bedside. The size of his scoops made me pity his throat. I twitched about my seat as they conjured up images of refugees in my mind. He finished the first bundle of *fufu corn* and started the second one. He was eating like a born *Graffi* (one born in the grass field). A coastal like him eats *fufu cocoyam*.

We spent the rest of the day in a quiet conversation. Every utterance he made was a reconstruction of our fading relationship. He said nothing but declare his love for me anew. As for me, I kept responding like a nurse on duty. It was a deliberate choice. I was putting my ears, eyes, and hands at his service, pouring out the milk of human kindness. Nothing more.

However, it was an uphill task, trying to shield my heart from involvement in the process. I guess that's why it was just so difficult for me to leave. I had to wait for two more hours for the arrival of dusk, to intervene on my behalf. Even then, Mesape was still reluctant to let me go, not until I assured him that everything between us would resume with the original steam.

Unfortunately, that was hardly a choice for me. Besides, I couldn't be in a relationship and be lukewarm at the same time. So what next to do, lie or pretend? I reluctantly promised that I would be available, but on condition that we had something constructive to do together.

He stared at me, sighed, and shook his head.

"Akongshee, I don't believe you are killing me so easily. What have I done wrong?" he asked.

His hands fell to his sides in desperation while his fingers brushed his face.

His display of frustration was annoying. I felt a surge of outrage building up from below my stomach. How ungrateful and demanding! I thought to myself. My heart ached as if I was carrying a stone in my chest. Uneasy feelings were converging around me. I stood up and stared through the window, wishing I could stop the approaching darkness.

He was too wrapped up in his desire to share in my pain. Suddenly, he dashed out of bed, grabbed his album, and flipped through the pages for my ideal portrait, the photographer's idol, which encapsulated the beauty and heydays of our storybook romance. He stared at it while rubbing his fingers over it. Then he looked at me and shook his head again and sighed.

He looked at the photo again and hit it with the back of his hand.

"Akong, do you mean I will return these photos to you? Please, please, don't go away," he pleaded. "My whole life will be empty, dull. I can't imagine my life without you." He was imploring me.

"Akong, I love you," he said. Then, he grabbed my hands and looked into my eyes with tears in his. "Yes, I do. I wish you knew just how much I love you."

He pulled me to himself and examined me all over as if we just met.

The pleas went on and on. The more Mesape insisted, the more the heaviness of my heart weighed down on my shoulders. Was I in a trap? I tried to hold back the tears, trying to be firm.

My head turned towards the door. I began wondering if it was wise of me to have come for his rescue in the first place. I regretted it.

"Akong, what am I going to tell my friends? What will I tell my mother? Oh, please, change your mind and stay. I'm going to take good care of you," he went on.

Meanwhile, I just listened. Then, I mustered up some courage, took a deep breath, and stared at Mesape.

"Your future is ahead of you," I spoke, staring him right in the eye. "Sooner or later, you'd fall in love again. So, why don't you just wait?" I begged him.

"What about you?" he spoke up with a smile, like the winner of the debate.

"I'm a woman, maybe riper for marriage than you," I tried to explain.

He took a deep breath, turned around, stamped his feet, and dropped his hands by his sides, helplessly.

"Two things you should not forget, Akong," he began, holding onto my right hand.

"Firstly, I've seen all kinds of women from all over. None is like you. You are the end of the road for me," he said while nodding, and with a teary voice went on, "I'll never find another better than you." His lips were tight and he was breathing hard.

I looked away from his consuming eyes and felt a surge of anger creeping in me. Was he talking to a child? I wondered. I moved towards the window. Then I turned around and tried to put on a humorless appearance. Instead, I burst out laughing.

"Mesape, how much of Cameroon have you seen, let alone the world?" I asked, laughing dryly.

"Besides," he quickly interrupted, raising his right finger. "I believe I'm the best man for you," he said.

Instantly, a shudder went down my spine. I wanted to scream at his boastfulness, but instead, I frowned, raised my eyebrows to express my impatience.

"Look, Akong, a woman like you deserves a man who can treat her with affection and tenderness," he spoke while staring into my eyes with an air of self-importance. "I don't think there is any other man who can care for you better than I. My dear Akong, I can't withstand the thought of someone giving you a hard time." He moved closer to me as he spoke. He was relieved and began jubilating.

Somehow, he got me thinking that he could be right. I started reminiscing over the abuse I had suffered in the hands of other guys. None of them was as polished and as gentle as Mesape.

For a moment, it seemed to me that, given the right circumstances, Mesape would be my Mr. Right. Of all my campus potentials, he came closest to meeting my expectations. He was unique in holding my hand whenever we strolled around or went shopping downtown. He was kind. And best still, our friendship was very transparent. I was again sailing in those thoughts when he tapped my shoulders as if waking me from slumber.

My eyes began searching him all over, anew, but darkness was invading the escaping rays of the setting sun. I picked up my bag.

However, Mesape held it and tried to pull it away from me. I held on to it, insisting on leaving. He kept a steady grip until my changing tone obliged him to let go.

> *For a moment, it seemed to me that, given the right circumstances, Mesape would be my Mr. Right.*

He stood up suddenly. Then he moved closer to me and asked if we would continue to see each other and if we could meet the following day or so. I stared at him for a moment and nodded while proceeding towards the door. He caught my right hand and held me close to himself. He bent his forehead over mine and kissed me. I knew that if he kissed me again, I would be in trouble. I always loved his warm, gentle kisses. I used to call him "Toasty."

Finally, I escaped from his grip, turned around, and began staring through the window again. He soon realized the risk of nagging me any further. I hurried towards the door.

Meanwhile, he rushed for his keys and joined me outside. We walked the quarter-mile footpath towards the bus stop, engaging in a light conversation.

It was exhilarating to be outdoors; the gentle evening breeze caressed my ears. I felt freer, though still yet captured.

We finally got to the bus stop and started waiting for the bus. Mesape kept insisting that I should promise we would resume our relationship. I just stared into his face. Then, the nagging returned, as if his life depended on it. The arriving, long, blue *Sotuc* bus interrupted us.

He let go of my hand. I climbed in and took my seat by the window, on his side. The last passenger stepped in. I waved at him, and he waved back.

To my shock, I heard a man wailing. My head leaned towards the window. It was him. The woman ahead looked at me and then towards Mesape. The bus was taking off. I turned around and caught another glimpse of him.

The street light was reflecting on his pleading face; tears were rolling down his cheeks. Tears began collecting in my eyes, too. The bus joined the traffic. I stood up and looked back to ensure that he was not holding onto the bus. He just stood there like a pillar, wailing and oozing out torrents of hot tears.

The bus swerved around the junction and headed for Obili. I was relieved. Yet, I was concerned about his safety on his return trip.

What could I do to help him as well as myself?

Finally, I arrived home, relieved and confused at the same time.

CHAPTER 16

Love versus Lust

For two days, I managed to push back the thought of visiting Mesape. The distance between us shielded me, but I was far from free. Indeed, both of us were imprisoned by something complex and beyond our ability to overcome. First, was our education. Instead of empowering us we had spent three years in the capital city cut off from our families, and immersed in curricula material irrelevant to the needs of our community, to a large extent. Thus, we had become vulnerable. There was a disconnection between our bachelor degrees and the basic needs of our developing society. Neither was the socio-economic milieu conducive to a wholesome love relationship. Even showing affection in public was almost unwelcome. Life was empty and boring. How were we going to know each other in a more profound way without opportunities to express ourselves in multiple activities, especially outdoors? With what were we going to feed our love? We had no hobbies, except being mere spectators staring at a movie screen in a theatre or watching a soccer match at the stadium.

Secondly, apart from accumulating knowledge, we were not trained to take up temporary positions as economic actors like in painting, plumbing, electricity, driving, cooking, gardening, dressmaking. Worse still, the superiority complex that was typical of graduates prevented us from even thinking of becoming apprentices.

Mesape's bilingual degree (in English and French) and my English major limited us to administrative jobs, with the government as the near exclusive employer. Our innate talents and other skills laid fallow. That lacuna constituted a barrier to our personal growth. What else could render our relationship more exciting and enriching? Would our love for each other survive in such a vacuum?

I got home late, on the third day, and saw Mesape's note. It was good to know he was doing fine, strong enough to visit me. I was equally thankful he came in my absence.

Nothing happened the following day. I began thinking that he had taken a step closer to my stance. That was not the case. The next day, I got home late again, and there was his note waiting for me. He had come two times within two hours. How long was that going to happen? I wondered. For how much longer was I going to evade my own home? I was getting weary.

On Saturday afternoon, he arrived and caught me right on the spot, entertaining a few guests. I ushered him in with a deliberate, mechanical smile. Hardly had he stepped in when he began forcing his way into my room, with the old familiarity that always reigned between us.

Whatever his intention, I didn't even give it a second thought. Spontaneously, my hands were pushing him out, without intending any rage or disgrace. And of course, I made no fuss over it as soon as he got seated with the rest of my guests. I didn't think that there was any need to apologize, either.

Maybe I had made a mistake. I thought it over for days, but nothing was clear to me, except the emptiness invading my being.

As for him, he just laughed. Smiling was an outstanding gift we both shared. The laughing veins would take over his forehead. Go-lucky guy, my dear Mesape, I thought to myself.

The following week, Mesape didn't call. At first, I was happy that he was falling in line with my request. Another week passed, and I didn't see him. Fine, I beamed.

By the third week, I began counting the days. To my utter surprise, I started missing Mesape. I continued missing him and wondering if he shouldn't come back. Maybe I had made a mistake. I thought it over for days, but nothing was clear to me, except the emptiness invading my being.

I got up in the morning with a desire to see him. As the day wore on, it persisted. On the third day, a Friday, I got up with a compelling desire to see him again. I was on my way to grocery shopping. So, I sent him a note inviting him for lunch. By then, my sister, Mangwi, had moved in with me.

At 2 pm, I stepped out of the door to empty the trash, when I sighted Mesape taking the bend leading to my quiet abode, located at a discrete corner, some fifty meters from the main road.

Our eyes met. I felt warmth in my bosom. Mesape smiled, and a childlike shyness came over me. As he moved closer, I quickly rubbed my palms against each other. He hugged me tenderly.

Lunchtime was a little quieter than usual. All three of us were cautious, like guests in the house of a total stranger. We spent the rest of the afternoon together, chatting from topic to topic. Mangwi was happy for me.

Our friendship was making slow strides towards a balance. We seemed to have picked up from where we had left off. However, the level of excitement was decidedly lower. Neither Mesape nor I was complaining. So, we left it at that.

Within the first month, the determination to pursue my studies abroad started becoming more pressing. I knew, like everyone else, that it was a daunting task to make all the necessary preparation. And even then, success was no guarantee, not even for those who had enough money for all the basics.

As for me, I needed lots of help, which wasn't forthcoming yet. So far, I had completed several application forms sent by Munga. Besides, I spent lots of time at the American Cultural Center library, looking through the profile of one school after another.

The following month, I took the TOEFL. My scores were good. All I needed was money. I had to save most of my monthly earnings to buy an air ticket—hopefully within a year. Otherwise, I had to wait for a more affordable opportunity at home even if it did not quite suit my ambition. Even that too would only come about as an act of faith. Nevertheless, I kept reminding Mesape, from time to time, about my desire to study abroad. He was still the same old Mesape, without an interest in that direction.

So, part of me maintained our old lifestyle while the other longed for something else, howbeit very far away from my grip. We went to the movies and the stadium for football matches while I imagined myself, shortly, exploring a new world.

Of course, we celebrated our reunion. Nothing could stop me from wishing, in the depths of my soul, for something to push me onto a higher plane.

Mesape was yet to land a job. He started trying his hand in selling a few men's items for pocket money. We went on like that for months. It was not fun. Meanwhile, I was learning and growing in my new position at radio, daily reporting, and editing for the news.

His visiting pattern continued as before. This time around, he did it more out of need than leisure. Nguti's changing attitude was not friendly at all. The emotional pressure weighed down on Mesape. After all, Nguti wasn't paying a franc for the apartment of his uncle's house, which, as family, he was not required to pay rent.

His friend's indifference or whatever put Mesape in a tight corner, and at a time when I needed an outlet myself. What could I do but attend as many seminars, conferences, and screenings as I could, especially at foreign cultural centers, scattered all over Yaounde? That left me with less time to spend with him, except when he visited me at my office or over the weekends. So, he kept calling at home for brief moments.

Suddenly, there was a new twist to it all. On Tuesday evening, I found two notes in my message box, one from him and the other from a former university mate, Moussa. The latter stated that he came to welcome me into the neighborhood.

Moussa was handsome, tall, with a dark brown complexion. He was equally brilliant—one of the few who managed to sail through the drowning waters of the faculty of Law and Economics, an institution as daunting as hiking to the top of Mount Cameroon.

He was an attentive and engaging speaker. Besides, he was looking for a school abroad, along with scholarship opportunities. What a beautiful coincidence! I celebrated. He had already had admission for graduate studies in one school in the US.

On the day of Moussa's departure, I joined the farewell crew at the airport. He had promised to assist me in looking for a school in the US.

I stood there in a small circle of guys, chatting while my soul was weeping with separation anxiety. My only consolation was hopes of joining him in the US, hopefully, by the following year or two, especially since he had promised to assist me in searching for more appropriate schools.

The overhead announcement started blasting through the loudspeakers. We each took our turns to hug Moussa. I regretted not having a souvenir for him. My bright white handkerchief, trimmed with a delicate variety of pastels, came in handy. I offered it to him, with a few words of appreciation and a wish for a safe flight. He looked at it, and then he looked into my eyes, smiled, and gave me another hug.

The following day, Mesape reprimanded me for showing affection to Moussa in public. He was visibly upset as he held on to his frown. Meanwhile, I listened, wondering which of those guys had come to the airport to pry into my personal affairs.

The story was so exact; I could not ignore it.

His investigative report left me with mixed feelings. For the first time, ever, it crossed my mind that he had gone too far. I detested the flavor of something which amounted to control. I felt liberated enough not to fall for such restricting behavior.

Yet, my friends kept insisting that Mesape acted out of pure love. Maybe they were right. Nonetheless, being in love then wasn't my priority. Pursuing a career and or further education was all I wanted, period.

However, little did I know that Mesape had been observing every inch of my moves regarding academic pursuits. On Friday, I was unpacking my trunk and realized that my passport was missing. How could that possibly happen? Imagine the sturdy maroon zinc case, placed out of view, and close to the ceiling. No one was in the house while I was concealing it, in between clothes and papers. So how did it disappear? I was devastated. How could an item as precious as gold vanish from my apartment, when I was the only one entitled to use it? I was lost. Profuse sweating streamed down my face. It was impossible to get another one, not even within the next decade.

To lose a passport then was like losing a loved one. Back then, not up to one percent of the population possessed a passport. Exiting the territory was highly restricted. A married woman, for example, had to produce a duly-signed, writted permission from her husband to be allowed to travel abroad. I searched for it in every bag and suitcase in vain. My sister, Mangwi, helped in the search. Our efforts were in vain. I burst into hot tears.

When Mesape came calling later in the afternoon, I recounted my misfortune to him. First of all, he faked ignorance. But he seemed to be getting a kick out of my sad story. I became suspicious. I didn't know him to be a sadist. Then he burst out laughing, to my relief, though I was disturbed by the fact that he had searched through my personal belongings without my permission.

It was no laughing matter, though. Unfortunately, I treated it like a simple matter. I never reexamined Mesape's action. Nor did I absorb the full strength of the statement he was making. I guess I had never felt any need to be on guard with a gentle person like him.

However, while I tried to reclaim my property from him, he spent his energies building springboards wherever he stepped foot. Each day, he would try to talk me out of pursuing an imminent friendship with Moussa. He pleaded that I should not respond to Moussa's expected first letter.

After a whole month of waiting for a simple "I got here safely" letter, I gave up. Several weeks after that, Moussa's friend invited me to a diplomat's house, to wait for a call from Moussa. Our conversation was barely cordial. I could tell that he needed to make peace with his soul. How about his promise to help me search for a school? No mention. Then and there, I realized that the man was incapable of differentiating between business and sentimental matters. Either he had reduced me to the level of his dependent former girlfriend, or my independent spirit had scared him. I turned over a new page, confident that another opportunity would come my way, certainly not through Moussa.

My sadness lingered for a while. There was no energy to waste, trying to catch the wind. Mesape could go on mounting his stepping stones to my tortured heart. My resistance was downhill. I was more willing to let him have his way. He had earned his honor.

As for me, I needed a balm of consolation. And Mesape was closest to my heart. I could use some of his unbending determination. After all, he was still offering a hundred percent, hoping I would take it, wholesale.

Our friendship took off as if it had barely been on hold; the original sparks and fireworks returned. Mesape seized the occasion to bluff about his persistent efforts to rescue our relationship. I was grateful for his steadfastness.

Hardly had we had time to reset our priorities when something unplanned happened.

CHAPTER 17

The Fruit of Love

Mesape came to my office, directly from Motor Park. He was returning from Victoria, where he had spent a week with his parents. I had just filed in my 3 pm report for the national and world news.

As soon as I set eyes on him, I dashed out of the studio and rushed into his open arms. Quickly, I dragged him outside and led him to the yard, right close by the hedges. Immediately, I whispered the news into his ears. I had been prudent not to break it to him by telephone.

His eyes glowed with delight. He looked at me anew, with the freshness of our first meeting. Then, he smiled until the veins on his forehead were ready to burst.

Meanwhile, he kept rubbing my back. And as he did, my anxiety dissipated in his warm, accommodating embrace. Our merging feelings wrapped us together at that sacred moment. We held onto each other while our hearts communed.

However, soon after he left, guilt feelings began invading me. I started thinking about my parents. I was genuinely sorry for having deprived them of the honor to walk me down the aisle of our church in Santa. As for the baby, poor little one, I sighed. How sad to be coming into a harsh world without adequate preparation! My heart ached.

My younger sister, Mangwi, was the first family member to learn about it. I was sore with regrets, having squandered our most cherished dream. Pursuing studies abroad became as elusive as the clouds.

Mangwi was so disappointed, to the point where she was deaf to my cry for mercy. Her face went from frowning to blankness. Without a word, she left me standing in our living room and dashed into the bedroom.

Her sobbing permeated our little apartment. I was lost, with nothing to say or do to soothe her agony. I just scratched my face and stared at the beige walls.

In less than ten minutes, she dressed up. Then she rushed past me as if she was afraid of contamination. The exit door swung open and banged after her; I blinked in shock. My heart started beating faster.

Communication between us dwindled to almost nothing within days; distance between us grew by the minute. She grumbled and complained. Soon, her impatience turned into contempt. Mesape was obliged to change his visiting hours.

Several months passed. Yet, Mangwi's disenchantment remained stiff. It was time for us to separate. No other option was negotiable, at least, not within my ability.

Our cousin, Evelyn, accepted my request for a temporary stay in her one-room apartment.

On Saturday morning, I was packing my personal belongings when a fight erupted between Mangwi and myself. She held on to my stuff.

"I don't want to see your boyfriend here," she yelled at me.

"Stop pointing that finger at me," I shouted back.

"What can you do to me?" she said, pushing her whole body into my face.

"Get out of my face, nonsense," I shouted, struggling to rearrange my shoes.

"You guys are a disgrace," she screamed out her lungs.

"Yes, that's exactly why I am leaving."

Even then, she kept provoking while I struggled to zip a bag. I yelled to no avail. Our heated exchange of insults alerted neighbors. Some rushed out. She flung her hands on me. In the struggle, she tore the gown I was wearing, right over my stomach.

What else did she want? I wondered. After all, I was already paying the price for my wrongdoing by quitting my own house, to make her feel more comfortable. Wasn't it enough trouble to experience the eclipsing of the sun of my future ambitions? To what degree did I need to be humiliated? It was unfair to succumb to her guilt trips. Neither was I going to make "look-at-me-with-pity pleas" to whoever.

Thank goodness my cousin's home was only about six blocks away. Mesape helped to transport my stuff. Evelyn left for work while Mesape went to get some groceries.

I dumped all my belongings on the floor, fell on my blanket, and started thinking of my mother. My welling tears poured out in torrents. I began imagining their reaction. If Mom heard the news, she would be sad and yet lift her pleading hands to God for care and protection. If she met me, she would cry and, however, embrace me. As for Papa, he might just look at me with sympathy and say something like "sorry."

I picked up my handkerchief to blow my nose. It was wet. Tears started soaking into the blanket.

Suddenly, I heard approaching footsteps. Instantly, I got to my feet and rushed to the sink, where I steeped my face with cold water, collecting into the palm of my right hand. The freshness of it penetrated my skin. I felt better, much better, but my head was numb, like an empty box.

In a couple of weeks, I started receiving reactions from family members.

"You should be ashamed of yourself," one brother condemned me in his letter.

The stiff struggles of my life became intractable. My sense of insecurity increased by the minute.

"Akongshee, who deceived you into sleeping with men? Why didn't you ask me first? I should have told you how difficult it is for a man to commit after you surrender your rights to him," another brother wrote.

"How can you go so far, give us such high hopes, and then let everything crash, just when you are at the end?" a sister regretted.

Those piercing letters crushed me emotionally. Thank goodness for words of comfort from Mesape's mother.

"I'm sorry that this happened to you unprepared, but take good care of yourself," she wrote. "Don't allow anything to worry you. I love you," she consoled me in her second mail.

Her letters became a balm for my hurting soul. I shoved them into the inner pocket of my handbag, which I always had with me.

After the first series of rejection, I learned to expect curses rather than support in my time of dire need. Indeed, I made it a point not to read any mail before meals or close to bedtime.

The stiff struggles of my life became intractable. My sense of insecurity increased by the minute. The daily challenge was to manage a monthly salary of CFA 125.000 francs (approximately 70 USD) for all my needs, help my parents, and support my younger siblings through school. It was like toiling on two full-time jobs and earning only a part-time salary. I worked my regular hours during the day and stayed up late in the night to complete the layette for the baby. Similarly, I designed and sewed my maternity gowns, including beddings. Most nights, my weary body just crashed into bed.

Sometimes I succumbed to the pain, crying myself to sleep.

Yet, I had to keep working harder and, equally, maintaining a positive mental attitude. There was no giving up.

Eating balanced and regular meals were priorities. Creative pinching for survival became my daily skill practice.

Finally, I moved from my cousin's home into my studio apartment, in the new neighborhood of Biyem-Assi. It had taken dozens of trips to the government housing agency, SIC, spanning three months, to finally obtain a key. I moved in barely a month before expecting the baby.

Meanwhile, Mesape, who was still living with Nguti, visited me every day. He helped to do the cleaning, unpacking, and organizing in the brand new home, smelling with fresh paint.

One day after I fully settled in, my eldest sister, Mercy, arrived from Bamenda. That long trip to Yaounde was a rare undertaking for her. Mangwi accompanied her to my home; the two had spent the weekend in Mangwi's apartment.

As soon as the preliminary greetings were over, Mercy announced the purpose of her visit. She had come to mediate between us. Our tradition demanded that all family feuds, involving the pregnant woman, be resolved before the expected baby is welcome. I felt a deep sense of relief.

Mercy launched her peace-making mission with an introductory speech.

"This is a terrible thing that has befallen our family. It's time to end the hostility. You, both, should forget the past quarrels, and turn a new leaf," she stated firmly and went on for a while.

"Sister, I have something to say," I requested.

"Go on," she said, falling back on her seat, all ears.

"I know you have heard a lot about this issue. But did you know that Mangwi insulted me in public, tore my dress, and ..." I was still speaking.

"No, no, no, no. We can't start that all over again," said Mercy, shaking her head several times.

"But you've not yet heard my side of the story," I persisted.

"No, no more insults. Enough is enough."

"But I just want to explain what you don't know."

"I'm tired of it. Now is the time for peace. So, let's end it now," Mercy interjected again.

Meanwhile, Mangwi relaxed on the couch and just watched; indifference was written all over her face. She looked unconcerned like a cat purring in-between two soft pillows.

I felt so little, so lonely. Anger, shame, and self-pity surged up in my being. Tears overwhelmed me, but I had to stay healthy for myself and the baby.

Mercy's apparent indifference to my condition hurt me. She was treating me as if I was an unwanted stranger. There and then, I realized that the issue was not so much our conflict as my predicament. I had let them down, the whole family.

Finally, Mercy closed the meeting and requested a glass of water. I stood up and went to the kitchen. She took the long sparkling glass and placed it at the table before us. Then she started to lecture on the need to restore peace and foster unity within the family.

After her final speech, she paused and prayed to God. It was soon over. We responded, "Amen," in chorus.

She requested that I drink the water first. My younger sister sipped the rest, from the same glass. Next, she asked us to embrace one another.

Where was the peace? I wondered. The weight of emotional pain was tearing my body apart; my chest was stuffed and heavy. I felt like an outcast.

Soon, she stood up and announced that she was leaving. They each embraced me and left.

Despite the heaviness of my heart, I yielded and followed them outside. I stood at the balcony and watched Mercy and Mangwi cross the street for a taxicab. As soon as they stopped one, I waved and returned to the living room. I threw myself on the couch and closed my face with both palms. Oh, how I missed my mother's balanced approach to conflict resolution! Villagers respected my mother for her sense of sound judgment, especially for mediating between husband and wife. Sometimes they called her for emergency intervention, even as late as midnight. Indeed, one night, an angry husband rushed into his room and grabbed his gun to shoot his wife, who was hiding behind my mother.

Meanwhile, Mesape came out of his hiding place. He was carrying a carton of plates to the kitchen.

From the couch, I observed him anew, with a grateful heart. How thankful I was! He was more than my partner in crime. He was my brother, a shoulder to lean on, the family I was missing.

Every accusation I had leveled against him began melting away in my heart, like butter on piping-hot, roasted *yams*.

I leaped to my feet, went to the kitchen, and just stared at him without a word. He dropped the napkin in his hand, moved closer to me, and wrapped his arms around me. The welling tears in my eyes flowed to my cheeks. I looked up into his eyes.

"I need you here with me," I managed to whisper to him.

He looked straight into my eyes, wiped my cheeks with his right hand, and kissed me.

CHAPTER 18

A Baby Out of This World

Our financial squeeze persisted. Mesape's part-time job at the travel agency barely provided pocket money and transportation. It was just good enough to keep him busy, a slim opportunity to keep hope alive. Countless job search tours of the Ministries and State Corporations were still fruitless.

Meanwhile, the count-down to labor began. We arrived at the hospital by 6 am on Monday. The midwife immediately examined me.

"The baby is not yet ready. Dilation is barely a quarter way," he announced. So, he requested that we go home and only return the following morning.

When we got home, there was a note stuck to the door. My mother had arrived the previous night, and she was waiting at Mangwi's apartment. We immediately made a U-turn.

On our way, I had mixed feelings. How was Mom going to receive Mesape? At worst, I imagined her yelling. Even if she initially expresses her anger, her motherliness would prevail in the end.

Mangwi opened the door. Mama, who was looking surprised and happy at the same time, stood up and embraced me. Then she took the time to scrutinize Mesape, to the point of bypassing his stretched out hand, left hanging in the air. She stared straight into his eyes as if to remind him that though he had trespassed, she was still the one in charge. The stony silence pierced my heart, causing it to beat faster. My eyes repeatedly blinked at the collision between my mother's disappointment and Mesape's anger from her snub.

I felt sorry for both of them. Still, I did not know what to say. Mesape turned his face away to the white wall facing him, looking stiff like an object which would not budge.

My struggles of nine long months flashed before me, invading my being. Feelings of guilt weakened my knees.

"So, the person in question is still a youth? No wonder," Mother spoke while scrutinizing him.

Neither Mangwi nor I responded.

Mama turned around and started looking at me.

"Why did you join forces with him against your sister?" she asked again in *Ngemba*.

Words were not forthcoming, or I was trying to swallow them. I didn't want to aggravate my mother any further or put Mesape in a more awkward position.

Soon, my mother spoke up again. Her words seemed to be escaping from her mouth. The more she spoke in *Ngemba,* the more her tensed facial muscles relaxed.

She looked at Mesape anew; she began scratching her face, and her characteristic warmth returned. Then she stretched out her right hand to him.

"*Chartalaah*" (greet me then). A glow was radiating from her face.

Unfortunately, Mesape's beige eyeballs had turned reddish already. He shifted his glance away from her stretched-out hand. Tit for tat, to my mother? A cold wave ran through my body; I felt insulted. If it were possible, I would have plucked his hand and plugged it onto my mother's.

My mother glared into his face. With the fullness of her fury, and in a loud tone, ordered him to greet her. He did, though reluctantly as if blood supply to his sturdy, muscular arm had dwindled. It remained suspended midway.

Tear rushed to my eyes. How was I going to thrive in the divided loyalty? I needed both of them; any rift between them would place me at a higher risk. I was as good as wet logs; any additional water would prevent the sparks of fire of collaboration that I needed desperately, at the most vulnerable stage of my life.

Mama had left behind her untended crops in the soil, sacrificing her very last coin, to travel eight hours, on a rocky, unfamiliar highway to assist me. Though Mesape and I were crawling under a pang of shared guilt, I needed him to run all the errands. He needed to stand by my illiterate mother at the maternity ward.

Finally, they greeted each other—an impromptu session of abashed personal contemplation followed.

"We need to go home," I said. Mama stood up quickly and went into my sister's room; she brought back her traveling bag. Mesape took the bag from her. We walked silently to the street. All three of us hired a taxicab and headed to my apartment.

On the way, Mom spoke to me in *Ngemba* again. She remarked that Mesape was still probably immature. I explained we wanted to come and visit them before the baby arrived, but Mesape could not afford the means. She sighed and clapped her arms. However, she appreciated the fact that Mesape had stood by me, all the way.

"How come you were able to time your arrival so precisely?" I asked.

"Isn't God alive? I counted the number of months from the time I learned about it," she explained.

We finally got home. Mesape reexamined the diaper bag to ensure nothing was missing.

Meanwhile, I showed Mom around my small apartment. We jointly made a quick meal of rice, steamed potatoes, and tomato stew for lunch. Mama and I spent time talking about our family while Mesape kept himself busy around the house.

In the night, Mom and I shared the only bed I had while Mesape settled on the couch.

By 5 am, my contractions became unbearable. Mama and Mesape helped me to get ready. We walked out to the street, where we hired a taxicab for the hospital.

The midwives examined me again. Dilation was still too small. So they advised us to go back home and wait. When we got out of the delivery room door, Mom suggested that we wait within the vicinity of the hospital. We sat at the visitor's benches along the corridor.

In a couple of hours, my doctor arrived. He examined me again. Indeed, the baby was not yet ready to be delivered. So, he wrote a prescription. The midwives had to administer it after a couple of hours.

"You see, she's high risk, and her case is worse now that the baby is breech," he explained to the midwives.

"Have you done breech birth before?" he asked.

"Yes," she said while taking a deep breath and scratching her head.

He gave her further instructions on how to handle the intricacies. However, he asked the midwives to call him if it became more complicated than expected.

A tear began dropping from my right eye. My doctor turned to me and explained that my situation was more complicated than it looked a week ago. "I know you are scared, but everything will be okay," he said, patting my right shoulder.

I believed him and hoped so too.

He had to go; he was conducting a seminar for the students of CUSS, the medical school in Yaounde.

I laid in bed, writhing in pain and watching, baby after baby, being delivered. The midwives were frustrated. Five hours were gone. So they pushed my bed out of their way into the ante-room. I waited, cried, and pleaded for help.

Meanwhile, Mama, Mesape, and Mangwi were outside. I could see them only through the glass window, which separated us. I was in too much pain to focus on the sign language they were using to comfort me.

My doctor returned unexpectedly at noon and administered the IV solution himself. Barely a few minutes after, the contractions started increasing. The pain was excruciating as if a lion was munching me. I couldn't help wailing. The doctor patted me on my shoulder and continued to comfort me. He reassured me that the baby would come faster. On that note, he left again. I started vomiting. By 2 pm, one of the midwives pulled me back into the delivery room. She examined me and complained that progress was still slow.

"The women who came after you have had their babies," she remarked. "And you sit here, refusing to obey our instructions."

I looked at them with tear-drenched eyes. Couldn't they see that I was drowning and that their nagging was just plunging me further?

"You are not even trying. The baby must be too tired by now," the pregnant midwife said while looking at the clock and sighing. "I wonder if the baby will even come out alive," she grumbled.

I was horrified but not discouraged.

One of them opened the door and invited Mom in, even though they had earlier chased her out.

"Come and stand here," she pointed at the bed. "If anything happens, you will be a witness."

Mama hurried in like a threatened houseboy, dying to please his master before he issues his dismissal.

"Thank you. I will do anything, whatever you ask," Mom spoke in broken English, flinging open her hands.

They looked at her with renewed interest, and one of them smiled.

"Yes, even if you ask me to mop the floor, I'm ready," Mom said while pleading with a teary voice.

At that critical moment, I started throwing up. Mama rushed for the bucket and started cleaning after me.

After a long pause, the midwife asked me to push again.

"Help me, please," Mom entreated them.

The baby was not coming, not yet. I heard the delivery team sighing in a chorus of dissatisfaction.

Meanwhile, Mom began coaxing the unborn baby in a lively and gentle tone. She was alternating between *Ngemba* and broken English.

"Precious one, why don't you come and share the beauty of this world with us?" she said, gently clapping her hands like court poets at the chief's palace, ushering in dignitaries. "We've prepared for your coming as for a prince," she went on.

"Come, beautiful little one. Delicious meals, pretty clothes, amazing colors, warm hands are waiting to cuddle you," Mama courted him. "Come see for yourself what God has reserved for you," she began couching her invitation in prayers.

In the meantime, I started yelling and calling out.

"Daddy, Daddy, please come. Just come, Daddy, please," I wooed him without knowing the sex of the baby.

Suddenly, the midwife became more friendly. She placed her hands on my stomach and asked me to follow her instructions.

"Yes, I will do my best," I promised in a weary, teary voice.

"Push, if I say push, okay?" she requested.

After several trials and errors, they became excited; all eyes were staring at the miracle spot.

"The baby is coming. Yeah! That's not the head. The hand? Yes. No. The leg," the mixed voices went on and soon quieted down.

At that critical moment, I felt an overwhelming rush through the very essence of my being. Then, suddenly, a sharp splitting pain, enough to melt away my heart and dissolve my body, flashed through me.

In a second, I felt a warmth flowing through my lap, bearing a striking presence.

The midwife picked up the baby, wrapped him in a towel, and showed him to me. He was screaming with full strength. His face was growing pink as he wailed. I fixed on him for the brief display. He was the most beautiful baby I ever saw in all of my entire life. The precious little boy was as handsome as an angel.

"I have to make sure they do not exchange our little angel for another baby," Mom whispered to me in *Ngemba* as she ran after the midwives to the dressing room.

Her excitement was tremendous. My joy was unspeakable. Mesape rushed in; his broad smile plastered a permanent glow on his face.

Soon, the midwife transferred me to one of the six beds in the private ward—time for joy and celebration. I spent the rest of that night staring at my baby. He had well-formed features, handsome to perfection!

Despite the fatigue, I admired the baby all night long. I kept interrupting my sleep to adore him. I fixed into his face, examining his nails and

My children

touching him, countless times. Then I wrapped him gently. Just by beholding him, the pain from my aching body became secondary.

We left the hospital after two days. The three of us were happy to squeeze into our studio apartment, thanks to the baby. Otherwise, it was odd, especially for Mama, to share the same tiny apartment with Mesape. The baby's presence seemed to wrap us in an aura of warmth and reconciliation. Our faces glowed as if there was a little piece of the sun hanging over our roof. Mesape seized the moment to show his skills as a gourmet cook.

On the eighth day, we all returned to the hospital to have the baby circumcised. The new demands of taking special care of him kept us busy and excited. Unannounced urine was shooting out ceiling-wise. It felt like we were all in playschool. We all laughed, exclaimed, and rushed to help. Circumcision wounds healed within the week, and napkins resumed.

CHAPTER 19

Starting a Family on Rocky Ground

By the third week, we established what was going to be routine care for our baby for the coming months.

Meanwhile, my mother started preparing to return to the village. Aside from that, she needed to know what precisely to tell my father. She explained that she did not want my father to accuse her of condoning our attempt to dishonor our parents.

I bent my head down as she spoke. I was very sorry in my heart, but I lacked what it took to express remorse. Neither was I able, there and then, to correct the situation or determine its future.

> *Tears began welling up in my eyes. Did he still love me, well enough, to want to marry me? I wondered.*

Mesape was rather silent and evasive. He opted out of the discussion by saying that he had first to consult his parents. None of his family members had been present for the delivery. However, his mother had requested that we name the baby after her husband.

Mama sighed while I quietly chewed on my fingernails. Mesape was trotting between the balcony and the room like scared soldier ants, whose business was interrupted by human footsteps. It was easy to tell that he was trying to avoid any face-to-face meeting with Mama.

Tears began welling up in my eyes. Did he still love me, well enough, to want to marry me? I wondered. It was painful and embarrassing to consider myself a victim. My heart was heavy. I had failed, I thought to myself, sighing, despite my daily struggles to overcome the attendant obstacles to progress.

What was I going to do? It was not proper for Mesape and me to continue cohabiting without sorting things out with our parents. Yet, what choice had a man without a job? Whatever the outcome, Mom agreed that I needed Mesape close by for the sake of our baby.

"My daughter, what can we do? We love the baby, and so does he," she declared, lifting her eyes towards the ceiling and raising her hands in rhythm. "I cannot deny him his right as a father. He needs to spend time with his son," she said.

I looked at her and swallowed the dry air in my mouth.

"How can I love the baby and hate where it comes from?" she went on.

She had no clue what a burden those words lifted from my heart. I took in a deep breath of relief.

Of course, she could not force Mesape to act or make a firm promise. She could not oblige his parents either, whom she had never met.

It was time to address the quarrel between my sister and I. Three full weeks after the baby was born, Mom started probing into why, as she claimed, I had teamed up with Mesape to insult and to throw out my sister.

"That's unfair to blame just me," I tried to set the record straight.

Mom would not listen. She was very disappointed with me.

Mangwi must have recounted her tale with such passion that Mom believed her, I thought to myself.

Unfortunately, only Mangwi could restore peace by recanting the lie. The arguments became heated; I cried all night. The flow of breast milk was interrupted, and the baby was restless all night long.

Mama now turned to Mesape. She began accusing him of causing a conflict between my sister and I. Mesape was infuriated; he rushed into the room and started packing his belongings.

Mom stopped him before he folded the first pile of clothes. As a rule, my parents never let an angry child leave the house or stray into the darkness of the night. She often said that if a parent allowed that to happen, the devil would embrace such a child.

Getting Mangwi to set the records straight became an emergency. Incidentally, she did not show up for two days. I was obliged to get up early and go to her apartment. Before 6 am on that Saturday, I was knocking at her door. I pleaded with her to come.

She just looked at me and turned away. I tried to persuade her to do it for Mama's sake, but she was still very reluctant.

My pain was so wrenching that all hunger left me.

Finally, she dragged her feet, and came along, after a full hour of pleading. We hired a taxicab for my apartment, which was just about a mile away.

The house was dead silent when we arrived, apart from little giggling noises from the baby. Sadness and the absence of communication permeated our home. Mom and Mesape were sitting just a few meters apart from each other, yet fuming and confining themselves from one another; the bone of contention between them was squashing me.

Mesape's family and friends would vouch for his good qualities and sense of commitment. Alas, not Mangwi, who was more interested in garnering enough facts to oblige Mom to punish us. The fumes of her emotions prevailed over objectivity. She kept blaming Mesape for "separating her from her sister." The compliments she often lavished on him now turned sour.

I implored her to say something positive, being that Mom was undergoing unnecessary pressure. Instead, she tightened her lips and looked away.

The arguments dragged on. Mangwi started griping anew about our wrongdoing and beating her chest. Her vengeful spirit made her lose sight of the real need at hand, thereby confusing her in the process. She reported the same incidents from different, discordant angles.

Soon, my wise and open-hearted mama detected her glaring inconsistency and selfishness. Her eagerness to extract punishment was evident. And that is the reason she lost in her own game. "Put a lead over those taunts," Mama stammered. "I've already told you of the consequences of harboring anger. Enough is enough," she began yelling and pointing at her with her right forefinger.

Instead, Mangwi's voice grew louder; she stood up and walked back and forth. Then she stared at Mesape and me in disgust. "You guys think you will go scot-free? I have not forgotten all those things you did to me," she said. "You are the one who is finding fault between my sister and me," she was yelling, parading the room and pointing at Mesape.

Mesape did not budge.

Mama ordered her to shut up and control herself.

"This man is still growing up," she said. "He needs a second chance, and you can't oblige me to punish them," Mom went on in *Ngemba*.

Mama was exasperated. She complained about the waste of energy, love, and time. She also regretted the flaunted "collaboration" between my sister and I was quickly evaporating in the heat of the quarrel.

Meanwhile, Mesape kept mumbling like a child. Neither did he acknowledge the extent of his wrongdoing, nor did he attempt to appease the agonizing parties. Mama felt insulted by Mesape's apparent shirking of responsibility. My heart ached for her. No one ever sought her help and left without receiving some form of relief. In the village, she responded to distress calls willingly from neighbors. She mediated between quarreling or estranged spouses. She also counseled girls, pregnant out of wedlock, advising against abortion. She even accompanied them right to the maternity. "If I had gone to school, I would have become a judge or a doctor," she often regretted.

Soon, she abandoned the quest for Mesape's pledge to become the man in charge or a father worthy of the name. She began singing a lullaby for the baby dozing off in her arms.

One month after, Mama packed her bags; she had accomplished her mission. "I'm leaving everything in God's hands," were her parting words.

Mesape and I continued working hard to take care of our lovely baby.

Eventually, my three-month maternity leave of absence from work was over. We succeeded in getting a part-time babysitter. However, sometimes, Mesape took the baby to work for a few hours. Even though he took pride in the glaring eyes of onlookers in the streets while cuddling his baby, it was very challenging. We also took the little prince to the movies, our favorite Saturday entertainment.

As for those nightly parties, we turned down most of them. Sometimes, Mesape elected that I go to represent us while he stayed home with the baby. I was genuinely grateful, conscious that most friends would mock him for choosing to stay home.

In the meantime, he began preparing for his upcoming professional training course. He was one among a dozen recruits from the hundreds who took the competitive examination. Upon receiving the news of his success, we joked that the baby had brought along his share of provisions on planet earth. Authorities published the results the same month the baby was born.

We waited patiently for two months for him to obtain his first financial package, his monthly pay. We began talking about formally legalizing our union. He wanted it to happen later while I preferred a sooner date. I understood his reluctance. There was always fierce competition involved in wedding parties. Self-appointed critics took pleasure in rating events, sometimes relegating a wedding party to a birthday party. They analyzed and compared venues, outfits, the quantity and variety of food, the type and amount of drinks served, and the number of guests. Because of the number of attendees in any given party, no one could differentiate between a gate crasher and a formal guest.

Mesape and I kept arguing over our separate views. He desired a big wedding while I believed that it was more important to put the honor and respect for our respective families before a sumptuous party. I was not the type to allow idle observers to cripple my priorities.

The months filed past without setting a date. Other needs cropped up. We bought better furniture which called for a bigger house. Mesape insisted that it was better to do our wedding party while we were in a bigger house. The more we postponed it, the more our responsibilities increased.

For the time being, life was beautiful. We were living like a happily "married" couple. Mesape seized the opportunity to make me proud. First and foremost, he took a very active part in housekeeping, cooking, and doing grocery shopping—he was unique. On Saturday morning, he would go to the local market to shop. Each time women would confront him.

"I say, eh, where is Akongshee? Is she sick or what?" they fussed as if I had committed a crime.

Other self-styled commentators dramatically expressed their horror. They stopped, exclaimed, and gripped their waists while shaking their heads and as if accosting him. "Has Akongshee fixed him up with a charm?" they wondered.

The truth is, Mesape was a bargain hunter. He often got more for his money's worth than I, a task he enjoyed. Indeed, I was never sure of having made a bargain until he gave his approval. Even then, it was usually apparent that he could have done better.

Similarly, on Saturdays, I did the laundry while he took particular pleasure in preparing one of his exclusive recipes, which included *eru* and *waterfufu*, or *mbanga-soup*. Another rare dish, *timbanaboussa*, was the famous staple of the coastal tribes. All he asked of me was to chop, grind, and grate the condiments.

Then, when the flavor began escaping from the simmering pots, he invited me to taste for balance and consistency. After cooking, he set the table himself and got members of his family well seated at their places before serving us, one after the other.

He also did a thorough monthly cleaning of the house. On Saturday morning, he was removing the carpet from the floor when a guest arrived. "How come you are doing this? What kind of a man are you?" she screamed as if bitten by a snake. "Akongshee, why would you allow your husband to do this?" she queried me.

Mesape just smiled and kept on working.

Indeed, a week before that, my sister, Mangwi, was so embarrassed that she complained that it was not fair for him to indulge in household chores. She wanted to seize the broom from him and do the job herself. I quickly warned her against disrupting the order of our family unit. She fidgeted about for an excuse to sneak out of the house momentarily, while Mesape's "ordeal" lasted.

None of them could stop Mesape from what he embraced as his duty. He made a more forceful statement during my absence. For example, I traveled to Paris for a month-long course and returned to a sparkling, cozy, and almost new house. He had moved the drapes around, changed potted plants, and did all of the grocery shopping and cooking by himself. Indeed, he turned the occasion into a royal homecoming dinner.

There was indeed a deep affection between Mesape and myself. We shared almost everything, including letters from our secret admirers. "Akong, if I had not eaten the dust to convince you that I still loved you, you would have dashed everything away," was his usual statement.

Of course, I was happy, especially seeing how much more he appreciated me, as time went by. After our first baby was born, he kept admiring my body just like he did before. He often joked that if ever something terrible happened and we suddenly lost our jobs he would suggest I be a cover model. At parties, we freely introduced our colleagues and acquaintances to each other. Indeed, one night, he held up my hand for a rock-and-roll dance partner. Dance was not his thing, but he knew how much I enjoyed it.

Besides, I didn't know any other woman whose husband was her wardrobe manager. Mesape routinely examined my hairdo, outfit, handbag, and shoes before I stepped out through the door, each morning. He took off time and window-shopped for the best pairs of shoes for me. He had good taste and preferred top quality. Indeed, his bosses gave him compliments while colleagues brought their ties to the office for his knotting expertise.

Nevertheless, we did not always agree on sartorial matters. Mesape would not give me a break from official suits, even on uneventful days. He frowned at my choice of casual wear, a simple dress, or a basic skirt and blouse on ordinary days.

"What would colleagues say if they see you like this?" was fast becoming his singsong.

Often, I just turned a deaf ear, underestimating the depth of his concern—or was it the degree of his obsession—until I finally tasted the bitter pill.

During the period when the media corporation was launching trial operations, demanding long hours at work, I brought a lunch package for him. As soon as he saw me, he snatched the bag from me and immediately forced me back into the elevator without a word.

I was prodded towards the street, upset and concerned, at the same time.

"What would people think?" he responded when I confronted him later in the evening.

"I'm not Princess Diana," I retorted

His request for a permanent professional look notwithstanding, I refused to yield to his misplaced priorities. Consider this: It was just ridiculous to wear high-heeled, delicate, expensive shoes and either trudge on gravel, march through blinding dust, or meander in mud puddles to go to work. After that, imagine going up and down the stairs and bending over several times for eight long hours.

The loudest advocates of facial and hair sheen for the sake of attractiveness were seizing every opportunity, from their office to any public appearance, to catch the attention of men, including unavailable ones, in high places. My main contention was the attempt by friends and colleagues to impose their choice of make-up on me. Their constant jeers got me weary in my struggle for social freedom and worthiness. I sensed something demonic in the subtle persuasion to attach undue importance to one's physical appearance while the mind stagnated, alongside a dying soul. As for me, my natural facial look served as a mirror, reflecting the current condition of my health—was I dehydrating, resting enough, eating properly, and enjoying peace of mind?

They dictated how a woman should appear in public. Thus, some friends and colleagues spent hours gossiping about what they considered "odd" looks. Yet, the same women, who dressed like Hollywood stars, wasted time and effort, failing to show ingenuity in all forms.

"Commot me for here with da ya Whiteman style" (give us a break from your western manners). They dismissed my creative recipes. Even more surprising was when they shunned me for measuring rice or beans before cooking.

"What's white about being precise?" I asked.

Rather than transforming my house into a palace with a gigantic Imelda Marcos-type wardrobe, I went ahead and bought gadgets, machines, and other kitchen appliances to save time and energy.

How I wished Mesape and I would jointly put up a common front against a creeping social epidemic!

Alas!

CHAPTER 20

Envy Creeps In

We finally set a date for a small wedding, almost overnight. Whatever prompted him, Mesape finally agreed that formalizing our union was more important than a big wedding. At last, we were in sync. There was no time to waste. Preparation took a barely week. Apart from a hat and a pair of matching shoes, my dress came straight from my wardrobe. It was from my collection of the previous year. The soft, cotton, gray outfit, with the hemline barely four inches below knee level, was a silhouette flaunter, designed *à la française* with hip gathers, delicately displaying contours, and showing all-front white buttons.

My dress matched my white, net hat, trimmed with gray edges. The brand new pair of white shoes and white handbag completed the costume to artistic perfection.

As for Mesape, he bought only a new pair of shoes and a matching tie for his shirt. Meanwhile, my dainty, pink corsage matched the pink blushes on his grey tie, thereby emphasizing the brightness of his white shirt. Overall, my outfit complemented his grayish jacket over a black pair of trousers. The mix blended very well with the sunflowers, hibiscus, and tulips in the background.

We stepped out with joy into a gentle, sunny, and pleasant Saturday morning. The location for the ceremony was Mfou, a neighboring village to Yaounde. Mesape and I joined eight other couples, anxiously waiting at the Governor's office, to publicly take their vows.

Each took their turn, accompanied by witnesses and family members. The signing ceremony was over in two hours.

Our camera crew was ready. Photographers guided us to the attractive spots within the background of the vast green and flower-filled lawn for our pictures. The elaborate picture-taking session, outside the office grounds, took more time and seemed to require more technique than the official ceremony.

We were about twenty in our group, including some of our siblings on both sides. The variety of colors composed a rainbow for a memorable performance immortalized on camera.

Unexpectedly, there was a scandal orchestrated by one of Mesape's high school classmates, Nerissa. She tried to disrupt the order of the group photos. Firstly, she had been forcing her way in a desperate attempt to stand closest to Mesape. Then, she positioned herself behind us and pushed her hand forward stealthily. So, when Mesape stretched out his hand, instinctively, to take mine, he caught hers instead.

"*Iii...ish*," he exclaimed. "I thought it was Akong's hand," he said, brushing hers off in disgust.

"Why is she so pompous?" two of my friends whispered in my ears.

I had no clue as to what was going on. It did not occur to me then that it could be something beyond bad manners. Since Mesape did not say anything afterward, I brushed it off as silly intrusion.

A month or two later, Mesape returned home in the evening, all excited. He started exclaiming and clapping his hands as soon as he stepped through the door.

"Akong, I've seen something today," he announced, pulling out the dining chair and sitting down.

He had met a very strange-looking woman at a friend's house. He explained that something about her figure was unsettling, a curiosity.

He couldn't even bring himself to capture the sight in words. So, he sighed, shook his head, and moved his fingers in the air, while I observed every gesture of his, much like a fly buzzing around a rotting mango for the right angle to nibble.

"One day you will see her for yourself," he said, resigning.

"But what is so peculiar about her?" I asked again.

"She is like this," he said, stretching out both hands and opening his palms, one over the other.

"And her neck, like this." He drew together in open palms, close enough to show the degree of contraction.

I looked at him, opening my eyes wider as he progressed.

"You need to see her for yourself, Akong. I cannot describe," he said, still shocked.

"From where is she?" I asked.

"Just returned from the US," he said.

A few weeks afterward, Mesape returned home in the evening, complaining about Nerissa.

"You women are dangerous," he lamented while loosening the knot of his tie, right in the kitchen.

"What do you mean?" I asked, halting the salad preparation to listen.

"Can you imagine what Nerissa did today?"

"What?"

"That woman I told you about some time ago came to the training center to visit her. After she left, Nerissa whispered something in my ears."

"What?" I asked, turning and looking into his face.

"She said that that girl is dying for you," Mesape reported.

"Really?" I took a deep breath and waited for more.

"You women are dangerous," he went on, pointing his right forefinger.

Nerissa, our so-called family friend, was a beautiful, chocolate-brown woman. She used to be notorious in the university because of her insatiable demand for men. "She serves it on a silver platter to any willing man," was the everyday talk around campus.

"Like father like daughter," her childhood friends were fond of saying, about her romantic exploits. They further disclosed that her father, a rich man, respected for his business savvy, was a sugar daddy, in whose addictive pursuit of young women didn't mind including his daughter's classmates in secondary and high school.

I complained about her undue attachment to him. He argued that they were former classmates; now, colleagues-in-training.

Even though she passed for a family friend, she showed no personal interest in me. Our conversations were often superficial and general.

However, she seemed to reserve substantial issues to share with Mesape. As soon as I left for the kitchen for a drink or retired to the bedroom, she would begin speaking in low tones. A few times, she requested Mesape to accompany her to the street at the end of her visit. He would return and share some juicy scandal or rumor.

With repeated visits, conducted similarly, I started questioning her sneaky manner. Why was she keeping me out of it? Mesape's justification was somewhat escapist. Next, I complained about her undue attachment to him. He argued that they were former classmates; now, colleagues-in-training. Besides, both of them hailed from the coastal area. Soon, we began arguing and quarreling about her ways. One day, instead of dropping the hot potato, Mesape refused to eat dinner when I condemned the secretive chats with Nerissa and linked them to her lewd acts.

What else could I do? I took a deep breath and wondered how to stop the latest avalanche heading towards my family. Nerissa was notorious; she had caused rifts in more than one marriage. Now, she was trying to match-make between my husband and her strange friend from the US.

For the time being, I took comfort in Mesape's characteristic sincerity. We were best friends and practiced open communication. Just by admitting the corrupting nature of her exclusive trademark of "promiscuous deals," gave me some relief. Also, becoming upset about her attempt to tempt him was an equally good sign. As husband he should have demanded a stop to that behavior.

We never discussed the issue again until one week before the birth of our daughter, Sweetie, when I stumbled over a landmine in my bedroom. That afternoon, I stayed home, all alone, to make the finishing touches to welcome the baby. There was a box of old magazines and newspapers suitable for discarding. I pulled it but somehow felt an urge to search it. I picked up one magazine and newspaper after the other, making a pile on the floor. In the middle of it, I found Mesape's daily appointment diary. I picked it up; its bulging cover tickled my curiosity. So, I opened it. An envelope fell out. I flipped my fingers over the folded sheets and scrutinized it. There it was, a photo lodged between folded pages, staring at me. I stretched out my neck and stared.

"Who is this?" I wondered while my heart began beating faster.

My curiosity turned into chills, rushing down my spine like an electric current.

"Is this the woman?" I wondered as my heart was racing. I could hear it loud and clear.

I turned the photo over, but there was nothing written on the back.

"One day, you will see for yourself," I heard Mesape's voice echoing to me.

My eyes scrutinized the picture for clues to the slimmest connection between him and her. What could be the attraction? I kept staring. Her pantyhose? The fact that she had lived in America? Her dress? A possibly affected accent? Her fascinating looks? What? Of course, the superiority complex of having lived in the US.

A cold wave started eating up my body from my feet upwards. I was trembling. How I wished it were just a nightmare instead! The thought of Mesape having an affair made me dizzy. The photo fell from my hands into the open diary. My eyes were dimming. I managed to drag myself from the bed to the floor. My hands tried to hold my bulging stomach to make contact with my baby. Instead, I collapsed to my side. My stomach churned. I wanted to rub it with my right hand.

After a long while, I opened my eyes. My right hand caught hold of the bed, and I pulled myself up to see if I was still dizzy. Maybe I wasn't. Anger was now surging in me; I had to do something immediately for quick relief. My first thought was to destroy the picture. It sounded like the best thing to do.

I picked it up and limped towards the front door. Then, I peeped out and surveyed the yard. No one was looking. I went to the kitchen and got some kerosene, newspapers, and a box of matches. I went out and chose a hidden spot in the backyard, behind the little pepper garden. Standing there, hidden from view, I closed my eyes and prayed.

"I don't know who you are or what you want in my family. If you are bringing evil, it will consume you first. You have no right to put asunder what God has put together. Wicked woman. Shame on you, the angel of darkness," I spoke with trembling lips while my breathing was pounding.

Then I placed the photo in-between the newspapers and sprinkled some kerosene on the heap. A single striking of the match sent up the flames instantly. I stood there and watched until it turned into ashes. There was a momentary relief. I took a deep breath and carried my body back into the house.

My feet dragged my body to the refrigerator. I selected a bottle and poured out some orange soda into a tall glass. It was tasteless. I could not even swallow a second gulp. I abandoned it on the kitchen counter and plodded to the living room.

My tired body surrendered to the couch; my eyes closed. The problem was nagging in the very roots of my being.

Should I address the issue with Mesape as soon as he gets home? Or should I wait for him to open the chapter? The questions were endless. But will he tell the truth? Should I wait until the baby is born? Or should I hold on to see how it unfolds? Was he already committed to her? Was this some kind of a "fatal attraction"? Just in case I'm exaggerating, why carry her photo, if he does not desire her? My mind was an expanding question box.

The more I thought about it, the more I dreaded Nerissa's involvement in it.

Mesape got home that evening after I had suffered three long hours of anxiety. He looked as cheerful as usual. He hugged me and rubbed his hand over my protruding belly. I smiled and went into the kitchen while he proceeded to the room to take off his work clothes. Then he followed me to the kitchen and carried his dinner to the dining table. He was enjoying his meal while I sat by him, quietly rehearsing my approach to the issue. When he finished and started sipping his wine, I thought it was time to open the box of piercing questions.

"Mes, I have something to ask you."

He stopped and looked up, all ears.

Meanwhile, I took a deep breath and paused, gazing at my brown, rubber slippers, which were gently kicking against the leg of the polished wooden table. There was a lump growing in my throat.

I raised my head again and started blinking without meaning to.

"I'm just asking," tears welled up in my eyes, and I struggled to contain the choking lump. "Who is this woman whose photo I saw in your diary?" I asked while looking at him, still unable to replace the blinking with sternness.

He fidgeted as if there were pins on his seat. He cleared his throat, turned around, and looked at me enquiringly.

"What are you talking about?" he asked, frowning.

"You mean you don't know what I'm talking about?" I stammered as my sight was getting blurred. He put down his glass and started blinking again.

"This is not just some photo from the countertop or something; you took the time to conceal it in an envelope."

"Poor thing," he twisted his face in a dramatic move to make me look ridiculous. "Why do you get so worked up because of a little thing like this?" he asked, forcing a smile.

"Little thing?" I asked. "You accept a strange woman's photo and call it a little thing?" I insisted while staring at him.

My voice was growing louder even though I wanted to keep an open mind to whatever convincing arguments he could advance.

"Akong, it was just one of those silly things you do without giving a second thought to it," he began explaining. "You see, I didn't want to humiliate her. So I just took it," he said with the sincerity of a child.

There was a growing pain in me. And he wasn't doing or saying anything concrete enough to stop it.

"If you had no ulterior motives, why take such pains to hide it? I don't know you like that," my voice began coming from deep down my soul.

"Why would I bother to show you if it means nothing to me?" he asked, picking his teeth.

The more he tried to escape, the more I was hurting.

"So, after accepting her photo, would you be surprised if she persists in what she wants?" I asked.

"I don't care what she wants. I didn't invite her to the Center," he insisted. "She came to visit Nerissa," he explained.

Mesape was becoming impatient. His tone was getting aggressive. He kept talking and trying hard to defend himself.

"I don't know why you are trying so hard to pin this thing on me. I've told you, and you will not accept," said Mesape, throwing his arms on his sides and sinking his body into the chair. Then he stretched his neck forward, right over the table, rather suddenly.

> *There was a growing pain in me. And he wasn't doing or saying anything concrete enough to stop it.*

> *"If you had no ulterior motives, why take such pains to hide it? I don't know you like that," my voice began coming from deep down my soul.*

"What do you want?" his eyes were ready to devour me. "For me to cut off my head and give you?" he demonstrated with his right hand.

I immediately threw the napkin on the table and stood up like an athlete, leaving him by himself. I went to the room, spun around for want of what next to do. My right hand reached for the closet while my eyes closed, I guess, to give my deepening breathing full rein.

There was a slight weakening in my knees. I hated it. Maybe I was tired. My left hand dragged my sleeping cap from the closet top. I just slumped into bed, clutching it in my hands, unable to go to the mirror, as I did each night. My body fell on the mattress, backward. Sleep was weighing down on my eyes. So, I pulled myself up and put on my sleeping cap to preserve my newly styled hair.

After a short while, I heard his approaching footsteps.

"Nerissa, the match-maker," I said, twitching in bed as he moved closer to me.

I wanted to give him the honor of telling the truth, or, at least, admitting that he had made a mistake. But would he?

"Would she force me to love her?" he grumbled as he fumbled in the closet, his back turned to me.

"Well, they say action speaks louder than words," I said.

"Akong," his voice was loud and aggressive. "I don't know what you want from me," he suddenly swirled around. "You keep trying to force this thing on me. I'm not interested. Remember wasn't I the one who disclosed it to you first?" he asked.

The shirt in his hand was moving up and down.

"How could I turn around and begin to cover it up now?" he asked. "Why don't you look at yourself and see that this is not the time to put yourself through this?"

He started calming down. "Please, don't take it too far," he pleaded. His face was dropping as if he was ready to cry.

My heart was still aching with disappointment and a sense of betrayal. I turned my back and tried to force back the tears.

"What was happening to Mesape? Wasn't he the one who used to tell me everything?" I wondered to myself. I had a feeling that he was not telling me the whole truth.

He took off his pants and flung them on the chair. Then he sat on the bed for a good while, steeped in his thoughts. Then, he sighed aloud and climbed into bed.

Meanwhile, I had pulled myself to the back of the bed, almost gluing my face to the wall.

There was a moment of silence. Then Mesape turned around and pulled me towards him while dragging himself towards me. My body was stiff, like a stone. He moved my arm while calling out softly. So, he carried his head over mine and tried to kiss me. I turned away. I wanted to go somewhere alone and cry. But he held onto me and kept calling as if trying to wake me up from a nightmare. I turned my face and looked at him blankly.

"Akong, I didn't intend to hurt you," he implored me. Veins were popping on his forehead.

"I can't have anything to do with her. I didn't think it will cause so much trouble," added Mesape, sighing and breathing deeply. "That is not the kind of woman with whom I would ever entertain close relations. Please, believe me. And I don't want this to bother you again," he pleaded.

I listened, but could I believe him? I truly missed the natural, unmistaken innocence of his voice. An alarm was sounding, deep down in me. I felt that the essence of my being was under attack. Yet, I was unable to do anything to protect it. For the first time in our relationship, I felt like I was alone in the world.

An alarm was sounding, deep down in me. I felt that the essence of my being was under attack. Yet, I was unable to do anything to protect it.

The long silence was soon interrupted by his snoring. Tears began to fill my eyes. Yet, what was the point of crying? I thought to myself. My mind started wandering into all the problems ahead, awaiting me.

CHAPTER 21

Moth and Rust Attack

After our baby girl was born, Mesape and I carried on as if home wreckers had not attempted to ruin our marriage.

However, I observed strange attitudes. Nerissa began visiting our home at unusual hours, earlier than 7 am. On Tuesday, she sneaked in while I was in the outer kitchen. I stepped out and barely saw her back, disappearing with Mesape into the street.

Two days afterward, she came again and invited Mesape to the yard, while waving to me like a stranger.

Mesape returned after some thirty minutes with little to say, except that Nerissa needed his advice to make some important personal decisions. How limp and porous! I thought to myself. However, I had neither time to waste nor facts to challenge them.

Gradually, I realized that Mesape was spending more and more time away from home. His excuse was assignments and research.

However, one evening, he came home much earlier, and we prepared dinner together. It felt like the past beautiful months again. We sat in the living room talking while he played with our son, Quydee. He informed me that the five anglophones in his school had created a *Ndjangui* club, a rotating, trust-savings pool of funds, whose members meet face to face monthly to hand over money to the current beneficiary. Shang, Tina, and Nerissa were members, of course. I went to bed that night, hoping for the best.

Two Sundays after the news of the *Ndjangui*, he dressed up and left, saying he'd be back soon. I could not complain because I had to care for the baby. Sunday was the only day I gave her breast milk at her regular meal times.

He returned in the night and told me that they had indeed launched *Ndjangui*. I responded fine, though wondering why he had not, at least, invited me. Hadn't he said spouses were an integral part of it? Whatever the case, I was tired of arguing.

The following Saturday morning, I met Tina at the fruit and vegetable section of the Mokolo market. She asked why I didn't show up for the inaugural meeting. She also informed me that everyone was present but for Shang's wife and myself. Then, some members were surprised that Zipora, whose picture I had burnt, had shown up uninvited.

"So, who did she come for when she is not your colleague?" I asked.

"Who knows?" she shrugged. "It seems it was Nerissa, who informed her about it. You know she comes to the Center all the time," she disclosed.

Sudden dizziness began overtaking me. I did not want to hear any more about Zipora's appearances. We parted company, and I went on shopping while trying to sort out things in my mind. The mere thought of infidelity gave me instant headaches. Feelings of helplessness engulfed me like giant ants, tunneling their way into bread crumbs, especially since I couldn't prove it.

A couple of months afterward, Mesape told me that Zipora had invited him to her parents' home for the blessing of her car.

"What?" I asked, staring at him.

"You remember Mullah's red car?" he asked.

I just stared at him.

"The one he wanted us to buy," he explained.

I nodded hesitantly.

My eyes fixed on him as if he was addressing my shadow.

"I don't know why she is inviting me," he went on as if he was speaking to himself. "She's not my friend," he said and then paused and picked up a chicken wing from the bowl on the stove.

"And I'm a married man," he added.

I just listened, without a comment. Mesape might as well have been confessing to a priest, listening to him behind a curtain or a tiny window.

I looked at him without moving my lips.

Meanwhile, the yams were drying up in the pot. My hands grabbed a spoon and a dish while my mind wondered if Mesape was on the verge of embracing something he always condemned. It felt like I was standing on blazing coals of fire, though he did not honor that invitation.

Barely a few days afterward, while I was still trying to cope with scary thoughts, news of a disgraceful affair began spreading in bars, the university campus, markets, and offices. I learned about it firsthand from Mesape. The culprits were his classmate, Shang, and Nerissa. The news spread. They were saying that Shang was no longer driving his wife in their family car.

Instead, Nerissa had taken over the passenger seat by him. They rode to and from the Center every day. Coworkers confirmed it. He even dared to park his car, for hours, in front of the apartment building where she lived, sometimes until late in the night. Tongues went wagging. Angry neighbors criticized her for openly provoking the man's wife.

Instead, she began publicizing the affair.

"Nerissa is truly dangerous," Mesape stated without question.

"Oh yeah?" I asked, faking ignorance.

"How could he do such a wicked thing to his wife?" he fussed, beating his chest and moving in and out as if the woman in question was his sister or mother.

I concurred and exclaimed.

"And he is doing this shamelessly," he went on. "No, no, we can't just sit back and watch this happen," he carried on, fuming.

In the midst of it all, he appointed himself as Shang's counselor. In the following weeks, he embarked on a "mission to save his friend's marriage." He routinely returned from the Center, dropped his bags, and left. He seemed all determined to put an end to the affair.

Meanwhile, I began wondering if he was going through some kind of a rude awakening himself. Whatever the case, I gave him my blessings. I was genuinely proud of him.

Before long, concerned women began gathering randomly, in groups, during meetings or at the square, Carrefour Obili, to brainstorm. Some predicted the outcome.

"That woman will grill Nerissa," they vowed. "Enough is enough."

We all watched the unfolding of Nerissa's disrupting craft, upsetting the fabric of the family of a prominent woman in the community. Everyone hoped that the latter would use her position to scare away the intruder.

Not so. It was not long before we started sighing and shaking our heads. Disappointment permeated the gossip.

"She is a weakling," women complained. "How can a whole university professor behave like a fool?" they questioned. Even men sighed.

She had missed the opportunity to step out boldly, assert her rights, and teach Nerissa the lesson of her life.

Meanwhile, I commended Mesape for his relentless efforts. Each evening, he returned home and updated me. He was proving himself to be a man of integrity by defending undermined families. He kept counseling Shang. His direct intervention had to be the saving grace to my situation. I beamed. The redeemed Mesape, was, indeed, the Mesape I had known, cherished, and respected for eight long years.

Our immediate community was still numbed by the shock of the stinking affair when rumors began spreading that Mesape was seeing Zipora. No, they were mistaken, I tried to convince myself.

However, Tina and others reiterated that she was visiting the training Center more often than before. They disclosed that she was as regular as any student, though arriving just before break time, sometimes bringing along snacks for the anglophones. Otherwise, she drove them in her parent's Mercedes-Benz home for lunch.

Nothing sounded right to me. Mesape never liked eating someone else's food. No wonder, he was turning down the lunch packages I prepared for him. He explained that he didn't want his colleagues to single him out in his class as stingy by bringing along his well-prepared lunch. It was better to patronize Nerissa's daily snack, made up of *dodo* (fried ripe plantains), fish, and drinks. How could he turn down my cookbook snacks for the same ordinary lunch daily? What could I do?

Whether the rumors of an affair with Zipora were true or false, Mesape quickly dispelled them.

"Akong, who are you referring to?" he drew nearer to me, asking with a lot of energy to his breath. "Let me ask you this," he began addressing me in a renewed tone, tilting his head and staring straight into my eyes.

"Have you seen her face to face? So you imagine that she is the type of woman I would go out with?" he emphasized, sighing, turning around and slapping his hip with his right hand.

He moved away and walked right back.

"You have to realize one thing, Akong," he said with a raised, right forefinger. "People tell you these things just because they want to destroy our marriage. Can't you see they are jealous of us?" he continued speaking, pausing and staring at me endlessly.

Each time I listened to him, I had mixed feelings. Maybe I was overreacting. Or perhaps he was just using one truth to conceal another. Whatever the case, I wanted to stop arguing over Zipora.

Unfortunately, my predicament turned out to be worse than I suspected.

Monday afternoon marked the beginning of the second week of my training as an intern for *Cameroon Tribune*. The wall clock in the Cam-news building, downtown Yaounde, chimed. It was time to go home. I stood up, stretched my body, and picked up my handbag. My steps were brisk. I stepped through the double door and stopped at the top of the stairs to sniff the gentle, soothing breeze. The afternoon sun was fresh and inviting.

The taxicab station was just across the street. I stood by the curb, waiting for the occasion to cross. Guess who was watching me from across the street? Mesape. He was strolling in front of the largest shopping center, T. Bella. He waved and smiled. I was happy. We began moving towards each other and met at the front parking lot of the news building. Spontaneously, he touched my hair and squeezed my palms into his. His usual broad smile magnetized me. He explained that he wanted to buy something at the store but didn't find it. Strangely, he did not tell me what. I didn't ask either. I was just happy to see him.

Our chat was lively. Suddenly, a tiny woman appeared at the balcony of the news building, facing me. My eyes wandered away from Mesape to the woman, who was trailing long news dispatches behind her. Mesape turned around and followed my glance.

As she approached, I tried to pick up the thread of our conversation. Instead, Mesape kept blinking and looking away. The woman marched briskly towards the red car parked next to us. I shuddered at my first close-up encounter with her. Her scanty figure provoked instant scanning. My head turned around while I said hello to her. She didn't respond.

Instead, she continued fumbling with her key. She seemed to need help in opening her car. I turned to Mesape to resume our conversation. He was even more distracted. Why? I didn't understand the pockets of silence and emptiness between us.

Suddenly, Mesape announced that he was returning to work. Without warning, he took a few steps away and rushed for the passenger seat of Zipora's waiting car.

A cold wave descended over me and began drying up my bones; my body trembled. My tongue seemed glued between my lips. I could have been dead in my tracks! Was I having a nightmare or viewing someone stabbing me? I stared on, frozen like a helpless child, watching her mother fainting. The car took off, without any motion from him, leaving behind a trail of blinding dust.

"Emergency, please," my soul cried out.

My shocked body was struggling to restore the balance between my torn spirit and shaken mind. It seemed like my body was falling apart in pieces. My eyes stared without purpose for five good minutes. I was afraid of falling.

So, I managed to drag myself across the street like a baby learning to walk. My body was shaking. I hoped no one was watching me as I pulled myself, one step after another. My frozen buttocks dropped on the white, concrete flower bed by the stairs leading up to the American Cultural Center. My mind went blank. I just sat there, hoping to regain my balance without any need for an ambulance.

I took a deep breath, and in a little while, I regained full consciousness. A family friend and colleague, Rose, arrived on the spot, on her way to the American Cultural Center. She sat by me, and we chatted for a couple of minutes. She bid me goodbye and climbed the stairs behind. Since she didn't express surprise at a possible distortion in my speech, or an oddity in my appearance, I felt relieved. I was okay and ready to go.

So, I stood up and strolled down towards the taxicab station. My jittery body was still jarring in my muddling thoughts.

CHAPTER 22

From Delight to Hollowness

When Mesape got home later in the evening, he didn't utter a word after saying hello. He needed to speak up, but he wouldn't. He ate his dinner and still didn't say a word. I needed to hear from him, but he was as good as dumb. My body was heavy with fatigue, but I couldn't sleep.

"You don't have anything to tell me?" I asked, after a long silence, while struggling to conceal a yawn.

He lifted his head from his wine-colored, brand new shoes, glanced in my direction, and then looked at the light brown carpet on the floor. He was brooding like a bird waiting for its eggs to hatch.

I stood up and flung the napkin in my hand on the glass table. Frustration was eating me up like a weary mother whose sick baby won't take medication.

"You want me to tell you what?" he roared, twisting his face like a spear, aiming at me.

"So, you don't see anything wrong with how you treated me this afternoon?" I asked calmly.

Storm or tornado, I was ready. Time out for his singsong claim to faithfulness, *"Oh, Akong, if you know what you mean to me. I will never forget that day when you went and bought that "mandate" (money order) for me, with your long belly."* Enough is enough. No longer was he going to lean on that rescue effort, that helped him to apply for a recruitment test, as justification for his faithfulness.

Chapter 22: From Delight to Hollowness

"So, you find nothing wrong in driving off in a strange woman's car?" I insisted, fixing on him while he blinked endlessly.

"And so what's wrong with riding in a colleague's car?" he asked with a stare to suggest that I was ridiculous.

My body slumped back in the chair. I took a deep breath and sighed. My brain reeled while I struggled to remain calm, but my stomach began churning. The looming calamity must not tamper with my heart and mind. Trying to extract the truth from Mesape felt like going through surgery without anesthesia. I was barely taking one more plunge to avoid hitting the wall that Mesape had become.

"If she is just a colleague as you claim, why didn't you introduce her?" I insisted.

He carried his head in his palms and wiped his face. Then he began picking his nails with his teeth.

"Why didn't you greet her, too?" he dared to ask.

A sudden wave of heat, or was it cold, began hitting my forehead. If my brown skin were colorless, I would have turned entirely red with rage. I clutched the scarf in my hand as shame was stirring overwhelming emotions from the bottom of my belly.

"What?" I shouted. "You expected me to greet her? Really? And after I went out of my way to do it, you say I didn't? What is wrong with you?"

"Ak, please, stop shouting," he said, moving forward in his chair and clinging at the edge.

"Oh no, this is so disgusting. Since when did I become a pig? Are you trying to rub me in the mud?" I asked.

My heart was throbbing against my chest so loud and fast that I feared that I would faint. I pulled the dining chair behind me and sat down. My head dropped between my legs while my palms pressed hard against it.

Meanwhile, Mesape kept wiping his mouth repeatedly in circles with his left hand. Yet, he looked somehow unconcerned.

I lifted myself from the chair and dragged my feet away. I went into the kitchen, put away the leftovers, and cleaned the countertop. It was over between us. That much I knew.

The kitchen door clicked behind me. I walked passed the living room, where Mesape slumped into the chair like a beggar, waiting for dawn. I mumbled good night and hurried into the room.

My home after divorce

One question lingered in my mind while I waited for sleep. Will a man give up an affair after his wife uncovered it? And if yes, is that why he is not admitting to it? Again, I had no idea.

Exactly one week after that incident, Mesape, the defensive dog, went back to its vomit. I left the News Building at practically the same time. Mesape seemed to be window-shopping again at the same T. Bella.

As for me, I was humming Chiquitita by ABBA while strolling out.

He quickly crossed the street to meet me. His smile warmed my heart. I gave him a good one too. Then he held my hand and led me back across the street, where he had been standing.

After a short chat, he offered to walk me down to the taxi stop. Dozens of commuters were struggling like bees to get into the next car.

"Akong, let's get that car for you," he proposed.

"Thank you. But what am I rushing home for?" I asked like a little girl bathing in her father's love.

He had such a pleasant attitude about him that I wanted to spend some time with him before he returned to work. Besides, the fresh evening air was so refreshing. I didn't mind taking a walk through town to a less congested area.

Chapter 22: From Delight to Hollowness

Suddenly, wrinkles began forming on his forehead. I searched into his face for clues.

Instead, he looked at me and smiled. The instant mental erasure on his face was disturbing. I pulled away from the center of the crowd, fixed my eyes on a pair of glittering, brown, high heels, in front of me, and started thinking.

"Akong, come on. You should get into one of those brand new taxis," he proposed again while dragging me and pointing at the sparkling, yellow Toyota cars.

My hand eased off from his while I shook my head in disapproval. He left the priority spot in the crowd and followed me. Our eyes met and didn't connect. I didn't like the strange look on his face; it bore the touch of animosity.

Suddenly his face dropped. He looked rather impatient or perhaps angry.

"I don't know why you are behaving like this," he said. "You want to go home, and yet you don't want me to help you get a cab," he blurted out.

"But how does that bother you? I can take a cab by myself," I said while staring straight into his face.

"You are behaving these days very strangely," he went on.

"You mean you or me?" I asked, stealing a glance into his menacing face.

He walked a few steps away from me and strolled back. We just stood there, doing nothing and not talking. A cold sweat started invading my face.

I was still struggling to make sense of it all when suddenly a red car pulled up towards us. It slowed down but instantly accelerated. It was Zipora.

She quickly took off with a screeching sound. Heads turned while eyes stared. She disappeared beyond the curve of the central flower bed by the tall government buildings. About two people in the crowd turned around and looked at us. By then, Mesape was trying to smear his anger over my laughing face. It was a nasty victory for me. The clumsiness of it all was gross. I bent down to contain the burst of laughter choking me.

Mesape stood in front of me, immobilized. He was wearing the innocent look of a child, scared of imminent punishment.

My laughter quickly dwindled into a bewildering smile. Yet, I was giggling like a child, totally unaware of the danger.

I wanted to see the end of the drama. And there was no time to think or analyze. So, I just followed him from one street to another. He ordered me to stop, but I just kept trailing him.

After a while, he stopped without warning and started scanning me, as if he was just discovering a beautiful new me.

Meanwhile, I remained steady like a picture. My eyes fixed on the button of his mustard-green, check jacket. He could even proceed to paint me if he so desired, I thought to myself.

"Akongshee, I don't like the way you are behaving," he said in an angry tone.

I was unmoved, still as a doll, hoping for a look of his admiration. Regrettably, he was distracted; he just kept looking back and forth and sighing.

"Do you feel like a drink?" he asked suddenly.

He waited for my response as if we both had something to celebrate.

I raised my eyes to his, paused, and nodded in approval.

"*Oui, bien sûr, Monsieur*" (Yes, of course, Sir), I responded with a smile.

We walked to the café, just a few steps from where we were standing. The red, yellow, and purple flowers in bloom and the white chairs, in the green lawn, were inviting. We hesitated and then chose the table at the far end.

It was my very first visit. Nevertheless, it brought back vivid memories of the beginning of our relationship. I recalled how we used to spend leisure time at outdoor cafés on Central Avenue, Saturday evenings, after the movies. It was something we did, right from our university days until when we had our first baby.

"Ak," he called out to me.

My eyes looked up from my handbag. A gentleman in a white shirt and khaki shorts was waiting to take our orders. Mesape displayed a familiarity with the waiter. I couldn't help imagining him and Zipora, sitting there for a drink.

Nevertheless, I decided to be just a sweet presence. No one needed to counsel me that my future was in my own hands. Our relationship was showing cracks. My heart ached while my eyes brimmed with tears. A harsh lesson was imposing itself. I had to learn how to wrestle without absorbing the full intensity of the blows. The good in me would and should always prevail. My love prevails, no matter what, I decided. My resolve was firm.

"Back to your fountain," my mind ordered the collecting tears.

Chapter 22: From Delight to Hollowness

Mesape's ready and steady communion with me was evaporating. His heart was becoming my desert. Oh, how it hurt! There was hardly room for self-pity. Life, to me, was fast becoming a battlefront and not a charity camp.

He poured our drinks and lifted his glass to me. I smiled. Our glasses touched.

"*A ta santé*" (To your health), he proposed.

"To yours, too," I said, forcing another smile.

By the time we finished our drinks, the fighting had resumed. I announced to Mesape that I was coming to work with him.

He frowned and tightened his lips. I could only imagine him wishing he had the power to ban me from the premises. Impossible. Though a full-time student at the Yaounde-based Advanced School of Mass Communication, I was still an integral part of the broadcasting corporation, where all three of us worked, including Zipora. So, the choice was mine to come and go, according to my assignments. I had a year barely to graduate.

He collected his change from the saucer. We both stood up.

"I don't like that," he said, frowning.

I didn't respond immediately.

"But I'm not going there to visit you," I said, finally.

"Then, don't come with me," he busted out.

I didn't answer.

We got to the taxi station.

"*Télévision, s'il vous plaît*" (Television, please), he bent down and said to the first cab driver.

I signaled for the cab driver to move on, showing him two fingers. Mesape turned around and stared at me with blood-shot eyes. It was like standing on burning coals with naked feet.

However, the curiosity in me refused to give up. I was nearly as inseparable from the man as the clothes on him.

Finally, he gave up after several attempts. So, we wound up taking the same taxicab, home-ward bound.

On the way, he blamed me, complaining and grumbling. He was vague. Neither did he admit his wrongdoing nor say anything that could promote the wellbeing of our family.

As for me, I collapsed into the tattered seat of the car, sitting calmly like a dumb observer from the north pole. My relaxed posture seemed to annoy him. He was rumbling like a storm. The more I maintained my calm, the more upset he seemed to be.

Finally, we arrived at our destination. We walked the rest of the two-hundred-meter distance, hardly acknowledging each other's presence.

As expected, the evening was dull. Mesape's continuous grumbling invaded the house like choking fumes.

Nevertheless, I went about my domestic duties undisturbed as if his daggers targeting my chest had been hitting at my breastplate. I even smiled, from time to time, whenever I recalled scenes from the narrow escape of Zipora.

The truth is, I had fallen too low to fear to sink any lower.

CHAPTER 23

A Stormy Relationship

I went to bed that night, expecting chunks of our crumbling relationship to free-fall from any direction. Nonetheless, I wasn't going to surrender myself as a piece of stale bread just waiting for someone to toss it into the trash can. If I didn't believe in myself, who else would?

I began counseling myself whenever I was alone, sometimes out loud, reciting some famous literary lines we had studied in literature class. At other times, I made gestures with my hands, head, and feet. Notably, I encouraged myself by forming the letter V with my fore and middle fingers, the nodding of my head for self-assertion and approval while taking a walk of fame on the red carpet like a Golden Globe star. After all, life was ahead of me beckoning. If Mesape walked away, he didn't deserve me; I made up my mind.

Besides, I quickly recalled that my mother was fond of saying that my real first husband was my education. "Knowledge builds up, and each challenge is an invitation to soar higher," she often added. However, I wondered what I was going to learn from the ongoing family tragedy that could propel me to higher heights.

Or maybe I was going to have to abandon the torturous ruins of a failed relationship and fall back on my achievements. Six good years as a broadcaster, news editor and anchor on national radio, correspondent for television from the presidency, was enough ground to build on. Also, I was looking forward to my upcoming graduation from the highly competitive professional graduate program in economics. In terms of hierarchy, I was at the national pinnacle of my profession, ahead of either Mesape or Zipora.

So, was Mesape suffering from some kind of inferiority complex? The thought crossed my mind several times. He should have done well to take Ndifor's advice, I mused on how my life would have been had I not met him.

Otherwise, I was the problem—too short-sighted to see that I've been a social misfit. Mesape had been prompting me, for years, to flaunt my mettle, at least, for his glory. Stubbornly, I kept shoving some of the outfits he cherished back into the closet. Maybe, I look to him like someone wearing their dress inside out. The thought crossed my mind.

If, indeed, I was indirectly the cause of our sour days, I was willing to work towards a revival. I resolved on the spot.

Alas, as I was on the point of stepping out into the sun again, the trickster was back at work fulltime. On Thursday, I returned from school, two hours earlier than scheduled, and my sister informed me that Mesape had just left the house to see off a guest. Zipora had come right to my home, with the pretext of seeing our newly born baby. Why choose a moment when her mother is absent? A sinister feeling filled the air with the news. I became dizzy as my sister was speaking.

By the way, wasn't Mesape supposed to be at work? I thought to myself. If he could stay away from work to entertain Zipora in our home, things were out of hand already. How many more headaches did I owe Zipora or Mesape? Should I allow their ruthlessness to consume me or focus on the tons of assignments and term papers craving my attention?

What was going on with Mesape? How much money and material gifts had Zipora promised Mesape? Having confessed her desperation to friends, was Mesape the only man willing to offer his services to a woman with distress calls?

Supposing there was a grain of truth in reasoning, a cozier house would set things right again, or so I imagined. Though born into a culture where it was the husband's duty to provide a home for his family, I was facing a travesty of role reversals, imposed by the denigrating reality. Immediately, I began thinking that it was time to move out of the three-bedroom, *calaboat* (plank) house into a cement house in an upscale neighborhood. If we could afford one with a bathtub, I could swear that my nightmares were over.

Also, we needed a family car. On Sunday morning, I took advantage of the relaxing atmosphere to make my suggestion. Mesape was in the kitchen, preparing breakfast. Our babies had eaten already. Mesape and I settled on the couch with our cups of tea in hand. Life was good. So, I seized the moment.

"I think it's time," I said.

"For what?" he asked.

"To buy a car," I said, looking at him somewhat earnestly.

He laughed and brushed off his ear as if a fly was bugging him. He blinked and remained silent for a while.

"Where will the money come from?" he finally asked, with raised eyebrows.

"How come colleagues who earn less than half our salary buy cars?"

"Is that the kind of car you want?" he asked, with eyes widely opened.

"What do you mean?" I asked, frowning.

"Akong, you want an *eckete* (Pidgin for a battered car)?" he asked, staring at me as if I was drunk.

"But don't they drive? We should be ashamed of accepting rides from some of our colleagues who don't even earn up to half our pay," I argued.

"Well, your idea is good. I've been thinking about it, too. But we have a long way to go, Akong," he pleaded.

"A long way to go. How much longer?" I asked. "Are you not tired of taking taxis?" I pressed on.

"I know, but please, don't push yourself too far," he cautioned, shaking his head while placing his cup on the side stool.

Needless to continue arguing. Instead, I made up my mind to begin to do something about it immediately.

Before retiring to bed in the evening, I sat up for an extra hour. I made a list of snacks and soft drinks to sell at my job.

It was somewhat a messy and exhausting job. I kept it going, juggling between the studio, the conference hall, and my office, to attend to customers. Finally, it paid off. Our savings swelled by CFA 700.000 francs by the end of seven months, an amount that was worth more than an *eckete*.

Mesape's eyes lit up with the news.

On Thursday, he returned from work with car magazines, the first time. By Sunday, he came home smiling.

"Akong, I've seen something," he announced.

"Tell me about it," I responded, pulling my dining seat closer to him.

"Today, I was speaking with this guy about his car," he began. "Let me see what he is asking," the story went on.

He was talking about a friend's sparkling, white Mitsubishi Gallant, pre-owned by his doctor brother.

Within eight weeks, I took the driver's seat of that same car. Between the two of us, I was the one with a driver's license. Mesape realized that indeed I had been bracing up myself for this day, more than a year ago, when I had initially invited him to come with me to driving school.

My shaking hands gripped the steering wheel while I struggled to control my nervousness. Balancing the steering wheel at a nine-to-three position felt like a giant promotion from trekking to flying. I took a deep breath. Happiness, peace of mind, rising self-esteem was all I breathed in. Welcome to a piece of technology, equipped to weed out intruders from my family; I beamed. Exit my husband from Zipora's passenger seat. Exit Zipora and her mini, red car from our life. Enter our initiation into a marriage of peace, quiet, and growth. My soul sang on.

Now, what next? We had to bridge the communication gap between us during service hours. Everyone in the country knew just how difficult it was to install a telephone at home. Only the rich, famous, and influential were able to skip over the labyrinth of discouraging bottlenecks at the office in charge.

> *Exit my husband from Zipora's passenger seat. Exit Zipora and her mini, red car from our life. Enter our initiation into a marriage of peace, quiet, and growth. My soul sang on.*

So, Mesape advised that we should hold on a little while. He didn't mind sending those purse-sized messages, indicating when he was due to return home during delays. I understood him. As for me, the choice was here and now.

I plunged without looking back. It finally took two months of unreported, sporadic absences from work, queuing up on long lines, in front of discriminating customer service representatives at P & T, and enduring abuse, to hear that buzz in my own home. At last! What a delight! Welcome to the era of on-demand direct and express communication! Even the pulse of our romance started rising.

The daily "hello, just-calling-to-check-on-you" calls, during tight schedules, was the balm that our dehydrating hearts needed.

However, hardly had we enjoyed it for up to three months when I detected bugs on our family line. There were incoming calls from Zipora into our family home, as late as midnight. My soul lamented.

Indeed, one evening while we were preparing supper and indulging in an engaging conversation, Mesape left me for the bathroom and stayed away for almost an hour. So, I went to check on him. There he was, lying in bed, and caressing the telephone.

As soon as he saw me, he started stuttering. I continued staring straight into his face. Nothing made sense to me. Was he "speaking in tongues" or what? I refused to budge. My gaze fixed on him while I tried to decipher his private talk. He tried some more coinages and babbling in vain. He finally dropped the telephone without a formal end to the conversation.

Barely a few days after, the telephone rang. Our seven-year-old picked it up from the room.

"Mommy, why is Zipora changing her name?" he ran out of the room with the question.

What could I say but regret that when elephants fight, the grass under their feet suffers?

It was not long before rumors started spreading. There were rampant reports of both of them, spotted in our family car, at clubs, restaurants, and even hotels. I was devastated, yet hoping that they were all exaggerations. How could something as outrageous as Zipora driving our family car to her church for choir rehearsal, be real? Yet how could I justify Mesape's long absences from home, especially during weekends? The charging demon seemed unstoppable.

On Sunday, Mesape promised to pick me up from the National Assembly, where I was assigned for the month, to cover the long parliamentary sessions.

"Make sure you wait for me. I will be listening to the radio for when the session wraps up, okay?" Mesape's instructions were firm when he dropped me off that afternoon.

At the end of the session, I stood at the entrance alone and waved good night to two friends, who were riding in the assembly bus to their respective destinations. My eyes kept moving between my watch and the lonely streets of administrative buildings. Thirty minutes was too long to continue waiting after midnight. My cold, weary legs trotted to the dimly-lit road, where I waited for up to five minutes for the first taxicab.

The driver's attitude during the solo ride, through the dark streets, scared me. He was fidgeting and breathing like a horse, all through the trip. He drove and slowed down, from time to time, without an apparent reason. Was he hatching a plot for instant execution? I couldn't help thinking. Indeed, my eyes began collecting tears. His loud breathing caused chills on my arms and face. My heart was palpitating. It was difficult for me to sit steady.

Thank goodness I was sitting in the back seat. We passed by an electric pole, and my royal blue blouse reflected the glitters. What a betrayal! I regretted.

Finally, he got to my destination. Instead of slowing down, he accelerated. I screamed, and he halted abruptly. The door flung open. I jumped out.

Only opaque darkness surrounded me. I could have walked away without my change, but it was about four times the fare, and I badly needed it because it was my last 1.000 CFA note for the rest of the week.

Under normal circumstances, I could have requested that he drive me home, the remaining quarter-mile distance. It would have been unwise to take the risk.

My stretched arm ventured through the open passenger seat window for my change. The driver was fumbling in the darkness. Finally, I saw or imagined his buried head rise suddenly. He stretched out his hand to me and raced away. The note seemed a little too hard for money, but it wasn't the time to bother about deceit. Or maybe I was too scared to think straight.

I took a deep breath and dashed into the engulfing darkness. My giant steps displaced meters of the partially tarred road, leading to the exclusive Quartier Fouda neighborhood.

Toads were croaking endlessly in the stillness of the night, from the valley behind me. Yet, I had to be careful not to wake any sleeping dogs. The concealing darkness was a timely blessing, too.

When I got to the first electric light pole, I opened my palms and looked. Alas, the hard money was a pre-cutout and well folded, cardboard paper instead of CFA 500 francs. I shook my head and sighed. A sudden fear gripped me. I started running through the rest of the quarter-mile distance.

The following day, Mesape and I had a long, fruitless argument. We stopped the bickering only for our children's sake.

"Akong, I will never forget that day when you went with your protruding belly and bought a *mandat* for me," Mesape's voice was echoing to me, later on, at work, while I edited audio tapes for the 3 pm news.

Yet, in the other ear, friends and colleagues were complaining.

"That guy is a pretender, Akong. We are sick and tired. You have to do something to put an end to this insanity," they advised.

Meanwhile, others, especially women, called my bluff.

"Of what are you afraid? That short woman is nothing," they urged me.

"Just squeeze that short neck of hers and she will stop," fingers were pointing all over while tempers bubbled.

"Maybe you are the one who is encouraging this nonsense," onlookers condemned my reluctance.

Undoubtedly, I could pounce over the dwarfish Zipora and give her the beating of her life. However, she happened to be physically closer to the earth than I. Besides, I was on the losing side, while she had nothing to lose. What's more, we were no longer in elementary school.

Above every other consideration, my real fight was with Mesape, and not with her. Yet, each time I visited the corporation headquarters, it was said that workers "held their breath," waiting for the ensuing screams from my attack. How comforting to know how many supporters I had, I thought to myself. Practically every co-worker was behind me.

Despite their massive support, the emotional torture was devouring me where none of them could reach. My brain could explode from the stress I endured, with all three of us, sitting at the same round table, every Monday morning, for the "Chief's Meeting." Each time I walked into the hall, I paused to spot Zipora, before taking my seat.

Why did we even bother to discuss the private affairs of foreign celebrities while I was passing out, right under their nose? I languished. Was there a curse associated with the world labeled "third?" I ached from the indifference of others.

One half of me listened to the directives of the Director of Information, while the other was managing the rising internal tension. The mere sight of her, her audacity, and the hot gossips tore me apart. My challenge? Seal my anger in summoned self-control against the pulsating temptation to unleash on her, right there. Two long years of crawling under that burden were simply too much fire for one soul.

Finally, one afternoon, I sought an audience with my Director-General. I was shocked to learn that he, too, already knew about it. I was disappointed by his long silence and inaction.

"What did you expect?" my colleagues responded, almost in chorus.

I looked at them and sighed, with tears swelling up in my eyes.

"Are his hands clean?" was the rhetorical question they kept repeating. I agreed with them as I tried to analyze the outcome. Was it fear of reaction from Zipora's uncle, who was a former cabinet minister? I wondered.

Despite all I heard and endured, confusion surrounded the imbroglio. Mesape was known as a good father, meticulous artist, and a gentleman. So, one conclusion was that jealous idlers were framing him. Another was that I was either paranoid or just exaggerating.

Some days, my emotions rose like a vapor while on others, they turned into a waterfall. So, what was I to make of those stories? What about those days I could not track him at work? What about telephone calls in his office and to the studios, to no avail? Were they all fabrications? I had no answers.

Yet, Saturday night, I went to bed without knowing where Mesape was. On Sunday morning, the whole production crew arrived, in two cars, to prove that indeed, they had spent the night in the studio. I came out of the house with swollen eyes, into the yard, to greet the six men, smiling and entreating me. They even showed me their empty drink cans and used snack bags. How could I not believe them, especially since the first-ever TV anchor was with them, a man of honor and my relation?

My emotional battles were truly over, I thought to myself as I heaved a sigh of relief. Maybe, after all, those stories only existed in my mind, I celebrated.

However, barely a couple of weeks, I stumbled on another call to order. That afternoon, a television announcer, Endallé, came to my office, for the first time, with an odd or out-of-place question.

"Akongshee, what's your secret?" she asked as she peered into my eyes as if to pluck out a treasure.

"What a question!" I said, short of crying in front of the young woman. Not only did she know my shame, but it was worse than anything she had ever heard. I began biting my fingernails. Her question was like an invisible dagger, chopping at my bleeding heart.

"I know this may sound strange to you," she resumed. "But, please, tell me how you do it," she pleaded, throwing her hands in the air while fixing on me.

"How can you continue to do such a wonderful job and keep smiling?" she went on.

Her head swayed from left to right in enquiring poses.

"It's tough, yes," I spoke up and paused to control myself.

"But what should I do? Give up? My children need me to remain healthy and emotionally balanced," I tried to explain while my right hand moved the family photo frame, on my table, from left to the center.

"You see, the reason I'm asking is that someday it may happen to me, too. I want to learn from you," Endallé spoke with eyes full of admiration.

The more she applauded my efforts, the more it seemed as if I had become a bundle of firewood, around which ropes were tautly tied.

Pain, shame, and anger crushed me anew as the door closed behind her. Was it possible that I was sitting on an anthill without realizing it? The question tore me apart.

Her compliments that she had intended would lift my spirit, somewhat crushed the little self-esteem left. All along, I had thought that my mess was stinking only to those close to me. Now, I felt like a failure in front of the younger generation.

What I didn't tell Endallé was that the emotional pressure was so intense that it was becoming more challenging to return home at the end of each day. Indeed, I envied my colleagues, including newly recruited reporters, who could not yet afford a cozy home like mine.

Take away my salary and give me peace of mind ... my soul pleaded.

CHAPTER 24

The Game of Disloyalty

My whole world was falling apart. Random counseling from friends no longer sustained me. So, I began taking refuge in what seemed to be the only source of comfort—our social group of professional women, called the Tenas, for "Tenacity." Ten of us came together, every other week, for two hours. Our purpose? Find ways and means to support each other.

We shared our joys, perplexities, talents, ideas, and opinions. We also prayed together. Most notably, we dined and wined together. We treated our husbands to dinner parties once a month. We equally organized picnics for our children.

We pledged to be one another's ears, eyes, and mouth as the need arose. The Tenas brainstormed over my problem more than on any other issue. Two of them eventually confronted Mesape on my behalf. However, unfolding events proved that the challenge was beyond all of our efforts put together.

Short of just resigning myself to the situation, I had a growing need to be by myself. If nothing, I had to pursue my personal goals more seriously.

However, the idea of moving into a better house was still tempting as a possible solution to our family problem. Mesape refused to do anything about it. So, I resumed my contacts with real estate agents. There was no luck. I kept pressing on until he accepted to evaluate a couple of mediocre ones. None was satisfactory. Disappointed, I suspended the search, especially after he won a scholarship for a professional training course in Japan.

In his absence, I decided to prepare a pleasant surprise for him, for savoring upon his return. I began searching for a house with upgraded

Chapter 24: The Game of Disloyalty

features to include a new bathtub, a modern kitchen, a tarred driveway, and space for a flower garden. And all of that in a classy neighborhood.

After a long search, I succeeded, except that that project consumed almost all of our savings. I began wondering if it was worth it. I took comfort in the French saying, *"Qui ne risque rien n'a rien"* (Nothing ventured, nothing gained).

Meanwhile, from Japan, Mesape entertained me with the juiciest love letters. They were so pleasurable that I started doubting if there was such a thing as an affair between him and Zipora. I even carried some along in my handbag. Nostalgia for our past romance filled my days. My hopes were rising to the sky.

The following week, one of my colleagues began gossiping about Zipora, being "so excited because of mail received from abroad." Indeed, he disclosed that Zipora was "preparing for the return of her boyfriend."

All I could do was rebuke him.

Two days before Mesape's return, he telephoned me from Japan. He made two requests: Firstly, "Don't tell anyone, especially Nerissa and her friends, of my due date of return." Secondly, "Please, don't bother about coming to the airport for me. It will be too much of a hassle for you."

How considerate of him, I thought, after hanging up the telephone. Considerate? Think again.

How considerate of him, I thought, after hanging up the telephone. Considerate? Think again. First, why did Nerissa and Co. come up at all? Just why should "Nerissa and her friends" form part of the equation?

Well, if they were imposing themselves as desperate intruders, then he has drawn the line, the other voice reassured me.

The suggestion not to go to the airport dampened my enthusiasm. We could hire a taxicab. Why not?

Nevertheless, it was time to polish up everything in the house to welcome my Romeo, in person, rather than dwell on the "family shortfall." It was the homecoming of a prince, separated from his sweetheart by rumors of fabricated feuds. Or so I consoled myself again.

At 2 pm., a strange *Peugeot* car pulled up our driveway. From the bedroom window, I spotted a woman coming out from the passenger seat. Isn't that Nerissa? I wondered. You must be kidding. Next, Mesape stepped out from the back seat. Everything took less than a minute. Before my feet had time to step into my slippers and rush out, the car was already reversing. As for the driver, I did not recognize him.

My guts were splitting between shock and excitement, even as I hugged my husband. It was like pretending to be dry and warm when I was dripping wet with emotional rain, under the crushing of hailstones. Meanwhile, our son and daughter were dancing about in excitement and holding onto the hugs.

As for me, I rushed to the kitchen. The dinner table was full in less than ten minutes. The children took their places, giggling, laughing, and calling him. Mesape came out of the bathroom and joined us.

We prayed and started eating one of his favorite dishes, *eru*. The conversation at the table was lighthearted.

However, anyone with eyes could tell that Mesape was miles away from us. Indeed, he rushed over the tiny piece of *fufu*, which he had scooped into his plate. Halfway into dinner, he pushed away his empty plate.

"What's going on? Is that all?" I asked.

"Yes, I have to go," he said, wiping his mouth and dropping his napkin on his plate.

I searched him over for clues, in vain. Instantly, a numbness began coming over me. Woe betide the food descending into my stomach, I cursed. My energy was abandoning me. I could feel it. I clung onto my seat and just stared while he rushed towards the room.

In seconds, he was ready to go.

"Akong, I'm sorry. But I have to deliver an urgent parcel to someone," he announced, clutching a big, beautifully wrapped package between his left arm and side.

"I will be back soon," he added.

Before I had time to ask any further questions, he dashed through the door.

My children and I spent the rest of the evening wrestling with more questions than answers, every passing hour. Where was Mesape? What was taking him so long? Whose package was it, anyway? I tried to push back negative thoughts, if only because he had brought me a whole suitcase of gifts: dresses, suits, nightwear, underwear, perfumes, and more. Why carry so much for me and so little for himself? A puzzle. How could I doubt that he loved me so much? Was I naive or not trusting enough?

10 pm. We got tired of waiting. So, I put the children to bed.

Then I went into our room and put on my nightdress. Was Mesape safe? I began worrying.

Otherwise, just thinking about him, sitting close to Zipora, cut through my heart like a blunt knife. Minutes and hours passed in vain. It began to look like an emergency. So, I started calling up friends, one after another. None of them had seen or heard of his return.

I switched off the lights. But I could not sleep.

In the dead of night, the doorknob clicked. I flipped the blanket from my eyes and looked at the bedside clock. It was precisely 2 am, eleven hours since he left.

I made a quick decision—no accusations whatsoever, no guilt trips either.

Within minutes, he took off his clothes and slipped under the blanket. Immediately, he started touching me. No movement. Then he started shaking my arm and calling. I remained immobile. He tried to turn me around towards him.

"Too late for the bride," I thought to myself.

My body was motionless in our king-size bed.

"Ak, Ak, Ak," he kept calling while rubbing my shoulder.

I was as good as dead. Mesape finally gave up and started sighing and complaining.

Nothing about our relationship mattered anymore to me.

I woke up the following morning with a resolve: act fast or become a scapegoat.

It was Saturday. I took my children to a friend's house for a play date. Mesape's absence was very welcome. I spent the whole afternoon alone, pouring my energies into thorough house-cleaning, and organizing my wardrobe. That physical exercise turned out to be more therapeutic than I had anticipated.

However, I wanted more than just relaxing my muscles. At the end of scrubbing, dusting, and polishing, I suddenly broke down into tears of self-pity. As my tear-drenched blouse turned cold, I began thinking aloud to myself. Did I deserve to become a victim of Mesape's choices? When would the vicious attacks stop? What would be the consequences of inaction on my part? What changes should I bring into my life, for the moment, while waiting for the grand solution to materialize?

As my mind wondered beyond myself, I grabbed a sheet of paper and pen and started recording the fleeting, loose, raw, and sometimes contradictory responses. It was challenging to get hold of what path to follow.

Suddenly, it struck me that I should talk directly to God. So, I started addressing Him as if my Creator was standing right there.

"Lord, I feel completely lost. I have hit rock-bottom, despite my repeated efforts, to help myself and keep my family together. If Mesape is not the right choice for me, I am willing to go on, even as a single mother. Please, God, my Father, forgive me for sleeping with Mesape, in the first place, without permission from my parents. Lord, I need Your help. Please, free me from this net. I cannot help myself. There is no one to turn to for help. Please, help me."

At that point, I burst out into more tears. I cried until there were no more tears. It was amazing that my eyeballs did not fall out after their fountain dried up. My energy was waning, too. I could no longer cry for lack of strength. So, I managed to pick up my broken body by my knees and sat at the edge of the bathtub. I turned on the water and dabbed my face with warm handfuls, pressing down my swollen eyes.

It felt a little better. I grabbed the towel and wiped my face. Then I picked up my note pad and pencil again. I tiptoed into the room and came back into the bathroom, where I shut myself in.

Nothing was exact and attention-grabbing. But my pen kept scribbling.

Suddenly, I had an idea. I made two different columns, one for my qualities, ambitions, and positive accomplishments: and the other for my weaknesses, wrongdoings, and lack of foresight. In asterisks, I started highlighting what I would love to accomplish intellectually, professionally, and financially in the long run.

By evening, I quietly resolved, in my heart, not to expect any miracles, any time soon, from Mesape. I knew that separation and divorce were complicated matters to handle, especially with children.

"Please, God, protect my children and me against any impending dangers," I prayed some more, to seal in my resolve.

CHAPTER 25

Shaming the Home-wrecker

Just before leaving for work on Monday morning, I telephoned Zipora. My heart began beating faster while I waited for her to pick up the receiver from the other end.

"Can we, please, meet for a short talk today," I proposed.

"I do not have time today," she quickly snapped back.

"What about tomorrow?" I suggested.

She paused for a while.

"Any time tomorrow, as you want," I pressed on.

"No, tomorrow is not possible," she said dryly.

"Okay, choose any other day that's convenient for you," I pleaded.

"No, I don't think I will have time," she answered.

There was a pause. Then Zipora started complaining about being too busy. I knew then that I was not going to get anywhere with her on this. So, I gave up, hoping that my request would signal something to her.

After that, I resigned myself to the situation, creatively coping, howbeit with lots of sighing and crying.

Then, after a long while, I got up with unexpected news. I was pregnant with our third child.

Anxiety hit me like a thunderbolt while Mesape pulled a long face and looked away. Vulnerability crept into my bosom, weakening my knees.

Gradually, our denial gave way to acceptance. We started making initial plans for the baby. Health and strength began returning to my bones. By the second term, we started making good guesses of the baby's name.

Suddenly, Mesape became very scarce, hardly having lunch with us. The new routine went on week after week. He complained about tight schedules and the need to meet datelines with unique productions.

Lunch break became a moment of torture for me. He would pick me up from work, drop me off at the drive-way, and reverse the car, saying that he needed to go back to work. I argued in vain.

I would sit at the table, trying to cheer up my children while struggling to hold back the tears. My appetite was gone.

After lunch, I would leave the children and sneak into my room to ponder over my predicament. It was difficult to escape from my current woes. Help seemed to be oceans away. My body ached from emotional anguish. I needed more rest and sleep, yet both were elusive.

On Monday morning, after the news conference, my francophone colleague, Estelle, walked up to me and asked why I was looking so sad.

I looked at her, a little embarrassed. I didn't realize that anyone could tell by just looking at me. Even then, I was not ready to share my personal life affairs with someone beyond my close cycle of friends.

Nevertheless, I managed to shake my head and force a smile. My lips were tight while my eyes tried to dodge her inquiring eyes.

"*Comme ci, comme ça*" (So, so), I finally responded, twisting my face, without meaning to.

> *Estelle's hand was still on my shoulder. It began to seem as if my body was gathering energy from her soothing touch. I was not alone; after all, I thought to myself.*

Immediately, I felt a lump blocking my chest. I bent my head down and dragged myself towards the window. She followed me and placed her hand on my right shoulder.

"Are you okay, Akongshee?" she inquired.

At that moment, I was dumb and deaf to the lively chats going on in the newsroom. I didn't feel like speaking either. My eyes just stared at the trees beyond. Estelle's hand was still on my shoulder. It began to seem as if my body was gathering energy from her soothing touch. I was not alone; after all, I thought to myself.

So, I turned around and faced her.

"*Ça va aller*" (It will be okay), she consoled me.

Her words succeeded to extract a smile from my stressed soul.

She smiled back and started talking some more.

"Take heart, Akong, whatever it is, okay?"

I looked at Estelle with appreciation. Her look was full of compassion.

Meanwhile, my right leg was kicking the edge of the table next to us. Tears started collecting in my eyes. I squeezed my lips together to push them back into their fountain.

The slim, chocolate brown, above-average height Estelle was a respectable woman. She did not get involved in chatter. And being francophone, I was convinced that she did not know about my mess.

The following day, she came to my table and said hello. I smiled excitedly and stretched out my hand to her.

"Akongshee, *je suis contente pour toi*" (I'm happy for you), she said, smiling.

"Do you believe in God?" she bent over my table and whispered.

"Yes," I nodded several times.

"Do you want to pray with me?" she asked somewhat timidly.

"*Oui, bien sûr*" (Of course), I responded.

Immediately, I picked up my bunch of keys from the desk and grabbed my brown handbag as if I had been ready, waiting for it.

Estelle and I hurried through the circular corridor leading to my office. She was admiring my freshly styled hairdo while I touched her royal blue velvety dress.

We got to my office. I opened the door and closed it behind us. I turned the key again to make sure it was locked. As soon as we took our places, Estelle opened her handbag and pulled out her Bible. She flipped through in a flash and opened a page. Then she started reciting verses, more from memory, in French.

Meanwhile, I looked at her as if it was my first day at kindergarten. She turned her Bible round to me, but I seized the maroon, dust-ridden one from the pile of books on my table. The pages flipped like a fan and stopped at the corresponding text and chapter.

Then she pressed her pink-polished nail on the exact verse, in Psalm 23, verse 3. I read it aloud. It was reassuring to imagine that words could heal my battered body. She explained the rest of the text, using a few more verses. Then we joined hands together, and she began praying.

"*Dieu tout puissant,*" she started.

"Almighty God," I repeated in a whisper.

Then I listened intently, trying to make the connection from sentence to sentence. Chills were coming over me even as Estelle was speaking.

I shivered as she led me through the excellent experience of speaking directly to God on my behalf.

"Akongshee has a burden, Lord. I don't know what it is. But I know that You do. Please, lift that burden from her shoulder. And whatever Your will is for her, I humbly ask that You give her peace of mind, and especially wisdom...." she went on.

"Amen," I concurred at the end.

She squeezed her warm hands over mine. I smiled and looked at her with tear-filled eyes. My vision seemed to be clearer like a driver's view after torrents of rain have swept away, swirling dust from the atmosphere.

The ten minutes were deeply refreshing, far from gossip sessions with friends, which always left me emotionally drained and more miserable.

I locked my door and rushed after her to the newsroom. Work resumed with editing for the 3 pm news. Meanwhile, she joined other reporters going out for various news beats.

Back home that evening, dinner preparation and other chores went on at express speed. Dinner, cleaning up, and tugging the children into bed succeeded one another as if I was a machine.

Finally, I grabbed my Bible while still struggling to catch my breath. The house was quiet, and the living room was all mine.

For the first time in the twenty years, I was going to use my Bible for bedtime prayers. I still recalled that first Monday of secondary school, in Our Lady of Lourdes, when each student received a tall pile of required books from sister Ann.

So far, my Bible had served me well for religious knowledge. My grades never dropped below 90%. Thank goodness, I had carried it along with my personal belongings from one residence to another.

And here I was, trying to acquaint myself with it. I held it tightly in my hands, cherishing every impression my fingers were making on it. It almost seemed to me like an admirer living next door, whose requests I had ignored for two decades. Finally, matured enough to realize that, of all the "men" in the world, that one was the perfect match. I turned over the pages from book to book. Genesis, Exodus, Proverbs, Psalms, Revelation, all stared into my face for attention.

Albeit, I had first to review the verses which Estelle had given me. I couldn't retain all of them. So, I began scribbling a few words and phrases from here and there into my notebook. Estelle had to explain how those verses directly concerned me, I promised myself.

I read them over again and closed my Bible. Then I knelt, in front of the couch, and started praying.

"Heavenly Father, thank You for life and this day. I put my problems into Your hands. Please, bless us as we sleep. Amen."

Sleep overwhelmed me the very second I closed my eyes. However, each time I turned around in bed, one of the verses kept flashing through my body like lightening. It was like a neon flashcard waving at me in the darkness of the room.

"For God hath not given us a spirit of fear, but of power, and love, and a sound mind," Estelle's voice kept echoing.

What book of the Bible did it come from again? I wondered. I couldn't name it. Yet, the mental search went on since it made a lot of sense to me.

I was paralyzed by fear at several levels: The fear of infidelity, of a broken marriage, of humiliation, of disappointment, and untrustworthiness. My worst fear was the impact of domestic violence on my children. I was helpless like a baby, abandoned to itself.

The love of my life was sour. Neither fresh air nor salt, pepper, or any spice could render it palatable again. The one, who once swore that I was his end-of-the-road, had abandoned me in the middle of nowhere.

"For God had not given us a spirit of fear..." the verse was soothing. I took several deep breaths as if attempting to digest it.

The following morning, I stood in front of the mirror and scrutinized myself. A pale-looking figure stared back at me, causing me to shudder. Painful and conflicting emotions were draining my physical energy.

I was dying to speak with Estelle. Gladly, she came over to my table just before the news conference started.

"Akongshee, I prayed for you last night," she whispered.

We were still shaking hands when the *chef de rédaction* (editor-in-chief) began calling for silence, to open the meeting. We clicked our fingers, and she rushed back to her seat. I smiled and waved to her as we agreed to meet later on.

Meanwhile, two anglophone colleagues were watching us. I caught them exchanging inquiring glances. Many people avoided Estelle because of her saintly demeanor. My eyes moved quickly from them and focused on the *chef de rédaction*, who was sounding very formal, as usual, in his opening remarks. The various news teams of the previous twenty-four hours were receiving cheers and jeers.

Estelle went home for the lunch break and returned thirty minutes later while I crossed the t's and dotted the i's of my news bulletin.

The technician played the jingle at the end of the national and world news. I opened the door of the burning studio and dashed out. Then I raced up the flight of stairs to the second floor. The newsroom was empty except for Estelle and a male colleague. I dropped my folder on the desk while Estelle commented on my presentation. I appreciated her remarks, even though the call for the report from Bamenda didn't go through the first time.

While still panting and sweating, I tried to catch my breath. I signaled to Estelle. We hurried to my office.

"Estelle, how do these verses apply to me as an individual?" I asked, placing my opened Bible in front of her.

She pushed it back to me and pulled hers from her handbag. Then she closed her eyes and took a deep breath.

"Akongshee, *la Bible, c'est la parole de Dieu*" (The Bible is the Word of God), she began, holding her hand out towards me while her head tilted in rhythm to her talk.

"God speaking?" I asked in amazement.

"*Tout* (everything), from beginning to the end, is for you and me, everyone," she said, holding the Bible with her left hand and flipping it with her right thumb like a pack of cards in the hands of a professional.

Each word was slipping in through my deep breath as if my brain needed to open up a new territory of comprehension. My hands brushed over my face as Estelle went on explaining.

"So whatever the Bible promises, that applies to me, too?" I asked.

"Of course, Akongshee," she answered with deep conviction. Her head was moving in rhythm with her speech. "Everyone who hears or reads it," she went on.

"But Estelle, how do I get this power, love, and sound mind?" I asked.

"God is love, the Bible says. He is full of power, also, no doubt. *En plus*" (plus), she said, "H can recreate your mind, too," she spoke slowly and paused to accommodate my surprise.

"Can you imagine the Holy Spirit bringing new ideas to you just like you are reading the news to someone you don't know, in a far off village?" she threw the question at me.

I couldn't help laughing. My eyebrows rose to their full height. I've never before heard anything like that. "*Ah bon!*" (Really!) I exclaimed.

"Oh yeah, *oui, oui, Dieu est tout puissant*" (Oh, yes, God is Almighty). She emphasized every word, lifting her right hand in the air and looking up.

"Almighty God, indeed," I cried out to her, my right hand stretched out to hers.

She flipped her wristwatch over and looked. We barely had two minutes to go. So, she opened another page of her Bible and pulled out a list of new verses she had prepared for me. Then she stood up and held my hands. I jumped to my feet. We closed our eyes, and she began praying.

In the end, she embraced me and left.

Each day, I became more aware of my ignorance. My spiritual life was like a parcel of unfertile land lying fallow. Estelle was like a horticulturalist, weeding the garden, and pruning the plants. As I quietly reviewed the Bible passages and explanations, I realized that I was part of the expanse of the universe, the cosmic reality.

I recalled that the local priest had baptized me as a baby in the Roman Catholic church in the village. I had passed my confirmation soon after learning the church doctrine and correctly reciting critical sections of the Cathechism.

Later, in secondary school, religious knowledge was a compulsory subject, in which I always had excellent grades. Our Lady of Lourdes students attended mass every day of the week as a requirement. Five of us, all Form 5 students, read the Scriptures on Sundays.

> *Each day, I became more aware of my ignorance. My spiritual life was like a parcel of unfertile land lying fallow.*

However, as soon as I graduated from secondary school, church attendance became monotonous to the extent that I stopped attending church regularly. Was cessation from weekly Sunday mass the cause of my ignorance? If so, how come I did not know a single Bible verse from memory, let alone understanding the meaning behind any one of them?

The Bible conversations with Estelle revealed my total ignorance, not only of the Bible but also of God.

A few years ago, the obsession with or excitement about Holy Mary sparked up stories of her appearances in forests and on tree branches. A handful of women, loaded with unsolved life mysteries, spent weekends or moved house to the wild forest in Nsimalen, a few miles from Yaounde. Though the media covered the story, I was still unable to relate to it personally.

The following day, I asked Estelle to connect the claims and promises of the Bible to my personal life.

"Believe what they say, Akongshee. Anyone who accepts that Jesus is the Son of God has a claim to each promise," she explained.

"I know, but are they not history?" I asked, scratching my head and looking at the ceiling as if I was on my first visit to a planetarium.

"You are right, Akong, they have existed since the beginning of the world," she said with a nod.

"Yes, I always thought so. But exactly where do I fit in this picture?" I asked, leaning forward on my table towards her.

"Whatever you learned before now is the truth," she said. "And that still applies today," she went on. She sounded authoritative like a professor.

"Really?" I exclaimed.

"I cannot count all the miracles that God has done in my life," she was getting excited. Estelle's eyes suddenly lit up. She started sharing stories of specific instances when God answered her prayers. I listened and stared in admiration. My mind wandered into the unfamiliar realm of supernatural blessings.

Unfortunately, I was more acquainted with the existence of the powers of darkness. As a child, witches used to beat my father in his sleep, though he was a staunch church member and even sang in the choir. We would hear him crying in the night in his room, repeatedly screaming, "Leave me alone." He knew the witch since he recognized her flimsy figure arriving and leaving his room through the wall.

The more I learned Bible verses with Estelle, the more I became inquisitive; I asked her a lot of questions.

"Why does God allow bad things to happen to me?"

"The devil is the one causing the problem, not God." She quickly pulled out her Bible and started searching for appropriate verses.

"But why me? I know people who are in worse relationships than mine. But nothing as terrible as mine ever happens to them."

"Satan does not bother the mediocre ones. They are his already," she emphasized. "He knows that you have a heart of gold. He wants to turn it into gall, so that you begin to curse God, and turn other women's lives into a living hell, too."

"What?" I exclaimed.

"Yes, he allows the wicked ones to rot eventually, while he attacks the loving ones," she went on.

"Is that really it?" I asked with a gaping mouth.

CHAPTER 26

Discovering Everlasting Love

My friendship with Estelle grew steadily. Each time we met, we explored more territory within the spiritual realm. Each spare minute, I sneaked from the newsroom into my office in addition to break time.

Whenever she was absent, I locked my office door to read the Bible—my opportunity to ponder over life, profoundly. Time was becoming more and more precious. Ten minutes was enough to rush in and learn a new or familiar verse.

Soon, Estelle invited me to her church for the Sunday worship service and prayer meetings on Tuesdays. I gladly accepted it. How prestigious to attend church at the Hilton! I thought.

On my first day, Pastor Claude's sermon directly addressed my problem. When it was over, I asked Estelle if she had talked about me to the pastor. She said no. Whether she had or not, I felt a significant emotional weight lifted off from my heart. So, I kept attending regularly.

The next Sunday, the Pastor preached on another aspect of the same subject. My life, again? I was stunned. How could this just be a coincidence? I couldn't explain. Yet, how beautiful! The more I listened to him, the more I felt at peace. I loved it when he said that each person was precious in God's eyes. I had always thought so.

For two months, I attended regularly. Each time, I took notes religiously, like a verbatim reporter.

On Sunday, after six weeks, Estelle announced that she was quitting. She said she wanted "more solemn and tranquil worship." She could no longer focus due to growing distraction. I agreed with her. Pastor Claude no longer seemed to have a clearcut goal. Soon, he stopped wavering.

However, he instead drifted from uplifting sermons into bitter complaints about his former partner. He went berserk, denouncing the entrepreneur, who failed to honor his promise to build a church for him. For the next three weeks, Pastor Claude delved into the saga of his past dealings with demons. He recounted the slightest details passionately. It seemed as if he still had connections with his murky past.

Nevertheless, I was not yet ready to quit. My cup of blessings was barely half full. I wanted a permanent solution to my problem. So, I prayed that the pastor would soon overcome his leaning towards the abominable acts of the devil and resume with stories of victory in Christ, that he had started out interpreting to a congregation that would clap and shout for joy.

Alas, the preacher carried on, relating his involvement with the agents of the devil. It was depressing. I waited for a more positive message, but in vain. So, at work, I began asking my colleagues, randomly, where and how they worshipped. I was still searching when Pastor Claude himself invited all his members to attend an evangelistic meeting in another auditorium, in the same hotel.

That Sunday, I left his auditorium at 2 pm and transferred to a larger one at 6 pm. There were more than 1,000 people inside. A lot more people crowded outside, peeping through the windows, which were flung open for their convenience. We all waited in high expectations while some choirs entertained us.

Finally, half a dozen men ushered in the speaker, a Nigerian, called "the man of God," amid rousing applause. He strolled in majestically like a king, arrayed in overflowing white robes, the traditional Aguada, trimmed with golden embroidery, with excess material folded in layers on both shoulders.

Firstly, he made lengthy introductions, beginning with his wife, whom he showed off proudly, holding her hand and spinning her around, in her luxurious light green, dainty *wrapper* outfit. Spectators clapped, some men stood up and bowed. Next, he introduced two of his assistants.

Then, it was time for his message. He cleared his throat, moved from one side of the stage to the other, with a microphone to his left, while his right hand kept adjusting his drooping traditional gown.

He asked one of his assistants to read aloud the chosen Bible story. It was about the experience of a widow during a famine, whom God chose to care for Prophet Elijah. Upon the latter's arrival, the widow had a tiny bit of oil and the last measure of barley flour. She was fetching wood to bake the last cake for herself and her son.

After the reading, the man of God took over. He made a few comments about the text, comparing the famine to a generalized shortage of funds within a given population. Incidentally, Cameroon had just started its plunge into an economic recession. Jobs were dwindling, and money was scarce. Not even current account holders were sure to withdraw cash for weekly groceries from their banks. The assembly listened in rapt attention.

Then, he asked the mass audience if anyone needed money. "Let me hear you," he said repeatedly. People shouted, yes. "Are you sure, if so, let me see your hands." All hands went up while some stood up. He assured us that God was going to make twenty millionaires out of all those gathered there that evening.

Nothing could be more tempting, more captivating, as well as timely. Yet, the event was barely starting. Suddenly, the man of God stopped and raised his right hand towards those sitting to his right. Instantly, all the five hundred or so people in the row fell to their backs at the same time. They all came back up like one man. He walked towards the left side and did the same. Not even one person resisted, including me. I had never before, in all of my life, witnessed such a command of power.

Next, the man of God asked those who believed in the capability of God to transform their lives, to lift their hands. All hands went up. On that note, his assistants ushered some people from the back of the stage. They were about a dozen of them, mostly mature men and women. One after the other, they moved forward and testified about how the man of God had prayed and miraculously healed them. Some said they came in blind, but now they could see. Two others brought their walking sticks, which they flung away, to demonstrate their restored ambulatory ability. The rest reported that they had received healing and total restoration from cancer, chronic stomach aches, blindness, and more.

The enthusiastic audience responded with thunderous applause. It was the first time that almost all of us were hearing that simple prayer could heal someone, especially from a chronic disease.

Unknown to us, the man of God had reserved the best for last. First, he explained that the moment for his raison d'être had arrived. He noted that neo-colonialists had siphoned the wealth of the country abroad.

Those responsible were corrupt and shrewd businessmen. The exploitation had been going on for a long time. God was about to put an end to the gnawing injustice, eating away into the economic fabric of the nation.

He proceeded to make an analogy between the widow in the Bible text and the people of the Cameroons. Prophet Elijah had promised the widow that neither her oil nor flour would get finished until the famine was over.

Similarly, God will bring back the stolen wealth of the country. He would raise millionaires from within the participants. The audience screamed while those watching from outside danced.

The man of God had set the stage. He proceeded to announce that "tonight, twenty of you will become millionaires." People couldn't stop clapping and shouting.

"If you want to become millionaires," please, stand up and come forward. People began streaming out. Even some prominent public figures, including ministers, joined the line. He invited them, one after the other, to the stage. Standing face to face with him, he described the specifics of each person's business. Then he raised his hand and touched the man's forehead, saying out loud, "Receive your blessings." Each beneficiary automatically fell backward into the stretched-out hands of helpers, waiting to catch him or her.

I went home that night and felt like I had just been to the moon. My mind was still to realize that my body had already regained its place on planet earth. Despite the lingering excitement, great regret overwhelmed me, like tons of rocks, thrown on my chest. Why didn't I walk up to be crowned a millionaire, too? Indeed, the bitter regret over the missed opportunity obstructed my sleep in the form of sharp painful spasms cutting through my stomach.

Desperate for my share of blessings, I began thinking of how to snatch back the lost millions. I was relieved that the man of God was checking out of the Hilton at noon the following day.

By morning, I had a swollen face from the nightly emotional stress. The obsession with regaining my blessings gripped me even as I dressed up. There was neither time nor desire for breakfast.

I arrived at the radio station earlier than usual. When it was time, I went straight to my editor-in-chief's office. I opted to cover the story that was bringing hundreds of people to the hotel. He said it was more appropriate for the Religious Programs Service. So, I gave up and went straight

Chapter 26: Discovering Everlasting Love

to that department. The boss gladly gave me the equipment I needed. Armed with the twenty-pound recorder strapped to my shoulder, I invited two of my colleagues who were dying to meet "the man of God" face to face.

It was impossible to wade through the crowds of people waiting to have an audience with the man of God. We tried to comb through the moving walls of adults, an exercise that caused instant perspiration.

Finally, we spotted one of the ushers, clad in a white shirt, white shorts, and a red badge around his wrists. As soon as he saw the recorder and our professional identity tags imprinted with the CRTV (Cameroon Radio Television) logo, he signaled to us. There and then, he opened both arms widely and managed to pave the way. Soon, we were standing at the entrance of the hotel suite, where counseling and individual consultations were taking place. He unlocked the sealed doors and ushered us in. Then he proudly introduced us to the most desired man in the city of Yaounde that day.

The man of God smiled and opened his arms as soon as I requested an interview. I sat down and set up my equipment with the help of my colleagues; they were journalists turned technicians for the occasion.

> *I pressed my eyes tightly and wished for three things: to become an author, to own a brand new Pajero Jeep, and thirdly, to be reconciled to my husband.*

The man of God finished with the last guest and turned towards us. The interview lasted about fifteen minutes.

"Excellent," my friends concurred with nods. We wrapped up quickly. However, we couldn't leave without requesting our share of blessings—the reason for going on the assignment. We waited for his response while our hearts were beating faster. What if he dismissed us, for whatever reason? Happily, he invited his wife to assist him.

We each took our turn, standing in front of him. I was the last. He asked me to close my eyes and focus on my request. I pressed my eyes tightly and wished for three things: to become an author, to own a brand new Pajero Jeep, and thirdly, to be reconciled to my husband.

"Are you ready?" he asked.

"Yes," I said.

"Receive your blessings," he shouted out and lightly pushed my forehead with his right hand.

Instantly, I started falling backward, losing all control to resist or help myself. Thank goodness, the waiting hands of the wife of the man of God caught me in time, from behind.

Our joy was overwhelming. It was as if we had just won the lottery. We thanked him and left. The afterglow brought endless smiles to our faces. Great expectations. We, too, had become lucky winners. We beamed. Meanwhile, my companions thanked me and hugged me.

I got to my office and took a deep breath, smiling triumphantly. My mind went wild, conjuring spectacular changes in my life, filled with shiploads of packages that would soon land in my lap like manna. Would I have enough space for them? I was mesmerized.

Weeks rolled by, but nothing extraordinary happened. Instead, a gaping emptiness began invading me. I was so discouraged that I did not attend the series of meetings in the new church, which the man of God was launching in Yaounde. Neither did the highly publicized inaugural meeting of the women's wing catch my attention.

Even then, I still wondered if I wasn't passing up the second chance for real blessings.

Nonetheless, the disapproving opinions of some well-respected Christians consoled me. Their reports were disturbing. One of them had identified one of the two guys who had flung away his walking stick, wrongly claiming that he used to be lame. Thus, they insisted that most of the avowals of the grand night at the Hilton were fake. Also, they recounted gruesome scenes during the launch meetings, wherein people were falling on the floor, shivering, shouting, and convulsing, on the orders of attending evangelists. They suspected that it was more of magical tricks than the power of miracles.

I listened to them and wondered whether the man of God was not just one of a million businessmen, good at tantalizing vulnerable people. The unanswered questions went through my mind. Maybe a follow-up interview with the man of God would have exonerated him, but it was too late. He was already on his merry way to his next port of call.

Nevertheless, I still held onto my three requests. Instead of waiting for a miracle, I was determined to work hard to attain my goals. Wasn't the burning desire to succeed, in and of itself, a miracle? Wasn't being a journalist the gateway to becoming a prolific writer? I tried to convince myself.

As for reconciling with Mesape, I had to be realistic. A common adage stated that it takes two hands to tie a bundle.

Until then, I still felt a pressing need for the right place for worship. I had since left the prestigious location of prayer and worship at the Hilton. I continued my tour of Christian churches, in the company of friends and neighbors. On the sidelines, I began researching on the Muslim faith. It was an easy task for me. I got help from Ali, who produced religious programs for our radio station. He gave me an introductory lesson on the teachings of Mohammed. When he realized that my interest was growing, he lent me a copy of the Qu'ran. He also gave me other gift books.

Back home, I turned over the pages and the smell of frankincense or some other spice invaded my breath. Nevertheless, I kept reading, a little here and a little there. Soon, I began imagining myself, clad in colorful lace *wrapper* with a scarf over my head, sitting beside other Muslim women.

However, some recurring questions deterred me. Did I want to become part of a culture that bars women from entering the mosque? Even in cases where men allowed women to enter the mosque, did I want to be forever a silent participant?

Besides, my personality did not suit the place of the voiceless and the invisible reserved for women. Why should I anchor the national and world news, reaching some fifty million listeners, interview foreign dignitaries, stand side by side by with VIPs, including the President of the Republic, and then suddenly disappear into obscurity? Why should I be equal with men in the daily execution of my job, but become insignificant in approaching God, my Maker? I wanted to ask God hard questions, boldly and directly, about my personal life.

When I recalled how Estelle's touch comforted me the first time, I craved the touch of God's hand. There were hurtful, pent-up emotions, like gravel, stuck in my heart that He only could reach in and shake off.

I needed a radical change in my life.

CHAPTER 27

Tragedy Junction

One Sunday morning, after my tour of non-Roman Catholic churches, I returned to my best-known denomination, where a priest had dedicated me as a baby to God at the village chapel. I was among the first to arrive at the Eligefa English church, breaking my childhood record. When I was a student at the faculty, it was fashionable to get to the churchyard, not necessarily on time, but while the service was still going on. We preferred hanging out, chatting until the mass ended.

That morning I behaved like older men or women who walked straight in and took their places before the massive crowds invaded all the seats.

I marched in and stopped at the fifth pew from the front. It was empty. I sat right in the middle, where I could listen to the priest uninterrupted. Quickly, I took out my notebook from my handbag. My pen was ready. I was determined to be an active participant in the mass. I wanted to be the best student of the priest's sermon.

Of course, I did not bring along my Bible. I didn't want to be the odd one out, especially at a time when I was avoiding any form of distraction. My pen danced across the page of my notebook as Father James preached. It was as if I was going to report on the sermon of the priest.

During the time for singing, my voice chimed in with the choir. It was not only loud but distinct. Some members turned around and glanced at me. I might have been off-key, but what did I care? Church for me, at that given moment in my life, was the one place where embarrassment and I parted company at the door.

Soon, the service was over. I was delighted to see so many of my old friends. I couldn't wait to get home to pore over my notes. After that day, reviewing and analyzing sermons became a must.

However, several weeks went by, but progress seemed rather slow, if there was any, at all. That personal touch, experienced from the Hilton pulpit, was absent. However, quitting was still the furthest thing from my mind. So, I kept trudging along with the weekly Sunday masses.

Three months went by. The gaping emptiness was now sounding like an alarm that would not turn off. I had to take action.

The first thing I did was evaluate myself. For the three preceding months, I had been presenting myself to God as a woman trying hard to attract the attention of a man. Yet, no response; the taste of unrequited love was bitter on my lips.

However, I had to do more than just pout and sigh. I did a critical analysis of all the churches I had attended so far. The Baptists were closest to my needs. In addition to teaching the Bible in an open class, I enjoyed the interaction. Also, I liked the creativity that they brought into singing. So, maybe I could write a song one day and teach it.

Meanwhile, nothing got better between Mesape and me. Instead, one Wednesday, in a matter-of-fact tone, he proposed to me to seek transfer from the broadcasting house to the Ministry of Communication. Was I dreaming, or was he speaking triple Dutch? His words hit me like thunder, but I mustered up the courage to probe further.

"Why?" I asked with trembling in my voice.

"It's not proper for husband and wife to work in the same corporation."

Not only was I taken aback by his insistence, but his measured tone felt like a sledgehammer hitting my head. Did I deserve to be punished for his misdeeds? I wondered. I should turn down my career for administration—what ruthlessness! I took a step backward to scrutinize the fellow, who was going crazy by the minute.

"I'm telling you the right thing to do. Think about it," Mesape lashed out, picking each syllable and looking grave.

Had he finally hit the edge of the cliff? The Zipora invasion was going way beyond curable insanity. He wanted me to walk away from my acclaimed career, and close shop, just when customers began to flock in, right? If that wasn't insanity, hitting at its peak, I didn't know what else. I had to hold on to that analysis, at least, to maintain my own sanity. I continued to ponder over the worsening situation, day and night. So, what next?

"Zipora has been hounding the editor-in-chief, trying to persuade him, to block your transfer to television, as a news anchor," said a sympathizing colleague, who pulled me to the corner the following week. She divulged more of what my husband and Zipora were concocting behind my back.

The mystery was still to unfold; the snake was still to lash out its fangs. I began noticing something unusual about Mesape's movements. He seemed to be following an alternating pattern of moments of presence and absence from home. For one or two weeks, he would spend more time out and only arrive by or after bedtime.

Then for the next couple of weeks, he would return promptly from work, giving a hundred percent dedication to his family. He would cook, clean up, and join in family activities full swing. He would indulge in our company so much that his job seemed undesirable. He would even be reluctant to pick up the telephone.

That alternating pattern went on for months.

Strangely enough, those moments of withdrawal also created a feeling of guilt in me. I reexamined myself. Have I been accusing Mesape mistakenly? Were people making up stories about us? Though nothing was definitely as sure as before, I began granting him special favors and endeavoring to focus on positive thoughts.

Before long, he relapsed. It struck suddenly like the sting of a bee. Indeed, we had hardly had enough time to rebuild the torn family nest before he dropped all and flew away like a migrating bird, scared of a sudden change in the weather.

That left me exasperated and perplexed. I groped for what to believe, much less count on, as the way forward. My mind darted like pendulum of a wall clock, without hope for a definite positive outcome.

For how long could I survive the sudden and radical swings? Gradually, I became a mere observer, sometimes too calm for his liking.

Yet, he wouldn't leave me alone. Suddenly, he started complaining about Estelle. "I don't want to see that woman here again," he said, to my utter surprise.

Estelle had been home only once, for lunch, and in his absence.

"What is wrong with her?" I asked.

"Is she behaving normally to you?" he asked, frowning.

Too bad, I thought to myself. Mesape's proposal was non-negotiable. How could I possibly give up such a kind, gentle, polite, friendly, classy, hardworking friend? As far as I was concerned, the most significant difference between her and most women was her sparing use of make-up. In the domain of faith, Mesape was clearly, and obnoxiously, out of balance. I couldn't, wouldn't, and shouldn't turn down my steady connection to the source of divine peace, especially in a corporation of 1,500, wallowing in intrigues and competition.

Meanwhile, my pregnancy had, so far, been smooth. The Tenas ladies were fond of asking me to stand and show off my sexy maternity gowns. I made most of them myself, progressively increasing the girth as the baby grew more prominent. During my last meeting with them as a pregnant woman, I had on a floral dress on a gray background. I had personally designed it to maintain a sexy touch. There was a three-inch band above the knees, supporting a slit at the center back.

"*Nyango* (young lady), give us a break," they started laughing and exclaiming as soon as I arrived.

I glowed in their admiration and proceeded to treat them to a fashion parade *à la française*, before taking my place.

Apart from relaxing moments like those, I was miserable. My morning devotions gradually became a conscious effort at educating myself in overcoming or, at least, coping with, the fear of the unknown. Nevertheless, I was looking forward to a safe delivery.

However, a week before the next doctor's appointment, I got up in the morning, feeling a slight pain in my stomach. I guessed that I had eaten something to which I was allergic. By late morning, I began feeling weak. That Saturday, I was unable to do my routine shopping and housekeeping. I stayed in bed most of the day.

It seemed to be a rhythmic pain. But how could it be? I was struggling to sleep, yet waking up, time and again, to hold my hurting stomach. It grew worse by evening.

On Sunday, I stayed in bed practically throughout the whole day. Mesape left a number at which I could contact him in case of an emergency. Thank goodness I survived the day until he returned from work.

However, by 2 am on Monday, the pain was tearing my stomach apart. It was excruciating. I groaned in bed, writhing like a snake, hit with a blunt knife at its belly.

Mesape looked confused, hardly knowing how to help. Then he rushed to our next-door neighbor. Within minutes, he returned and helped me get into the car, which was steaming in front of our door. They rushed me to Clinique Fouda, the private clinic, where I consulted my doctor.

Before the car slowed down, in front of Emergency, the pain was unbearable. My wailing voice was reaching atop the trees in the yard. Better off dead than endure the searing pain. I surrendered my life.

The midwives rushed me to the nearest bed and telephoned my doctor at home. I couldn't wait. Something had to be done and immediately to save me. All I could do was scream.

Suddenly, a gush of warm liquid began drowning my thighs. One of the midwives bent over me and requested that I part my legs. I couldn't. It didn't make sense to me.

So, she pushed up my gown and tore away my underpants. The rest of the staff joined her, requesting that I push. What? Was the baby coming out? No, impossible. I tried to resist, in a desperate attempt to retain the unripe fetus in my womb, or was it the womb of my mind?

Yet, the pain was growing worse. The end had come for me, I feared.

Suddenly, I felt something pushing its way through me. The baby forcing its way out? Unbelievable! Two more midwives came closer, with outstretched hands. Puff. Exit. Instantly, I took a deep breath of relief. Life flowed through my body that very second. The pain started subsiding.

I lifted my head from the bed and stared. Our seven-month premature baby was lying helpless. She was pretty and fully formed though her head was slightly out of proportion to the rest of her body.

They kept me in bed for examination and recovery from shock while waiting for my doctor. He came and explained that the baby had very slim chances of survival. Besides, we could not afford the incubating equipment. My heart ached as I cried out of desperation.

It was a tearful homecoming two days after the loss. How was I to explain to Quydee and Sweetie what had happened to my bulging "stomach"? I, myself, was barely wrestling with the fact that she had evaporated into invisible air so suddenly.

Despite the unfortunate outcome, and Mesape's presence for quick intervention, I was still not confident of my safety.

Nevertheless, I hoped that the misfortune would serve an urgent signal to him. I hoped that he would soon realize that he was treading on dangerous territory. My heart yearned for a radical change from his dual lifestyle.

The following day, friends came from work to visit me. We talked about my loss and the shock of it all. We also made references to Zipora. It was then that one of them disclosed that Zipora had spent days, off work, long before the miscarriage, hearbroken at the news of my pregnancy. Having another child would jeopardize any chance of her getting married to Mesape any time soon.

It was time for my guests to go. I smiled as they each hugged me. I truly appreciated their concern. As soon as they left, I began pondering over our conversation. How happy would Zipora be to receive the news of my loss! I wept under my sheets.

Three months before, Mesape had come home with news that he was receiving anonymous calls in his office. He said that the telephone would ring as soon as he stepped into his office. The unidentified caller would proceed to announce to him that he was not the father of our expected baby. The person, he said, would state the exact age of the pregnancy. How perplexing! I thought to myself.

Above all, what bothered me was his calm and composure in the face of the queer report.

"Who does this person sound like?" I asked.

"I don't know," he answered reluctantly, shaking his head.

"Is it a man or a woman?" I probed.

"The voice is too heavy to be a woman's voice and yet too light to be a man's," he responded, like a confused child.

Two weeks after his scanty report, he announced that he had received the exact copy of the message in type-written form. When I asked to see it, he said he had already disposed of it. He added that the writer did not sign it. The only peculiar thing was the misspelling of his name.

Where was his sense of horror? I kept asking myself. Neither had he attempted to do something about it nor was he budging.

"So what shall we do?" my troubled soul worried aloud.

"What can we do?" he asked with raised eyebrows.

"Find out who is behind all this."

The minutes left to detonate the time bomb began ticking louder in my brain. After the blast that caused the miscarriage, did I need another reminder that I was facing a raging battle against a legion?

"How?" he asked, throwing his hands in the air.

The minutes left to detonate the time bomb began ticking louder in my brain. After the blast that caused the miscarriage, did I need another reminder that I was facing a raging battle against a legion?

Unfortunately, I had neither tested ammunition nor battlefront experience. Yet, enemies could strike anytime and from any direction.

It was urgent to reinforce my self-defense. The loss of the baby obliged a deliberate effort on my part to search for the truth.

CHAPTER 28

Seeking Truth for Freedom

On Saturday morning, barely two weeks after the miscarriage, I got up earlier than usual. I was going to become an investigator in my own case.

I took advantage of Mesape's deep, snoring sleep and edged myself out of bed. Then I slipped into the bathroom and barely threw water over my body. Quickly, my hands fumbled for my clothes. I couldn't turn on the lights, meaning that I couldn't use the mirror either. There was no time to brush my teeth with toothpaste. Besides, running water was too high a risk to take. So, I grabbed a chewing stick and slipped it into my skirt pocket.

Then, I tiptoed back into the room, where I crawled on the floor and quietly pulled his bunch of keys from his side of the bed. I managed to hold my breath until I left the room. A gentle turn of the key at the door did it. My body slipped out through the crack of the door. It was not an occasion that warranted driving.

It was fresh and chilly. Birds were chirping away in distant trees. I looked at my watch; it was hardly 6:30. My quick steps mounted up the stairs. I stepped onto the tarred streets, and in less than three minutes, I sighted an approaching taxicab. I motioned the driver to stop. He accepted my destination, and I rushed for the door.

Within twenty minutes, the driver pulled right up to the main gate of the Television Corporation headquarters in Mballa II. There were three to four colleagues in the yard, apart from the night watchmen. My presence did not raise any suspicion. What freedom one enjoys when one is respected and admired by others! I beamed.

"*Bonjour*," I said with a wave of my right hand and hurried on.

Chapter 28: Seeking Truth for Freedom 179

CRTV—my office at that time

The elevator was waiting for me; my trembling hands pressed level six. I stepped out and glanced left and right. There was no other soul on the floor but me. My shaking hands fumbled with the key at his office door, which swung open. My giant steps dashed in. Immediately, I locked the door behind me.

The fact-finding process proper was on. Any form of interruption was prohibited. Work had to proceed at express speed. It was demanding to control my racing heart and trembling hands. File after file flew open. Loose papers were falling on his table and some to the floor.

After looking at the shelves, it was the turn of the drawers, followed by the closets. Both hands and eyes dug into files. Video cases yielded to authoritative fingers. I opened and scrutinized folded pages; I opened envelopes while glancing at empty spaces like a sniffer dog.

Finally, the search began yielding fruits: two Valentine cards with Zipora's signature. My heart threatened palpitations while my legs wobbled. I managed to put them aside and began scanning the last file.

There was no big surprise, just greeting cards from girls and women, about whom I cared less. I picked up items of evidence and put them into the brown paper bag I brought along. Then I dropped the carefully wrapped bundle into the black plastic bag, which I placed at the bottom of my twine market bag. Mission accomplished. Exit.

In minutes, another taxicab was driving me to the Mokolo market. On the way, new strategies began brewing in my mind. First, I had to situate my find within context. I noticed that indeed, Mesape and Zipora had covered more territory than I had allowed myself to imagine. Now I believed our mutual colleagues, who disclosed that a few months ago, Zipora had accompanied a media team on a mission led by Mesape; her name had not featured on the official mission list. The hotel bill that I had recovered from Mesape's shirt pocket, over which we argued, finally made sense. Cold sweat rushed down my face as I contemplated his mastery in deception.

The more I perfected my plans, the faster my truth-seeking mission took on a life of its own.

The following Tuesday, I called at the home of Zipora's parents. Her mother, a dark, average height, sturdily built woman, opened the door. She led me in with an inquiring look and showed me a seat opposite hers.

"I've come to see you because your daughter is wrecking my home," I announced with a tremble in my voice, as soon as I sat down.

Then I proceeded to introduce myself. There was hardly any need for it, though Zipora's mother claimed that she never knew that Mesape was my husband. She said she thought instead that he was my brother.

Barely a minute or so of recounting the opening details, she stopped me.

"No, no, no. I can't take in all of this by myself," Zipora's mother complained and quickly stood up. " Please, just hold on. Let me come," she moaned and left, trotting away, up the adjacent staircase.

Within minutes, a short, youthful man, with a delightful demeanor, descended the stairs of the cozy, three-level mansion. He had a note pad in his left hand and a pen in his right.

Introductions were rapid. I recommenced my story from the very beginning.

"Didn't I tell you?" he asked, staring at his wife, with eyes pleading for help.

Then he turned towards me and explained that they had met my husband at their daughter's new apartment, after 10 pm, which was shocking. Zipora's father disclosed that, after Mesape left, they warned their daughter against the risk she was taking. He went on to say that even though Zipora had been defensive, she did come home the following day, crying and promising that she would reduce her contacts with Mesape to a professional relationship.

"Not only is she trying to destroy my family. She is responsible for my recent miscarriage," I asserted myself while looking straight into his face.

He took a deep breath and started tapping his legs.

"Lord have mercy," he kept saying.

He bent down his head, right onto his lap, and his whole body started shaking.

Meanwhile, his wife fastened her lips like a baby forbidden to cry. He raised his head and addressed me.

"I cannot say you are lying. But I raised my daughter in a Christian home," he confessed.

He paused and looked at his wife, and she nodded in approval.

"However, today, my daughter is an adult. And honestly, I cannot vouch for her," he went on.

Peace and assurance fused into my heart. I took a deep breath and looked at him in admiration. He was a respected person in the community, especially for his contribution to spreading the good news of the gospel. Indeed, he was an authority in the Born-Again church.

Before I went on, he specially thanked me for my "respectful attitude." He said that he truly appreciated how I showed them respect by coming directly to them. I could have caused a scene to disgrace his family, under the mistaken impression that they condone her lewd acts.

"My daughter," he said with renewed conviction while looking straight at me. "You stand tall in the eyes of God. Only He can repay you for such self-control, in your moment of pain and direct provocation from our daughter," he went on, dragging each word while lifting his right hand as if he was anointing me from his pulpit.

The details were still pouring out. Zipora's father was listening and taking notes. Surprisingly, he requested proof of his daughter's involvement with my husband. He stressed that it was a necessary element in my accusation.

Ha, ha, ha, a broad smile parted my lips while my hands quickly rummaged into my handbag.

Meanwhile, he and his wife looked on with open mouths. Finally, I pulled out the greeting cards and presented them to him. He quickly turned around and stared at his wife, leaving my hand suspended in the air. Then he closed his eyes and took in a deep breath.

Finally, he stretched out his hand and took the cards, as if it was a death warrant. He proceeded to scrutinize the first one, back and forth. He pressed his eyes into it and touched it with his forefinger. Then he stopped, looked up to the ceiling, and took another deep breath.

"I recognize this one," he said as he handed it over to his wife. "She got this from the family collection," he went on. "Yes, this is my daughter's handwriting and signature," he insisted.

He stared at his wife again, startled, speechless. Then he bent down his head while both palms cupped his face. He started sobbing.

Meanwhile, his wife began blinking, as if hot pepper had entered into her eyes. She was also breathing hard and fidgeting in her seat.

"Oh God, have mercy," his voice was teary.

He hit his lap endlessly as he moaned.

"This is the work of the devil. It is a curse to my family. What shall we do?" he turned to her while she just looked on and continued biting her fingers.

Suddenly, he fell back into his seat. Then he pushed himself forward again. He remained silent for a while. Indeed, no one spoke for about two minutes. He was in deep thoughts.

"I tell you what," he said while turning to her and then to me. "If my daughter does not give up, I'm going to disown her," he warned, dragging his words again. "Wicked, wicked, evil."

Meanwhile, I just listened and watched. My soul was taking a momentary rest after unburdening its heavy load.

"What else shall I say? I have warned her of the risk of this wicked act," he kept on.

He stretched out his hand and picked up the black, hardcover Bible that was on the table in front of us.

"What if you had hired someone to finish her off?" he asked. "You have the right to protect your family. And this is more than enough provocation from your colleague," he spoke out in a rising voice, filled with anger.

There was no doubt, by now, that we had become a team. So, Zipora's parents went on to disclose that their daughter had effectively invited friends to their home, among whom was Mesape. They had assumed that all of them were just her friend's classmates. They were referring to Nerissa. They said they had warned their daughter to steer clear of Nerissa's corrupting influence.

That particular disclosure obliged me to share more sordid details with them. They clasped their hands in shock. The distraught father grabbed his Bible again and began to read passages from the books of Romans and Corinthians. He stopped, from time to time, to preach and explain. When he finished, he invited me for prayers. All three of us knelt on the carpeted floor.

"Holy Father," he started.

He went on and on while quoting Bible verses from memory. Then suddenly, he burst out crying.

"Lord," he said, and stopped to blow his nose. "This is such a terrible thing," he went on but paused to cry. "Please, Father, have mercy... on my family. Please, deliver, deliver, my daughter," he pleaded from the depths of his soul. "When the devil takes over the heart, the case becomes complicated."

His wife's hands began trembling.

As for me, what was I to do? My heart was aching.

Two full hours had passed.

Before I left, Zipora's parents and I struck a deal to stay in touch. We needed to keep monitoring the culprits from our respective angles.

CHAPTER 29

Surviving in the Fiery Furnace

Mesape labeled me "dangerous" upon receiving the news of my meeting with Zipora's parents. He said I had betrayed him. How dare I undertake an unusual mission without informing him? He accused me of exposing his family to the criticism of strangers.

He could not dissuade me. I was the more determined to scare away Zipora by exposing her or proceeding to request a divorce if Mesape persisted in infidelity.

However, the following Sunday morning ushered in a gentler and more loving Mesape than I had known for months. He kissed and hugged me each time he passed by me. He gave me compliments at every turn. He made statements to the effect that I was more deserving than him. He even offered to cook a special traditional Douala dish, *timbanaboussa*.

After lunch, he implored me to stay home and relax while he accompanied the children to their friend's birthday party. He was due to leave for work in a few hours, but in enough time to take the children to the party.

"Okay, I will come and get them later," I gladly proposed.

"No, don't worry about it," he said. "Just take this day off and give yourself a good rest."

How considerate of him! I thought. He must be trying to compensate for all the trouble he has put me through. Or so I convinced myself.

Little did I know that all his "loving" acts were his express attempts at weakening my defenses. Indeed, before nightfall, the tables had turned against me.

I received my children into the house that evening, cheerfully.

However, as soon as I closed the door, my little girl reported that Zipora had given them a ride from the party to their father's office. Instantly, dizziness began dimming my sight. My precautionary legs started to move towards the couch quietly. A cold blanket of insanity was wrapping itself around me as if I had mistakenly stepped into hell, and was still struggling to back out. I could no longer contain myself. It was the onset of a panic attack, splitting my body into pieces. Inside me, it felt like I had inhaled poisonous fumes. They had to come out instantly, and by any means. My life depended on that.

I got up and searched all around like a drunkard, dodging an on-coming car. My body was trembling like a lump of jelly on a plate, waiting to be munched by the Zipora witches. Something urgent had to happen to arrest the creeping derangement taking over my whole being. My shaking body prodded towards the kitchen for the box of matches. Fortunately, or unfortunately, it was not there. I looked at tables, countertops, and closets. It was nowhere.

So, I spun around, desperate for some other means to release the fury. I went into the wardrobe, thinking of what I could do to destroy Mesape's clothes within seconds, having failed to set the house on fire. Yet, there was no luck. I sighed and turned around again.

Then, my hands fell on a new tee-shirt, which I could have sworn was a gift from Zipora. I grabbed a pair of scissors. In minutes, it became dozens of tiny strings. Then I hung it at the room door, to make for a welcome-back-home décor for a prodigal spouse.

Meanwhile, my daughter showed me a bag of cookies, which she said Zipora had packaged for her. I quickly seized it and examined it from angle to angle. Then I flung it on the table. There and then, I began rebuking the devil aloud.

The time had come to begin disclosing some of the weird stuff which my family was going through. I told them about their father's links with Zipora. I led them into Zipora's attempts on my life. They both listened, looking dumbfounded and helpless. My son wore a frown on his face, wondering what in the world he could say or do. I could only imagine.

As for my daughter, she was enraged. She grabbed the package of goodies and threw it into the trash.

That night, she cried herself to sleep.

She got up in the morning and refused breakfast. As soon as her father woke up, she approached him.

"Daddy, don't you ever enter into Zipora's car again," she said, frowning and pointing her finger.

Why should the devil attack a five-year-old head-on? I grieved.

My silent resolve was never again to allow Mesape to mislead me into romantic pranks. It was time to learn how to sleep with one eye and one ear open.

If I was still in slumber, the wake-up call was not long in coming. Wednesday morning, he got up unusually early and left the house at 5:00, claiming that he was going to the office. Mesape was not a morning person. And I knew that, better than anyone else. He was not one to offer to leave his bed, not even at 6:00 am. He said that he was going to hand over equipment to colleagues, who were departing on a mission. That wasn't his job at all.

However, my guards were up, high up in the sky, that day. My nose was smelling for news on all his tracks. At work, I began throwing hints, here and there. I returned from the newsroom without any leads. So, I mentioned Zipora to Sophie, who was now sharing my office with me. Immediately, she began donating information. Indeed, Zipora had left, early that same morning, for a vacation to a neighboring country. The news pierced me like a spear.

While she was away, the coast was clear and quiet like it had never before yielded to any disruptive activity. My mind, body, and soul also declared a vacation.

However, as soon as she returned, I resumed watching and sniffing every spot in the house for signs of "toxins." I went as far as searching into every object in the wardrobe, including pockets of shirts, jackets, and bags.

Finally, it took putting away four suitcases and digging into a trunk, which we opened only once a year, to hit the bottom of the dreadful truth. There it was, a brand new tee-shirt, carefully wrapped and placed in-between other clothes.

I seized it, and my heart starting beating faster. My buttocks dropped on the bare floor as I pondered over the increasing cases of excruciating torture. I held onto it lost in my thoughts. I just couldn't figure out how to go about it. Should I burn it or just throw it away? I continued brainstorming, later on, in the office with the sophisticated Sophie. We agreed that the smart thing was trying to trace the origin of the tee-shirt instead of destroying it.

On Monday morning, I dressed in my beige suit. Underneath was a flowery brown blouse, which I always wore with it. I got into the car and waited until we were ready to leave.

As soon as Mesape turned on the ignition key, I excused myself and rushed back into the house. It barely took seconds to exchange my brown blouse for the suspect tee-shirt. I hurried back into the waiting car while struggling to pull my jacket towards the center.

We drove off. Half-way through the ride, right in the middle of a traffic jam, I showed off my shirt to Mesape. He smiled dryly but didn't say a word.

"Doesn't it look nice to you?" I gently rebuked him.

He gave me a rather stony look and quickly fixed on the black car ahead of us. I stared at him, with the intent of communicating my utter disappointment.

"Yeah, it's nice," he said finally.

"I'm surprised you didn't even care to show me," I said while fidgeting with my purse mirror and rubbing my cheeks, up and down.

He dropped me off at the radio house and promised to arrive promptly to take me home for the lunch break.

By 10.45 am, fifteen minutes to the end of the television news conference, I hired a taxicab from the radio house.

I was breathing hard by the time I rushed through the long, windy corridor, leading to the newsroom. Incidentally, the first person I met, exiting the room, was Mesape. He was stunned to see me. We greeted each other. I deliberately resisted making any excuses for my presence. There was no time to waste. I took a quick step forward towards my destination.

He caught me by the arm and invited me, rather urgently, to his office. I promised to come up later. He insisted while squeezing and pulling my arm. I declined, snatching myself free from his grip. He was furious. He started accusing me, right there and then, of misbehaving and provoking a fight in public.

There was no time to lose. I wriggled free from Mesape's tight grip and forced my way into the newsroom. By now, my jacket was on my left arm. I pushed my chest forward and began an unauthorized one-person fashion parade in the newsroom from corner to corner, greeting friends and colleagues. Then I stopped in front of Patrick, who was directly facing Zipora. I engaged him in an argument. From there, I watched the witch.

The smile on her face abruptly turned into advancing dark clouds, desperately trying to consume the sun.

If eyes could discharge bullets, she would have been merciless that fateful day. The silent battle went on amidst the detached noise and laughter of other colleagues.

The drama that followed at home that evening was telling of the enigmatic nature of the deal between them. Mesape got home earlier than usual, looking pale. As soon as he stepped in, he demanded, as a matter of urgency, the tee-shirt. He started yelling in a harsh and stirring tone. He was trembling and fidgeting at the same time.

"Where is the tee-shirt? I want it right now," he demanded, flinging his right hand at me.

"Why? What do you want a dirty tee-shirt for?" I asked.

He explained that it had been given to members of his sports department by an advertising company. They wanted them back.

Immediately, I stood up, rushed into our bedroom, and began searching in the wardrobe. My hands pulled it from inside my jacket. Quickly, I dashed into the bathroom. Before Mesape caught up with me, I had soaked it in the standing water.

Mesape pounced over me and tried to seize it. It was clenched between my hands. So, a fight over the shirt erupted between us. He was breathing hard while I was panting.

He stood up and spun around.

"What shall I say? I'm in trouble, I'm in trouble," he mourned while dancing around, almost in tears.

My firm hands quickly surrendered the shirt into the bathwater. Then I ran out into the living room.

In two minutes, I went back in. Surprisingly, Mesape was trembling and forcing it into a plastic bag. I had hardly had time to begin to capture the mystery when he ran out of the house with it, firmly clutched into his right hand. I dashed out after him. I noticed that our Mitsubishi Galant was nowhere visible.

He started racing up the hilly driveway. I followed, in an attempt to at least see the rest of the picture of the unfolding pandemonium.

Then, I stopped and paused. A thought crossed my mind. Could it be that Zipora was sitting in my car by the corner, waiting for my husband? It struck me hard. I ran up the hilly driveway, a few more meters.

Then suddenly, I stopped. What if the two ganged up against me? And who knows if there wasn't a legion, standing by and supporting them? It was a terrifying thought.

Mesape returned home that night, infuriated. He was barking like a wounded dog. He blamed me for trying to make a fool of him, insisting that I had no right to use the tee-shirt without his permission.

What was the point of arguing with him? I considered to myself. I didn't respond. Even a child could tell that he had, indeed, become a cause for concern. Who could doubt that he was under the control of some evil, supernatural powers? How sad and scary!

Barely two weeks after the tee-shirt incident, he got up earlier than usual again. This time around, he decided to take our son himself to school by taxicab since our car had a breakdown for almost a week. I was relieved by his unexpected offer.

Little did I know that another shocker was underway. When our seven-year-old returned from school that day, he informed me that instead of a taxicab, they had driven in Zipora's car.

When I asked Mesape, he said it was some other friend's car. Meanwhile, he had parked the car overnight, away from the house.

Little did he know that our son had already quoted the car plate number, make, and color to me.

CHAPTER 30

In Search of the Home of the Privileged

On Sunday morning, I drove for almost an hour, across town, to formally join the English Baptist Church. The secretary duly registered my name among those studying for baptism.

However, that same day, a friend, Mary, my colleague and a member of the same Baptist congregation, invited me to attend a musical concert as well as health lectures sponsored by Seventh-day Adventists. The name was very familiar. I recalled that they had dental clinics in Buea and Yaounde. That was all I knew about them.

The event sounded like an everyday occurrence, so I was not particularly interested. I told Mary that I would attend if only my schedule permitted. I didn't go. The following day, a senior colleague, Olive, invited me to the same occasion. I appreciated their interest in my well-being. However, why were they so eager for my presence?

"Akongshee, it is so soothing, you don't want to miss it," she said.

On Monday evening, I drove to the event location, a walking distance from my job. I entered the chapel, facing the back street. It was the basement of a two-level building, hosting the offices of the headquarters of the Seventh-day Adventist Church in central Africa. The conference had been going on for a week.

It was my very first visit. I came alongside nine other colleagues, whom Mary and Olive had invited. Since we were a little late, we decided to sit at the back. We were waiting impatiently for the soloist, whose name had piqued our interest.

Chapter 30: In Search of the Home of the Privileged   191

Adventist Women International Conference in Babcock, Nigeria

A woman sitting in the pew ahead of us informed us that the star artist, who sang like a nightingale, was not available for the evening. Neither were there any more health lectures; the screenings were over. My colleagues and I sighed. Regrettably, the two reasons for which we had come were absent.

"Let's go," one of my colleagues proposed. Each of the ladies picked up their handbags and left. As for me, curiosity got the better of me, so I stayed back. "Who are these people?" I wanted to find out something about them. "Besides, I don't want to go away empty-handed," I decided.

At that same moment, a gentleman, the coordinator, went to the microphone and ushered in the speaker for the evening, for the scheduled teaching. Immediately, a young lady from the receptionist's desk behind handed me a Bible, a pencil, and a small cutout sheet of paper.

Instinctively, I began scanning the room for any familiar faces. Not a soul did I recognize, out of the thirty or so, gathered in there.

Pastor Duwona, tie knotted to his neck, in a grayish-brown western suit, came forward and announced the topic for the evening—Creation. So, what about creation? I thought to myself.

Each person, including children, began taking their Bibles in hand, in readiness, like spoons for an eating contest.

"If it is in the Bible?" the Pastor began chanting.

"We accept it," they responded in chorus enthusiastically.

"If it's not in the Bible?"

"We don't accept it."

Thank goodness, Genesis was the first book of the Bible to find. I listened to every word while struggling to search the cross references in the other books.

It was over in barely fifteen minutes. I had hardly had time to jot down some catching phrases. A guy moved up to me, there and then, and said that I should not worry about what I had missed. Everything was in the handouts. So, I continued listening to the Pastor.

Excellent, I said to myself while opening my eyes wide. So, it is possible to understand the Bible without graduating from a seminary? So, indeed, God has a specific plan for everyone on earth, including me? I had never heard such a simple, crystal-clear interpretation of the Bible. Yet it was so powerful.

Soon, the pastor started requesting questions from the floor. He invited the audience to answer the questions. I saw children, as young as seven, stretching out their hands and jumping from their seats. Some even had answers tagged to specific Bible verses, which they recited from memory.

What! I exclaimed to myself. Those children knew Bible facts, events, personalities, and places, and it was all at their fingertips. Some of them were going to the extent of relating the significance of the teachings to everyday life. Right then and there, I realized that, possibly, I was the most ignorant person in that hall. What a shame! I thought to myself. Even as they spoke, I was so awed that goose pimples came over my arms. My body shivered a little. I felt like I had just been tossed off from a strange island, far from human habitation.

I went home that night, satisfied but disturbed. The level of my ignorance about life—the place of God in human life, the creation of the earth, divine laws, facts about space and time, the source of love, the management of social relationships, the origin of sin, the meaning and the importance of salvation, haunted me all night.

The following evening, I was among the first to arrive. I took the front seat. I was all ears; I listened and jotted down notes at the same time. Back home, I read over the list of Bible verses before going to bed.

Chapter 30: In Search of the Home of the Privileged

On Wednesday, I swapped my working hours with one of my colleagues and rewarded him with three times the regular taxi fare for transportation.

Before leaving the house, I washed off all the make-up from my face and used a simple moisturizer. My earrings were no longer the dangling neck-sweeping chain, but just a gold-plated dot. Also, instead of flashy lipstick, I rubbed my lips with Vaseline®.

"Akongshee, you look much prettier without your make-up and jewelry," Pastor Gibbons remarked as he ushered me in.

How did he know my mind? I wondered. I was more than flattered. I had always longed to be loved and accepted with my natural look without make-up, or jewelry; those I reserved for studio appearances. I smiled while my heart fluttered. My steps were bolder as I walked right to the front seat.

That session of the evening seemed to be mine. More than half of the twenty questions answered were from the list I had placed in the quiz box, the previous day. Even while the explanations were coming forth, so too, layers of ignorance were falling off from my mind like a snake, shedding away its old skin.

Baptism featured among the topics for the second week. Immediately, I counted myself out; the priest of the village church, where my parents belonged, had baptized me when I was a baby. It was rather strange to suggest another baptism, and especially to an adult.

> *How did he know my mind? I wondered. I was more than flattered. I had always longed to be loved and accepted with my natural look without make-up, or jewelry;*

I drove home that evening with a lot of misgivings. For fear of being misled, I had to cross-check everything the pastors were teaching and preaching. I had to investigate the soundness of their doctrine personally. It wasn't enough to review the lesson of the day, and read all the flyers and magazines, from cover to cover. However, I had no clue how else to proceed. The following morning brought a brilliant idea. I was going to leave my car at home, take a taxicab, and walk back home after the evening session, in the company of members, going my direction.

On our way home, I asked tons of questions. My query covered a whole range of issues: What was the meaning of difficult Bible verses accruing from the lesson of the evening? Why did they join the denomination? What has changed in their personal lives? How were they dealing with conflicts with family members and friends with different interpretations of the Bible?

From the first evening of interaction with those simple women, less educated than myself, I had to swallow my pride. Their quick, precise, and spontaneous answers got me off my high horse of Madam News Anchor and Special Correspondent at the Presidency of the Republic to the level of a beginner in basics of life lessons. Their wisdom caught me off guard. One of them, Juliana, who was a high school dropout (mostly for financial reasons), stunned me with her knowledge and understanding. She quoted chunks of verses as well as passages from other books, to illustrate her point. Even as she spoke, a surge of heat was rising from the pith of my human essence. My enlightened mind was instantly discarding dense layers of ignorance that had piled up over the years.

It was a humbling experience. Whether I understood it or not, I was on the verge of exiting from one world into another, howbeit still on planet earth. A process was set in motion in me, which I could no longer arrest. My mind began to reevaluate my self-worth. My investigating eyes ran over my body, from my shoes to my dress. My beautiful and expensive outfits were nothing compared to the wisdom of those women. I had to admit it. The question imposed itself. What was the worth of six years of university education, given that I was still so ignorant? Ultimately, what was my purpose on planet earth? Where was I going from there? Why do good people suffer so much? Each of those women, including their children, had answered those questions for themselves.

As for me, there was no doubt that I would need a lot of help.

Each night, after returning home, I reviewed every verse, highlighted in the mini studies. Then, I proceeded to read the free magazines and pamphlets, from the first to the last page. Of course, I was gaining knowledge with understanding around the basics, especially those explained by the pastor. The more I read, the more questions popped up like mushrooms on wet, rotting tree trunks or dark, fertile soil, and taking their rightful place under the sun.

On Thursday night, I returned home and prayed with tear-filled eyes.

"Lord, these lessons are too good to be true. Please, if this is the wrong church, please, please, take me out before it is too late. You know that only You can stop me at this point."

As soon as I finished, a feeling of gratefulness came over me. I was thankful for the opportunity, the time, the quiet space, where I studied, night after night, close to midnight.

Meanwhile, Mesape explained that he was returning home late because of too much work, the reason for which he could not attend the conference, whose worth I demonstrated to him repeatedly. How extra polite he was becoming! I dismissed the reasons he advanced. Not only had he never shown any interest in religion, but he never as much as turned over the tracts, which I placed next to his dinner at the table. Whatever, I was careful not to seem to be harassing him.

By Sunday, I began realizing that the more I thought about the possibility of joining the church, the more I became excited about baptism. I had understood the difference between baby presentation or dedication and baptism. While the former is a parental decision, the latter is the conscious, personal commitment of an individual. A baptismal candidate pledges to abide by a set of laid-down principles.

As soon as I took the resolve to proceed with baptism, something supernatural began happening in me. A gentle and compelling voice from somewhere spoke to me. I heard it distinctly, without a trace of interference, as if through the ears of my soul.

"Akongshee, you must be baptized because this is your only chance. It is now or never. For you, it is a choice between life and death. It is now or never," it persisted.

The voice was unobtrusive and soothing. It spoke to me, first thing in the morning, in the daytime while I drove alone through a quiet area with trees, and just before sleep overtook me, each night. For days, it went on and on until the target day.

Countdown to baptism began. Caution was in order. No one or anything was to prevent me, I decided. Meanwhile, friends at work, whom I invited to my baptism, mostly responded with jeers.

"What's wrong with you? Were you not baptized as a baby?" they tried to dissuade me.

"Oh, no, not at all. That was just a dedication, not baptism," I tried to explain.

"So what's the difference?" they asked, some with taunting laughter.

"Can a baby decide to accept Christ as his or her Lord and personal Savior?" I asked.

Gladys ran and repeated my question to other colleagues. Some laughed and brushed it off while others simply dismissed me, saying, "Just leave Akong alone."

On baptism morning, I crept out of bed, long before dawn. I bathed in the bucket of water, which I had collected the previous evening, for fear of alerting the attention of Mesape with the sound of the shower. I dressed up with lightning speed.

My bag with a change of clothes, which had been safely tucked away behind the living room couch overnight, was waiting. I seized it and gripped it under my arm. Then, I tiptoed out of the house.

Safely on the street, I offered the first taxicab up to three times the regular fare. I opened the door and perched on the back seat. My heart was beating very fast.

As soon as he took off, I started looking behind to ensure that no one was pursuing me. Within twenty-five minutes, precisely at 8 am, I was standing at the open field at Mimboman, Yaounde. I was the first to arrive, one full hour before the debut of the event.

The vast empty field of reddish dust provided enough mental space to reminisce over the swift and dangerous turns my life had, so far, taken. I began searching my Bible and asking God for a special baptismal gift. My hands flipped over the pages randomly. Then, my eyes fell on Ezekiel 37. I read the whole chapter. It sounded more like I was dreaming. So, I reread it. It was the strange story of dry bones in a valley, being transformed into living beings. That was too much to fathom.

However, I was intrigued by the dialogue between God and the "son of man." Wasn't I also as ignorant and powerless as the man whom God was using to revive the dry bones? Or was he being humble? As I pondered over it, a heatwave seemed to be enveloping my whole body as a baby cuddled in his or her mother's tender arms. Was I being transported into the scene of recreation? Or so it seemed. Indeed, my weary bones were crying out for revival, having suffered multiple acts of brutality.

I looked up from my Bible and saw other candidates arriving. Their family members and friends were accompanying them. Within ten minutes, crowds of people of all ages filled the field. My eyes combed through the groups. Apart from those who had studied with me, at that particular location, I did not recognize anyone else. None of my colleagues had honored my invitation.

The more people arrived in groups, the more the feelings of loneliness chilled my body. I was going through an internal struggle between ecstasy and sadness. I missed my husband, the one who used to hold my hand wherever we went. I longed for my children, who were spending their vacation with my parents, hundreds of miles away. I knew that they would have been capering around me and making witty jokes. I yearned for my mother, who woke up each morning, between 4:00 and 5:00, to pray for her children. I craved the presence of my sister, Mercy, who, after getting fed up with powerless religions, invited her siblings to seek the omnipotent God among the Cherubims and Seraphims of Mutengene, each clad in white dresses from head to toe.

A burst of bright sunshine began shinning. Minutes before the start of the event, hundreds of people were filling the gigantic tent to overflowing. Large crowds of onlookers jammed the open field. Dozens of young boys climbed the surrounding trees, in readiness to watch the spectacular plunging into the giant tank of water, placed in the middle of the field.

Pastor Nlo Nlo, a famous and engaging speaker, was ushered on stage with thunderous applause. After greetings, he started preaching. From time to time, the massive audience would respond, "Amen," in chorus or laugh out loud, for Emmanuel Nlo Nlo was so comical in his illustrations. The Pastor's voice was beaming from the loudspeaker and reaching the houses and stores in the neighborhood, the highways, the hills, and the surrounding valleys. When he began making the alter call for undecided and potential candidates for the next baptism, the cameraman for the event shouted out, "Yes, I believe, and I'm ready now."

Indeed, LeDoux joined the 140 baptismal candidates that day. Each of them was in either the gray or maroon long, drooping gowns; mine was gray. Four pastors entered into the artificial pool. Then, they stretched out their hands to the first four candidates. After the pastors plunged them simultaneously, multiple foamy waves rippled in the tank. My heart leaped with excitement. The observing crowds sang and clapped, chanting, "Amen! Alleluia!"

Finally, my turn arrived. The new friends that I had met at my brand-new church looked up and smiled. One of them had taken my bag and stuff as soon as the first candidate went into the baptismal pool. Meanwhile, Jacob, a church member and professional photographer, armed with his camera, drew closer. "I can miss others, but not this one," he said.

I proceeded, step after step. My heart was beating with joy and excitement. Two women of the Dorcas Society, dressed in gold-colored uniforms, each held me on both sides and led me into the pool. I took hold of Pastor Gibbon's waiting hand, and he repeated the standard instructions to me. I nodded in approval. My heart started beating fast again with my palms pressed together prayerfully. He placed his left hand on my right shoulder. Who would have thought that the Bermuda-born US citizen would come to my country and perform such a life-changing ceremony? He looked at me and smiled.

"I baptize you in the name of the Father, and the Son, and the Holy Ghost," he said, lifting his right hand. Then he plunged me backward into the sanctifying water. A few seconds was enough for the kiss of eternal life. Up, out, and forwards, he pulled me. Quickly, my palms ran over my face at express speed, with eyes shut. As I opened my eyes, Jacob clicked his camera; the light flashed in my direction. I got out at the opposite end, into the waiting hands of two other deaconesses in golden yellow. They patted my back and showered endless praises to God.

I rushed to the bathroom for a quick change of clothes. Then I dashed back out and joined the celebrating members. My curiosity was at its peak. Not a thing did I want to miss.

> *"I baptize you in the name of the Father, and the Son, and the Holy Ghost," he said, lifting his right hand. Then he plunged me backward into the sanctifying water. A few seconds was enough for the kiss of eternal life.*

Meanwhile, my new friends came and surrounded me with warm smiles and words of encouragement. Each took a turn to embrace me. Tears of joy began filling my eyes. Books, flowers, and hugs were all mine. Love, cheers, and encouragement were mine, too, falling like showers for the grandest celebration. Some offered to help in carrying my bag and gifts.

It was time for an all-church potluck lunch. We began moving over to the Adventist college, chatting. When we arrived there, the first time that my feet touched the reddish-brown earth of the campus, I stepped back and considered my new, large, extended family. It was, indeed, an initiation into a fresh new community. The trend of the latest and unfolding events, on a brand new side of life, was forever set in motion.

Meanwhile, the flavor of freshness filled the air, conveying the welcome smell of different foods. My mouth began to water.

Ushers guided us to one of the many classrooms, turned into dining halls, for the occasion. There were dozens of tables. The dinner looked somewhat strange; there was no meat or flesh food. I glanced into the basins and overflowing pots of rice, beans, fried plantains, *puff-puff, koki,* steamed vegetables, and salad, in vain.

Home-made fresh juices, from guava, soursop, foléré, and ginger, were on a separate table. Strangely, there was neither soda, beer, whiskey, nor any brand of French wine, which was the popular item on dining tables in French Cameroon. Yet everyone seemed satisfied, and ready to savor the food amidst lots of fun—sharing testimonies and laughing excitedly like children.

The last to arrive at the campus began taking their place at the benches. My eyes scrutinized each table and person in our room. Where was the high table for the officiating team? I left my seat momentarily and went to the other classrooms. They were all identical. Besides, pastors had similar plates like everyone else. Their size and variety of food in the rations were the same as ours. There was something wrong, I thought to myself. I looked at the faces of the friends at the table. No one was complaining or gaping like me. The pastors, who were seated randomly at different tables, looked as happy as everyone else. I took a deep breath and continued eating.

Mealtime was over. I joined my new friends in the schoolyard, some of whom were visiting students from the Adventist seminaries of Nigeria and Ghana, serving as interns. A lot of people were taking random group photos. Each group wanted me to pose with them. What an honor! I thought. I darted from group to group, laughing and cracking jokes with people I had barely met.

However, as the minutes ticked away, thoughts of the bad times between Mesape and I began creeping into my soul, quietly. I couldn't help thinking of the impending drama, awaiting my return home. The prospect of facing Mesape, with the news of my baptism, made me so uneasy that I felt like I had a full bladder.

Thank goodness, Pastor Duwona, the Ghanaian-born church leader, offered to give two of us a ride home. He dropped off the other lady before me, intentionally. I came out of his car with trembling legs and cautiously treaded towards the entrance door, which was open. My heart began beating faster. Fear would have paralyzed me, had Pastor Duwona not been so kind in anticipating opposition to my new spiritual status.

As soon as I introduced him to Mesape, I disappeared from the living room. However, I positioned myself at the room door, from where I overheard Pastor, struggling to calm down an irate Mesape.

"How could she do this to me? I didn't even know about it," Mesape complained.

"Of course, you have a point," said Pastor. "But, you know, it's not always easy to manage fear."

"Fear? What have I done to scare her?"

"Well, in the face of a major decision like this one, it's hard to convince someone who didn't study the Bible with you."

"You see how she has kept me out of an important decision in her life?"

"Please, don't dwell on that because this is just the beginning. Akongshee needs your support to carry on peacefully."

"Well, I bow to her decision."

The pastor went on, explaining that baptism was a very personal matter. "Each one has to decide for themselves," he reiterated. "Please, try to understand her. She must have been afraid that your authority would overrule her choice," he went on.

I was all ears, beaming, as Pastor interceded on my behalf. My mind was absorbing every detail while wishing that the chat with Pastor would arouse in Mesape the slightest curiosity in spiritual matters, as tiny as the mustard seed that I learned of regarding faith.

As for me, there was nothing he could do to erase the fact—September 5th, 1992, the most important day of my life, was forever etched into the records of heaven. I had no apologies to make, nor a smidgen of regret though anxiety was nibbling away at my nascent peace of mind. Come what may, *I was free*, was to become my resolve. If Mesape persisted in his dishonest ways, I would skip over them as stepping stones, leaving behind the chips to fall wherever they might.

I sighted his charming smile as he shook Pastor Duwona's hand, wishing him a safe return home. As soon as the door closed, I escaped into the kitchen and plunged myself into some chores. He followed me there and started complaining about how I had betrayed him. Guilt almost got a hold of me, but I quickly shrugged it off. I just listened, leaving him ample room to express his disappointment. Like a backing dog, stuck in between wires in the thorny path that he had chosen for himself, he began accusing me of disturbing the peace of our little family.

I had learned during the Bible study that accepting Christ creates a division between believers and non-believers within the family. So, his attitude neither surprised nor shocked me. Like a newly-born baby, not a word came out of my mouth.

Chapter 30: In Search of the Home of the Privileged

Otherwise, I was like a stubborn child, guilty of breaking the only drinking water calabash in the house. So, I began cleaning the countertop while glancing into his frowning face, attempting to match it with a remorseful countenance.

Gradually, his harsh tone softened. He began buzzing like a bee stuck into the folds of a massive window blind.

My newly revived soul was weeping for him. Yet, how could I reach his closed mind?

CHAPTER 31

My Foolishness, My Fortress

A few weeks after my baptism, Mesape's younger sister came visiting from Victoria. They had heard the news. "If you are not tough, you cannot join that church," she relayed her mother's remarks to me. Their family was sure that I would soon quit like others, whom they cited.

Each Saturday after church, excitement would turn into fright as soon as I began thinking of returning home. It was the dread of Mesape's anger, waiting like a pot of boiling water, to skin me like choice chicken for the fiesta of mediocrity and enslavement by sin.

On the way home, I would be celebrating the inspiration of the day while at the same time, praying that Mesape's anger would spare me.

"You are teaching these children the wrong thing," he would fuss, pointing at me with his finger. Then he would blame my new church for our marital problems.

Soon, my colleagues, including Estelle, joined the condemning crowds. Unable to convince me, she introduced me to her friend, Caro, who was a backslidden Seventh-day Adventist.

"Oh, Akong, you know that I used to be a member. Why don't you take my advice?" Caro pleaded.

"I appreciate your concern, but I believe this is the right path for me,"

"This Sabbath thing was meant for the Jews, long, long ago," Caro tried to explain.

"Poor thing, even her looks have changed," remarked Estelle.

Though an intense debate, it didn't bring the two sides closer to each other. While they were bent on proving me wrong, I pitied them for persisting in ignorance. We separated, each party flustered.

On Sunday, we met at Caro's house to compare appropriate Bible verses on the issue of contention. My illustrations and explanations met with strong arguments against obeying the Sabbath. We arranged two other meetings for Bible study. In the last session, I used only the Ten Commandments. They dismissed my point, stating that Sabbath did not mean Saturday. In the end, it was clear that we would not agree, given our different stance. Each day further increased my conviction while they sighed.

Thus, continuous arguments were ruining our friendship. We stopped meeting at Caro's house, but Estelle would shake her head at work each Monday when she found out that I had attended church on Saturday, not Sunday.

Soon, the number of critics began increasing. Other Sunday-keeping friends and colleagues started blaming me for destroying my marriage.

Indeed, one afternoon, a forty-year-old secretary, Suzie, my junior colleague, invited me to her office, to address what she considered my consuming malady.

"Akong, I have been a Christian from the time I was a child. But I don't think it's necessary to carry your belief all over you like this," she scolded me, visibly upset.

Was she my mother or a disciplinarian in a juvenile detention center? I listened out of sheer politeness.

"You are exaggerating. You are the one who has chased this poor man away from the house," she explained, putting on her glasses while fumbling for her Bible.

I couldn't help laughing.

She was not amused.

"See how plain you look," she said, shaking her head and pointing at me. "If you need earrings, I can give you some of mine."

"Am I not beautiful enough, just the way I am?" I asked.

"Without make-up? Please, put an end to this plain look and resume your old ways," she pleaded.

There was nothing I could say to reach her. Her receptors were out of order. Like most of the other women who were so scathing about physical appearance, she was directly displaying signs of low self-esteem. Instead of humbling herself and politely seeking to understand the drastic change in my life, she insisted on lecturing to me.

Suddenly, she stood up and started speaking aloud and pointing at me with a reprimanding finger.

"No man can stand this!" she blasted, hitting her hand on the table in disgust. "You are the one provoking him to follow that ugly thing," she went on.

Suzie was not the only one outraged by my new looks. Some colleagues at the higher echelons at my job did not welcome it either. Gradually, some bosses began excluding me from some duties and responsibilities. What a pity! They would rush to cover actresses the likes of Madonna for her outrageous outfits, to whom our immediate public could not relate, but disregard one of theirs, who was setting the pace of reform in fashion within each woman's reach.

What was wrong with wearing a skirt which was a few inches below the knee level as compared to exposing my hips? What was their business with my legs, anyway? I wondered. Even Mesape, who legally owned the legs and beyond, was shortsighted enough to join the condemning chorus.

Guess what? I still had a few skirts and dresses, whose hemlines I was loosening to creatively increase the length, dropping them down from above-the-knee to knee level.

On Friday afternoon, the Director-General invited me to his office. I had no clue what was coming. I was pleasantly surprised. I didn't know that anyone, much less him, cared that much anymore.

However, my heart was beating faster while I was waiting for his secretary to usher me in. I had been to his office a few times before, to receive special compliments for my performance.

As soon as he saw me, he pointed to the three seats in front of his desk. His mechanical smile spoke more of business than anything else.

He went straight to the point. He wanted my opinion about transferring my husband to another province.

"Wow!" I exclaimed. How nice of him! At first, I didn't know what to say. I felt so honored that I was speechless.

"I need to know what you think," he insisted.

It was not something to go home and think over. My opinion was just the icing on the cake. And I couldn't delay the eating any further.

I bent my head down, took a deep breath, and closed my eyes. Almost immediately, I began feeling a surge of anger, or was it indignation, building up inside me. How unfair, I thought! Tears began collecting in my eyes.

So, the boss was going to promote Mesape while demoting me? He would be the chief of station, with the rank of sub-director, while I would become a mere reporter despite being a senior journalist.

More so, Zipora would continue enjoying both the comfort and the limelight at the corporate headquarters. At the same time, I would have to figure out how to thrive on lean benefits within the obscurity of an outpost.

Besides, my life was more at risk in the hands of Mesape and Zipora within the confines of a remote, rural community where there would be no one to watch my back.

Also, it would have an immediate negative impact on my children. They would be obliged to switch to studying in French without prior preparation. We had not planned to raise them as francophones, anyway.

I raised my head and expressed my appreciation to the Director-General. At least, he had been thinking about rescuing my crumbling family.

I left his office and went straight to my red Nissan car, parked in front of the imposing edifice. It was neither the day nor time to call on my TV colleagues. I needed time by myself to ponder over the unfair perception of the authorities regarding our case. The more I imagined myself doing basic tasks from a remote village station, the more I thought how unfair! And what about health and social services in a cosmopolitan city compared to those in a village? There was no point in going over those details. I was more willing to divorce than be punished any further.

Meanwhile, Mesape was excited; the hierarchy had hinted to him. He began talking about the goodness that his promotion would bring to his family. I listened to him, amused. It was not going to happen any time soon. That much I knew.

I settled down to work, putting creativity into the challenging programs I produced. "Literary Half Hour" and "Success Hour" with Charles Landzeh, "Calling the Women" for Olive Shang, "Cameroon Report" renamed "Cameroon Calling," which brought together the nucleus of the English desk in investigative reporting, in-depth analyses, and commentaries on the week's national and world news, under the leadership of the editor-in-chief.

My colleagues, as usual, admired me for my brilliant performance. Except that they continued to criticize my "plain looks." One Tena lady,

Sally, suggested that the ladies should exclude me from the club. She just couldn't stand my strange lifestyle. The others concurred but hesitated.

Finally, Sally began mentioning that I was trying to make myself holier than them. Else, why was I refusing to drink beer anymore? What was suddenly wrong with red lips and short skirts, especially being that they were in fashion? If I was insisting on adopting my new lifestyle, didn't I think my husband would not desire me anymore? They bombarded me.

I doffed my hat to the excellence of their logic. It was pointless to carry on the debate. By the way, did they notice that I was more patient with them? I don't think so. Granted, they were justified since the change was radical, but who gave them the authority to decide for me how I should eat or dress? They were so enslaved by tradition that they couldn't see beyond the consequences of its dictates. At least, I could compare my past with my present. No one, no system, no laws could relegate me to my burdensome past. Not even formal education, on its own, had been capable of freeing my mind, releasing it to soar to a higher level of excellence and freedom.

> *The more they criticized me, the more I realized how precious I was. I was celebrating a new me. The value of time, like never before, meant so much more to me. I spent time pondering over the invigorating power of joy, mercy, and love.*

While they complained, I continued bathing in the engaging freshness and goodness of my brand new life. Even my smile was steadier than before.

They needed to be sorry for themselves, not for me. I was thankful for the courage to protect my "birthright" without harboring any resentment against my critics.

On Monday, I stood in front of my full bedroom mirror and heaved a sigh of relief. Life was good, and I couldn't feel any better about myself. Not even my dreams could convey such beauty and peace of mind. It was just exhilarating, daily tapping energy, and guidelines directly from heaven, the very source of the sun that rose and set every day.

How could my friends continue to miss the body-mind-spirit connection of human existence? How true that many perish for lack of knowledge! I pined for them.

The more they criticized me, the more I realized how precious I was. I was celebrating a new me. The value of time, like never before, meant so much more to me. I spent time pondering over the invigorating power of joy, mercy, and love.

On Wednesday, during break time, I sat in my office looking back. How on earth did I survive the heavy demands of pleasing others by respecting the unwritten requirements of physical appearance? For example, imagine a load of make-up on my face, alone: Brown liquid foundation under brown loose powder; blue and pink eyelids; pink turquoise on brown cheeks; black eyeliner; red, maroon or whatever lipstick. After that, a pair of dangling, drooping earrings to match my outfit. Then instead of proceeding to take my rightful place in an air-conditioned Fool's Paradise for display, I begin to run around on high heels with a twenty-pound recorder strapped to my shoulder. Above me, the burning heat of the tropical sunshine, cooking my body up to a sweat. I start wiping as the interview goes on.

Right away, I must rush out and catch the bus to the station. Oops! First, I need to dash into the ladies' room. A new layer of powder is on-demand, the original, now cracking from a constant river of sweat. Hurry up. The news is coming up soon, in a quarter-hour or less. The minute by minute countdown is on already. I must begin tape-editing now. But first, write my lead. Else, my story is not going.

Each time I looked at my jewelry box, I mused over that junk of social paraphernalia, all to meet standards set by others.

Two months after my baptism, I received an unusual invitation. The producer of the popular *Women's Development Magazine* wanted me to appear, as the special guest, on the national weekly TV show. I was going to represent the Adventist Development Relief Agency, ADRA, who had organized an international workshop in Yaounde on leadership skills for women.

The workshop, which brought together participants from ten African nations, had been sponsored by the government of Sweden. Both the sponsors and organizers had returned to their respective countries without television interviews, the proceedings having coincided with the first-ever democratic presidential elections in Cameroon in 1992.

I qualified on three counts. I had covered the occasion for the radio. Experts had trained me as Trainer of Trainees, during which I was also one of the interpreters. Besides, I happened to be the only English-speaking representative of the four Cameroonian participants.

The show came on air the following week.

"Ak, I know you are a terrific interviewer," Mesape remarked as he fell back on his seat and clapped his hands. His eyes lit up with excitement.

"However, I didn't know you were such a splendid performer from the other end," he emphasized, pulling his seat closer to me, stretching out his hands, and peering into my eyes as if he was discovering someone new.

How come the absence of jewelry from my ears had not spoilt the show? I just smiled and thought to myself. He didn't even make any mention of it. Maybe he had not also noticed that, possibly, I was the first Cameroonian woman to appear on national television with naked ears.

The thoughtful colleagues who had rushed into the studio, and offered me their earrings, had nothing to say, either.

Instead, they, too, were impressed at my ability to answer the interviewer's tricky questions without being flustered.

The next day, telephone calls inundated my office. Viewers were expressing their appreciation. "Were you one of the organizers or just a participant in that workshop?" one of them enquired.

Another lady wrote from Douala. She needed help to rally her neighbors for sanitation work in their immediate surroundings. I was delighted to help, even though I could only give her some general guidelines.

A month after, I received another letter from Angeline, reporting the good news. She had succeeded in organizing her neighbors, for the first time, after several failed attempts. Now her neighborhood was transformed into an inviting garden of pure, fresh air. She wanted me to visit, to see for myself.

Indeed, I was receiving professional crowns. Sadly, my life at home was still a mess. And I was getting fed up. So, one day, I started sneaking in cartons and arranging my books for eventual departure, to where I did not know. Like a rat, snatching one grain of groundnut after another, I took the full boxes to my office.

How sad that I was becoming homeless despite having a house of my own! Where was I going to go from there?

One sunny afternoon in June, when I least expected, my telephone rang.

"Can I speak to Akongshee?" a woman with an American accent requested.

The big news was that I had been selected to represent Cameroon, alongside professionals from seventeen other African nations, as a "Young African Leader" in the US.

Barely a week after that life-saving call, I received another invitation, this time in the mail, to travel to Denmark to take part in a month-long professional training course.

Indeed, on the day of my flight to the US, I was equally due to travel to Denmark, the very next day.

As I look back now, I recall Oprah Winfrey, saying in one of her television shows, that it is critical to do whatever it takes, to stand where the blessings would eventually fall. I recalled that about a month before the invitation, I had attended a conference at the American Cultural Center on American politics towards Africa. Among the authorities of the Center, other personalities, workers, and a few students, my former professor at the school of mass communication, Dr. Wete, was the only person that I recognized.

What was remarkable was the lifted eyebrows that turned towards me, all at the same time. My question was, at once, pertinent and stunning.

Someone turned around and asked, "Where did she study?" as I listened carefully to the answer to my question.

CHAPTER 32

Banishing God's Love

On Tuesday night, I returned from a prayer meeting with my sister, Awah. Surprisingly, Mesape had locked and bolted the door, as the key refused to turn. She and I immediately exchanged nervous glances as I pulled out the key and began scrutinizing it. I tried again and again, in vain.

Then I started knocking, gently at first, and then loudly. Nothing happened. We tried to peer through the window, but there was not even a ray of light in the house.

Meanwhile, Awah walked towards the garage. She returned and confirmed that Mesape's car was duly parked. With a folded fist, I hammered at the door, yet there was no response.

Why this, today? I began explaining to Awah. For four months, I have attended weekly prayer meetings without a problem. Why not speak directly to me?

> *"What? Open this door, please," I implored.*
>
> *Instead of the click sound of the door, all we heard was his disappearing footsteps.*

Awah and I were still waiting and complaining when finally we heard a movement. Mesape came to the window and spoke from inside without turning on the lights.

"Where are you coming from?" he grunted.

"Pardon me?"

"I hope you can take care of yourself out there."

"What? Open this door, please," I implored.

Chapter 32: Banishing God's Love

Instead of the click sound of the door, all we heard was his disappearing footsteps.

"Mesape, come and open this door, please," I repeatedly yelled, to no avail.

Awah looked at me. I was as helpless as a statue. We stood at the door for the next fifteen minutes or so, gazing into the darkness. Our contagious yawns took over the unfolding drama.

"Maybe we should go to Martha's house," I proposed. I was just thinking aloud. Disturbing the peace of other people or making a public scandal of a domestic issue was certainly not the way to go.

Awah looked at me with tightened lips and sighed.

I took a deep breath and shook my head from side to side.

"Let's pray about it," she requested, throwing her hands in the air towards me.

"Yes, we should."

"Doesn't this remind you of the study a month ago about the devil unleashing his wrath against those who have chosen to follow Christ?" she asked.

"Exactly," I concurred.

"Heavenly Father, we thank You for life and ..." Awah began praying, her hand in mine. In the end, we both took deep breaths after the *Amens*.

A long pause ensued. We just stood there waiting for heaven to either unlock the door or provide a hut, a sheep-pen, or stable for the night.

"Sis, what if we sleep in the car?" Awah burst out excitedly.

"Are you sure you can handle that?" I asked, staring into her face.

The bright fluorescent light tube above our heads was reflecting the tear trapped in her eyes.

We moved to my red Nissan hatchback. I opened it and began fidgeting with buttons and knobs around the seats. Finally, one of the places behind collapsed. Awah got into the car and threw herself in the back seat. Then she raised her hands and thanked God aloud for the seven feet wall, enclosing the yard, and protecting us from any intrusion from the street.

"If Josephine, Priscilla, and the rest at church hear that we slept outside just because we attended the prayer meeting," she said, shaking her head.

"Boy, that will be some news," I responded. Awah finally figured out how to collapse the other seat.

"We must begin to prepare for tougher days ahead, Sis," said Awah.

"You bet! Military Camp Training 101."

Silence crept in on us. I looked at my wristwatch. It was past ten already. My eyes began to close. We wished each other good night and began twitching around for a more comfortable posture.

I must have yielded to fatigue for the first fifteen minutes. However, after that, the persistent sound of toads got the better of my sleep. Also, mosquitoes were whizzing all around us, not to mention the bitter cold that wrapped itself around us like a frozen blanket. Our legs and arms were the worse hit. We kept stretching them for more space, and to generate some heat.

We struggled all night, sighing, moaning, swinging our hands in the air countless times to keep away mosquitoes. We must have slept again, out of sheer exhaustion. Then a cock's crow in the distance woke us up. We dozed off for a while. The sound of a barking dog began reaching us distinctly. We were not ready yet to open our eyes, but the day was breaking. Awah turned around and started yawning. Soon the car was filled with our yawns. Her eyes were bulging with fatigue. Mine, too. I stretched my body, and it cracked all over.

There was another dog, barking, then another, as if they were greeting each other.

"Sis, let's pray before he arrives," Awah proposed, and sat up suddenly. By the time we finished, daylight was in command. We were dying to get into the house and ease ourselves. Mesape was taking his time, obviously to aggravate our weariness.

The door finally clicked open. My children rushed out and fell on us. They seemed to have been waiting all night long.

"Mom, what happened?" my son and daughter enquired as we hugged them.

"They came back too late, and that's why they slept outside," Mesape interjected, stepping in on the scene, with a scowling face.

My big eyes scanned his figure from head to toe; I didn't utter a word. My bladder was bloated. I forced my way through the door and rushed to the bathroom.

I had lost time to prepare for work adequately. By the time I dashed into the room to dress up, Mesape had left. I was running late for work. I put on my shoes and hurried to the kitchen for a cup of hot beverage.

Alas, it was not possible to make a fire. The gas cylinder was gone. Even the backup was missing.

"Daddy put them in the trunk of his car," my son explained.

It was shocking, so shocking that I didn't know what to say. Mesape had given the children breakfast before leaving. Awah had to buy bread or puff-puff. Otherwise, she had to eat *coldwatergarri*.

I returned home at break time with a bundle of firewood, which I had bought from across the street. Quickly, I made a three-stone fire in the yard. I poured water in a pot, into which I put the fresh corn I had brought along.

Then I went into the room to change my clothes. By the time I got back out to check on the boiling pot, it was no longer on the three stones. All that was left was smoking firewood. Awah came out with surprise written all over her face. I was speechless in the face of the mounting hostility.

Meanwhile, Mesape had taken the children to the restaurant for lunch.

Before we finished exclaiming, he rushed in and brought back a bucket of water. I didn't know what was going on until when he proceeded to pour the water over the smothering wood. The wood soaked up the water and began dripping. I stood by in utter dismay. A nightmare or a war? I asked myself as my mouth began drying up.

Of course, I had expected trouble, but not to this magnitude. Anger and fear chilled my body; my limbs became stiff. Yet, what could I do but watch and sigh?

Awah and I ate some cold, leftover cocoyams and *ndjamandjama* (huckleberry leaves) if only to defy starvation. I had to return to work soon.

I returned home in the evening, hardly knowing what to expect. However, late in the night, Mesape brought back the gas cylinders. I was thankful that the cooking fire had returned to my kitchen.

A month after that incident, I returned from a regular club meeting of the Tenas and couldn't park my car. Mesape had parked the Mitsubishi Galant across, blocking the two-car garage. I honked, and the children rushed out. Then I requested that they get the keys to their father's car for me. They returned empty-handed. He had not said a thing, they reported.

So, I stopped the car and went in. As soon as I stepped into the bedroom, Mesape rushed behind me, banged the room door, locked it, and took off the keys. His action was as fast and unexpected as lightning.

I searched into his face for clues, totally dismayed at the ferocity of his reddening eyes.

"Akongshee, where are you from?" he yelled at the top of his voice.

"What do you mean?"

"Look, I'm tired of this nonsense," he began shouting and pointing at me with his forefinger.

"Don't you know I had a meeting?"

I had not had time to finish speaking when he slapped me; instantly, the light went out from my left eye. I hit back with my right fist. We began fighting while I screamed out loud. The children heard us and rushed to the door. They started knocking and crying. Yet, Mesape continued hitting me, even harder. Then he bent down and picked me up as if I was a little girl. I couldn't believe how easily my weight gave in to a man who was barely two inches taller than me. He was also a slim person; his pants fitted me. Was he possessed of supernatural powers? I wondered.

While I was struggling to wriggle myself away from his grip, he held onto me firmly and swung my body from left to right. I was yelling while trying to free myself from his strong hands. I couldn't; he completely overpowered me.

Abruptly, he gathered my obstructing hair into his hands. Then, he carried my head, directing it towards the thick plank edge of the bed, over which he lifted my head. He was getting ready to hit it while gathering momentum. He raised it higher and began dropping it rapidly, but he missed the mark. My head swayed away from his hands. My body continued struggling in his grip.

Finally, he dropped me down hurriedly like a bundle of firewood infested with ants. I managed to stand up; I could barely limp while panting and screaming. My arms and legs were hurting; blood was oozing out from scalding bruises. My whole body was aching.

"This is evil, wickedness," I screamed into his face.

Then suddenly, he burst out crying.

"Oh, Akong, I don't believe I did this to you. I'm so sorry. Sorry, sorry. I will never do this again," he pleaded on bended knees.

His reaction both astonished and confused me. Did he expect me to believe him?

I went into the bathroom and started examining myself in front of the mirror. There were bruises scattered all over my arms, neck, and legs. Mesape was still sobbing.

How could I ever trust him again? It was the second attempt on my life. The first time it happened was barely three weeks after my baptism. He had returned home that night while I was alone; our children were spending their vacation in the village with my parents, some 700 kilometers away. In Mesape's absence, his brother called from Maroua with an urgent message. I checked on Mesape in all of our friends' homes in vain. As a last resort, I called Zipora's house. Finally, Mesape got home around midnight. He opened the main door and crashed through the bedroom door, rushing towards me head-on. I was lying in bed, on my back, reading a novel.

"Who asked you to call her house?" he thundered over me repeatedly with blood-shot eyes.

Before I realized what I was in for, he went straight for my neck. He pressed hard, to the full extent of his energy. I laid helpless. So, I started crying for help. He kept pushing and making sounds like a woman in labor. I could barely struggle under his choking grip.

Then my breathing became interrupted. I could hardly speak. So, I started making sounds, pleading with Mesape to stop, but he kept on, forcing his full weight on me. Somehow, I was able to get my legs together. My knees clutched and kicked him at the groin area. Immediately, he let go. He moved backward and stared at me while I rubbed against my burning neck.

"Oh, Akong," he began crying, on bended knee. "Forgive me, please."

I stared at him from head to toe; my lips went dry.

"Oh, how come I did this to you? How can I hurt you so?" he asked while moaning.

As I recalled that first incident, I shuddered at the similarity of the violence against me, followed by his dramatized remorse, just minutes after.

The following morning, my eyes, especially the left one, was hurting so badly. I could not stand the light. I had to cover my left eye with my palm. My sister, Azuh, took a black clothe and folded it multiple times, which she placed over my eye. I had to put on a pair of sunshades. Meanwhile, there were swellings on bruised areas of my arms and shin.

I was desperate for medical attention. With a walking stick in hand, I managed to lean on my sister, and we tried to go out and hire a taxicab. As soon as I stepped out, the bright light pierced my eyes. My legs were unsteady. So, I got back in and obliged Mesape to drive me to the hospital. He did.

As soon as we got to the General Hospital, he stopped the car at the entrance. Then he came around and opened my door. I dragged myself out. He got back into the car, made a u-turn, and drove away without saying a word. I was left there by myself to limp, some two hundred meters, to the doctor's office.

Communication between us reduced to the minimum during the following week. However, within a month, things started getting better.

However, I became anxious when I overheard two women, in a large crowd, while covering a story for radio, talking about Zipora. My presence must have prompted their remarks; I was getting used to it already.

I could hear snatches of their conversation. They were saying that Zipora was using supernatural powers over Mesape. Indeed, they alluded to some Indians, who were going from office to office, looking for buyers of their charm. The men in question might not have been Indians.

However, in popular cycles throughout the country, magic or any reference to supernatural powers, practiced by Indians, always got people screaming, wiping the dust off their feet, and fleeing to safety. Indian films were popular, often fraught with their fascination with snakes, an animal cited in the Bible as the most cunning of all.

In any case, the whispering women said that the "Indians" used Zipora for their publicity; she was the perfect example of the effectiveness of their divination, charm, or magic. One of them disclosed that the magicians had come to their office.

"If that magic potion wasn't powerful, how could a handsome man like Mesape be running after Zipora?" said one of the women.

I listened, and chills came over my body while I rushed to my car; I barely had enough time to edit my story.

Eventually, I traced the office of the lady who had mentioned the visit of the magicians. By a stroke of luck, I found out that one of the reporter's colleagues was my acquaintance. I invited Julie outside for a chat. She confirmed that, indeed, some magicians had recently stopped at their job, trying to convince them to buy their charm. I shook my head in astonishment.

Stunned, I bid Julie goodbye and walked away. While contemplating my life, I wondered whether I was going through a nightmare or waking up to reality. Were the reports by third parties real or a figment of the imagination of our observers? Was I looking for an alibi to vindicate Mesape while smearing Zipora, and blaming her for using supernatural powers over him?

In any case, that quest marked the extent of my daring into Zipora's alleged demonic network. If Mesape was committing violent acts and asking for forgiveness immediately afterward, then he must have crossed the line of demarcation between the forces of good and evil. He had become an agent. A gentle Mesape had become a violent person.

The more I considered Mesape's seemingly intricate involvement in the whole shebang, the more I concluded that he was not innocent. No one could dismiss him like a dumb player; he had granted his accord. Otherwise, Zipora couldn't plan her wedding without the blessings of her supposed fiancé.

I kept calm and carried on with life as if nothing was the matter. On Sunday, I was doing chores and singing.

"What have you done to your body that nothing seems to bruise you?" Mesape howled as soon as he stepped into the house. I had no idea where he was coming from, but I bet he was having a hard time.

As for me, ever since my baptism, I had placed a premium on my happiness. Besides, life was too precious to waste. And my children needed me alive, I resolved, once and for all.

CHAPTER 33

Spiritual Warfare

On Monday morning, I opened my office and was taken aback by some strange stuff, strewn all over my table. It was a yellow powder scattered all over, alongside drops of a dark sticky substance like melting ground coffee.

Yaounde, downtown

Two other colleagues, Sophie and Dora, who had planned to use my office over the weekend, were as dumbstruck as myself.

As the weeks passed by, the variety of mysterious items took their turn at my desk. A rodent left imprints of its paws on white papers. Also, there were tiny bits of excreta on my table. Nastiest of all, stinking urine or whatever, dripping from my seat. Each morning, I replaced my chair; this went on four separate times. When there were no more spare seats, I began cleaning my stinking chair with disinfectant and detergent.

Next, was my drawer; each morning, I would find a mixture of nuts, grains- *groundnuts*, corn, beans, kernel, all blended in rat waste. How did those items get into my drawers or office? I locked up both at the end of each day of work.

After the items, a rat entered into my office. How did it find itself on the second floor of the modern complex? The lower part of the solid wood door of 107 was in direct contact with the cement floor. What was attracting rats, anyway? It was two years since I closed my office canteen. Besides, no one else on the same floor nor those on the ground floor had a similar complaint. So, possibly, that rat that was moving around my office, was the only one in the entire building.

News of my predicament started spreading among my colleagues. Some advised me to quit the office. I just shook my head and took comfort in the assurance of direct protection from God.

While I was pondering over the weird substances on my desk, I noticed that Mesape stopped visiting my office. Unlike when he used to stop by to chat with me on Mondays when he came to the radio house to attend the director's meeting, he began rushing away at the closing.

I informed him about the odd occurrences in my office; it did not seem to matter to him—he brushed me off. So, I urged him to come to see for himself, but he categorically refused. I insisted. Instead, he told me that it was none of his business while deriding me for trying to make a mountain out of a molehill.

On Monday morning, at a few minutes past ten, I was in the office, helping Dora to write the lead of her report. Something bizarre happened right in front of us. While we were speaking, I heard the flutter of what I imagined was a cockroach. The sound was not loud enough to interrupt our lively voices.

A few minutes later, there was a flutter behind me; it was a progressive movement. Dora and I kept on as if nothing mattered.

It grew louder.

Suddenly, something dropped from the wall unit behind me onto the leg of my seat. The movements were rapid. Without warning, it edged its way from beneath and sprang through the arm of my chair at lightning speed.

Before I had time to turn around, it quickly propelled itself straight into my face. Ugh! Too close, barely an inch or less from my nose.

My screams went beyond the ceiling. It dropped at lightning speed towards my lap. Swiftly, I stood up while my hand was brushing my dress in anticipation. The giant rat dropped to the floor, too rapid for my eyes to fix on it. Within seconds, it darted through the door. Dora turned around while I stared at it, but too late, its head was gone, leaving its six-inch tail following behind like an escaping snake.

Dora and I screamed for help. She opened her eyes widely and looked at me. We trembled with fear. A petrified Dora cupped her hands over her mouth in utter dismay. Then, she fell back into the chair and started crying. Hallelujah, was all I could say while clapping my hands. She looked up with tears in her eyes.

"Akong, now I understand what you've been going through. I had to see for myself to believe," she said, breathing deeply.

While we were still exclaiming, my office began filling up with colleagues from the newsroom. Dora and I related the chilling details to them. They were all astonished by our accounts. They gaped, sighed, and shook their heads from side to side. In the end, they agreed that something was amiss. Normal rats usually hide in dark, restricted corners of a room, ready to escape at any human sound.

When the dozen or so colleagues dispersed, Dora stood up and exclaimed, while clapping her hands, repeatedly.

"This is too much to handle for a day. I have to go home and talk to my mom," she said.

I was left alone, desperate for an explanation and what next to do. I looked around me for wisdom. I had to prevent a recurrence. Brainstorming with colleagues went on for hours and days.

"But don't you know how to catch a rat?" Azuh, my younger sister, challenged me, later at home, in the evening.

The following day, I launched Operation Hunt It Down by setting a trap. It was my final duty at the end of the day, before leaving the office. I would place the brand new trap at the very center of my table. Some colleagues saw it and mocked at me for what they called my naiveté. "How can you place a trap in the open?" they asked.

Each morning, I behaved like a hunter, inspecting for the game—Monday, Tuesday, Wednesday, nothing.

On Thursday morning, I arrived fifteen minutes earlier. My colleague, Ken, welcomed me at the parking lot. He opened my car door for me. Then, he offered to help with my handbag. Majestically, we strolled towards my office. When we got to the door of my office, I stopped and implored him to pray with me before opening the door. After the prayer, I took two steps forward, turned the key, and pushed the door while he waited to usher me in.

The gentleman and I halted in our tracks as soon as the door swung opened. My eyes sighted something that sent me screaming. I fell backward on Ken. The grotesque rodent stretched its foot-long body along the length of the piece of wood. The iron squeezed its neck tightly; its eyes were popping out. Its tail was longer than its total body length.

Immediately, a crowd of colleagues started gathering in my office. They exclaimed, clapped their hands, and shook their heads as they looked on in disbelief.

"*Tu as la chance que ça ne t'a pas mordu*" (You are lucky that it didn't bite you), commented two persons.

"*Vraiment*" (Really), the rest concurred.

When the screams and exclamations quieted down, one of my colleagues, Atem, nudged me. He pulled my arm and took me to the side.

"Akongshee, whatever you plan to do with that rat," he whispered while opening his eyes widely and lifting his right forefinger. "Burn it into ashes," he warned. "Else, if you release it, it will come back, and it may cost you your life," he went on.

Tears began collecting in my eyes. Of course, I took his wise counsel seriously.

Finally, the crowd dispersed. I picked up my handbag, went out of the building, and drove to town, where I bought a bottle of kerosene and a box of matches. Upon return, six colleagues offered help. We picked up the trap with the rat stuck in it and took it behind the building, in an open space. Others carried a pile of old newspapers.

Before we proceeded, I invited them to pray with me. It was a thanksgiving for me, and a final judgment of the rat. We poured kerosene on the rat, amidst old newspapers, and struck the match. All of us seven women stood by the flaming fire for the next twenty minutes, adding kerosene and twisted papers gradually. The fire consumed the legs, head, and tail, reducing them into ash. We stayed put until its stomach burst open. What jubilation!

The excitement buoyed in me all day and accompanied me right home. As soon as Mesape greeted me, I announced the news of the "arrest" of the "villain." His response caught me off-guard.

"Too bad, the person will die, then," he said, throwing his hands in the air.

Immediately, he bent down and grabbed his slippers, and headed for the room. When he returned, he grabbed his keys from the center table and left the house without saying a word.

I gaped. Mesape's sudden departure and weird pronouncements corroborated the warning that one of my colleagues had issued. What did that mean by "the person?" I stood up and saw his back rushing like a cheetah escaping for life. I turned around in the living room, alone. Then I slumped into the couch, my hand under my chin. I shuddered. A cold wave slashed through me as I wondered how much more he was concealing about the chain of vicious attacks. The mere thought of worse occurrences numbed my body with shock.

In about an hour, he reappeared, looking uneasy. He did not say a word. Silence filled the room.

From that day onwards, my middle name became Vigilance. I walked around the house, keeping my eyes open for hidden traps.

About a month after the rat incident, the second trap, which I had set in my office, caught a second rat. The second rat was much smaller than the first. It suffered a similar fate like that of its predecessor—incineration.

However, unlike the first time, I did not bother to inform Mesape about the latest catch. Our worlds were as far apart as the north from the south pole. Undoubtedly, he was concealing vital information from me. Our relationship was now a silent, deadly conflict.

Indeed, one night at 2 am, I woke up and realized that Mesape was not in bed. I got up and searched. He was neither in the bathroom nor the living room. Upon return to the bedroom, I sighted a figure in the opaque darkness of the night. He was standing out, alone, in the balcony, smoking cigarettes. What a signal of impending disaster! It was ten years ago, at the faculty, when Mesape had given up the habit. That was during our very first outing. I still recalled how as soon as I turned away my face from the puffing smoke, he asked just one question, turned around, threw the stump, and smashed it.

How thankful I was that my new-found faith was very engaging. More importantly, it was my shield. There was no more time to waste on worries or threats to my life. I just needed to be alert, watchful, and prayerful. I turned his long absences from home into unperturbed Bible study time, memorizing Bible promises like an army stocking up ammunition in wartime.

Also, I pored over pages of a writer I recently discovered—Ellen G. White—whose inspiring books terminated my drive for novels.

Despite the refuge I took in my solo spiritual walk, my emotional problems persisted. Bickering became a new element in our initial smooth-ride relationship. Indeed, on Thursday morning, we disagreed over a trivial issue before leaving for work. While at work, I didn't give it a second thought, supposing the passage of time had dissipated the ruffling up for both of us.

Alas, when I got home, Mesape was withdrawn. He responded to my greetings rather curtly, his eyes blinking and looking away from me.

Instantly, I had a premonition that something dangerous might be in the making. It was an eerie feeling.

CHAPTER 34

The Bomb of Wickedness

Mesape left the house, soon after he returned from work, without a word. The valley between us was widening. My heart ached.

That night, I decided not to sleep in our bedroom. I merely dashed in, selected a work suit, a pair of shoes, and accessories for use the following day. After that, I took refuge in the children's room, where I made a bed for myself with old clothes, pillows, and cushions from the living room couch.

> "Are you not afraid that I'll eat all you got in the name of flesh?" *it was signed, "The Monster."*

Mesape returned, and left again, within the hour. I took advantage of his second absence and sneaked back into our bedroom. I grabbed my toothbrush from the bathroom. It was then that I noticed a piece of white paper on the bedcover, with something scribbled on it.

"Akongshee, isn't it strange that you continue to share this bed with a beast like me? Are you not afraid that I'll eat all you got in the name of flesh?" it was signed, "The Monster."

Whether that signaled imminent danger or a real threat or it was expressing his anger at my escape, I was out. To me, it was no less than a warning to back off.

He returned after 9 pm and marched straight to the children's room, where he ordered me out. I refused to budge. He fell on me like a vulture swooping down on the prey. His strong hands grabbed my hands and began pulling me while grunting a string of accusations.

Coincidentally, three of my sisters were at home. Mangwi was on her way to meet her husband in the US. Awah had just arrived from the village to collect her visa from the American Embassy. Azuh had been living with me for years.

Mesape charged at me. He tried to pull the cushions from below me. I clung onto them. He kept on dragging me shamelessly in front of the children. I held on until my arms began hurting. Finally, I yielded and rushed into the guest room, where I joined my sisters.

He picked up his bunch of keys and stepped out again, banging the door after him. The car sped off. He returned in less than an hour.

Somehow, his sudden movements, in and out of the house, gave me the idea that he was not alone in what was an assault in the making. So, all four of us sisters became more alert and vigilant. We started scampering for ways to ensure maximum security. Mangwi advised that we reinforce the locked door by bolting it. Then, we pushed the dressing table against the door and placed the chair above it. Next, we piled all the loaded suitcases in the room, over the chair.

Without further warning, the direct strike commenced. Mesape yelled out, ordering us to open the guest room door. None of us responded. He started hitting hard at the door, loud enough to disturb neighbours.

Indeed, my daughter, who had earlier joined us in the guest room, was dumbfounded. She quickly stuck her fingers into her ears, in disgust, as if a bomb had just exploded.

"Can you subject Zipora to similar torture?" I asked.

He was enraged. He started cursing and hitting the door with some object. The impact was tremendous; it could crush the door. Mangwi rushed to the door and wedged it from inside. We joined her while Azuh carried our eighteen-month nephew on her back. After that, we began taking turns, standing with hands against the door, pushing as hard as we could.

"Mesape, what would Nguti and other friends say if they caught you in this action?" Mangwi dared to intervene. "Don't you know you can endanger your wife's life?" she added.

"I will kill and pay for it," he said, over and over again, with growing ferocity.

The question seemed to have enraged the monster even further. None of us could pinpoint the reason for the rage.

A short silence ensued. We heard the sound of disappearing footsteps.

Suddenly, the knocks on the door resumed. However, they sounded different from the first series. We exchanged inquiring glances at each other. We tried to strain our ears. With what was Mesape hitting the door? We asked each other.

Yet, the hitting went on and on, non-stop. Then we saw for ourselves, as if in a nightmare. A machete was cutting through the ply-wood door. While punching, Mesape was also trying to push the door.

In response, we mustered our strength to the maximum and began pushing at the edges and moaning. Sweat began popping on our faces and flowing like a shower.

Suddenly, the upper part of the door started caving in towards us. By now, profuse sweating was drenching our brows.

Awah instinctively gave up pushing the door and rushed for the window. She thrust away the drapes and lifted the shutters. Then she stretched her head out into the dead of the night and started screaming, "*Au Secours*! *Au Secours*! *Au Secours*!" "Help! Help! Help! We are dying," she went on.

Awah's crying for help further enraged the monster. The speed of his cutting of the door increased. Simultaneously, the dogs, all the dogs in the neighborhood, started barking. They yelped, howled, and barked unabated. The peace of the community was disturbed.

Meanwhile, my screaming sister ran out of breath. So, she fell on her knees, lifted her hands, and started calling on God for help.

No neighbor responded, not even our landlord, who was living on the ground floor. We were on our own.

Then suddenly, the monster gave up.

Gradually, the dogs ceased from barking. Silence took over the neighborhood again.

What a relief! We spent the rest of the night standing like soldiers on guard at the battlefront.

"Sis, remember Aaron holding up the hands of Moses?" Awah asked.

I looked at her, nodded, sighed, and took in a deep breath.

Wedging the door went along with praying and brainstorming. Where was the morning? Our hearts yearned.

Meanwhile, I packed a little tourist bag.

My sisters helped me to plan my escape while the final execution awaited the breaking of the day.

Finally, day dawn began taking over. Azuh cracked open the guest-room door. She peeped through it and stuck out her ear. Quickly, she closed the door, smiled broadly, and shook her waist, excitedly. We lifted our eyebrows. She gave each of us a high five. We couldn't wait to hear the result of her discovery.

"He is snoring," she whispered.

My bedroom door was ajar.

We clicked our fingers and thankfully lifted our hands to the ceiling.

Within minutes, Azuh opened the door quietly and tip-toed towards the living room. Her eyes were searching all over for any signs of danger.

She proceeded and opened the entrance door, inch by inch, just enough to allow for the passage of one person at a time. Then she closed it and returned into the room. We said a prayer of thanksgiving.

Azuh again tip-toed into the children's room and woke up my son. Quydee hurried out, wiping his face with his hand. We sneaked out into the security of the street in a single file. I dropped my bag and took a deep breath. Then I bent down and embraced my children.

My eyes brimmed with tears. I had to leave, but no, I couldn't.

"Mom, go. God bless you," Sweetie, my little girl, said while shaking her head. Fear was written all over her baby face; she was barely five.

"Mom, you will be fine," Quydee added with a nod of his head.

"Don't rush back here until things have changed. Do you hear me?" Mangwi warned, pointing her forefinger.

"Don't say you are coming back because of the children, okay?" said Azuh, looking at me directly. "I'll take care of them."

"Sis, please, leave before he stops you," Awah cautioned.

All I could do was cry; tears were streaming out of my eyes. I wiped my face and looked at them. I would never have budged without their permission.

I hugged my sisters and kissed my children again. Azuh nudged my shoulders, and our eyes met in blinding tears.

I picked up my bag and moved towards the waiting taxicab. I squeezed my lips tightly to suppress the urge to cry. Then I opened the door of the yellow car. With one foot in, I stopped and looked back. A smile forced its way to push back the sadness.

I loathed the separation, yet, I had to go. The taxicab, now serving as a mobile refuge, sped off through the escape route. I fixed my eyes behind as my children kept waving in the dim light of dawn.

They were now out of sight. A feeling of loneliness came over me. I picked up my handbag from the springy backseat of the taxicab and clutched it. Meanwhile, my right palm pressed onto my face to arrest a lump in my throat, which was obliging tears or threatening to choke me. Oh, how my neck hurt! I sobbed right to Martha's house, which was barely a five-minute-ride away, by car.

I entered the yard with gentle steps. Then, I went to her bedroom window and tapped it lightly. I can't explain how she heard the sound immediately while her husband was deaf to it. I don't know how she guessed that I was the one. Within minutes, she was standing in front of me. Darkness was still lingering; it was not yet 6 am. She stood by me, inches away, and shook her head from side to side repeatedly, especially after she noticed my swollen eyes and the bag in my hand.

"Has it come to this?" she asked. Nothing was new to her about my problem, apart from that nightly drama. She was a Tena member.

Tears filled my eyes and started streaming down my face. She whisked me away to her outdoor apartment, where she showed me a bed in the unused room of her boy's quarters. We spoke in low tones. Without hesitating, she excused herself and went out to bring a bedsheet from the main house. She returned promptly. She helped to spread it over the bed. Then she tapped my shoulder and advised that I should take a rest.

Fatigue was all over my shaking body. Alone and by myself, I bent down, knees on the floor, head on the bed, and cried out a prayer.

Delayed sleep was hurting my eyes like invading smoke. Then, I sank into bed.

However, I couldn't sleep; I began pondering over the awkward "hows" of my life—how to be vigilant, how to stay in touch with my children and sisters, how to keep my job, how to keep hope alive; and how to pursue a divorce.

CHAPTER 35

Sisterly Intervention

It was a week already, since I left home, with barely a tourist bag, running away for dear life. I left Martha's house after two days and went to another's friend's house. She offered me space just for the night. The following day, I began looking for someone else, willing to provide refuge. What a pleasant surprise awaited me! Pam welcomed me into her home with open arms. Though we were former mates in college, we weren't close friends. Yet, she was willing to let me stay until when I would find a concrete solution to my problem.

From my temporary base, about two miles from my house, I telephoned my children. As soon as Mesape heard them saying "Mom" excitedly, he seized the receiver.

"Akong, please, help us, please, withdraw that case, please," he went on pleading, with a teary voice.

I immediately realized that he had received the summons.

> *However, I just listened without saying a word, though his apology sounded as sincere as usual. The heaven and hell of our decade-long relationship were clashing and causing my heart to ache.*

However, I just listened without saying a word, though his apology sounded as sincere as usual. The heaven and hell of our decade-long relationship were clashing and causing my heart to ache.

He added that he was sick. He had been away from work two for days. A doctor had come home to visit him, he said.

The conversation was painful to pursue. Indeed, tears began streaming down my face. I looked towards the ceiling of Pam's house and wondered what to do. My eyes stared at the scars on my body, which were still fresh.

On a bright Tuesday afternoon, Mangwi took time off to accompany me for the hearing of our divorce case. We arrived at the court building, some forty-five minutes early. We chose a safe spot to avoid meeting Mesape, before appearing in front of the judge. We hid by a slanted angle of the unpainted concrete walls. People were passing by us and heading towards the offices.

Suddenly, we saw Mesape coming. Mangwi and I quickly turned our backs to the passageway. Despite that, he found us out. He came close and greeted me with a broad smile. I had to dig in my heels to keep a straight face. He moved closer and said hello. I responded dryly. Mesape wore his characteristic infectious smile; I again turned away my face. My sister's stern disposition provided an insulating wall between us, giving me a sense of safety and freedom.

It was almost 2 pm when we took the stairs and followed the directions. There were four to six courtrooms. Dozens of noisy people were waiting along the corridors. Most of them looked wretched, worried, and desperate. There was not enough room to move around and to allow the mind space to think things over.

It was embarrassing; practically everyone recognized me as a media personality. Others whispered about Mesape. Shame on us for squandering the opportunity to set a good example! I pined. Never, in my whole life, had the thought crossed my mind that I would, one day, be obliged to face a judge, not to help preserve our marriage or defend our family, but to protect me from my legal protector. Worse than that, I needed the judge to help save my life.

My thoughts were soon interrupted by the calling of names, from one judge's office to another. My heart started beating faster. I took in deep breaths from the cigarette-smoke-infested corridor. I needed the courage to face the judge with unstinting confidence. Mesape looked visibly unsettled, too.

My legs moved closer to the door, where our names were pasted, on three sheets of ledger paper. My eyes started scanning the names, but the door suddenly swung open in my face. A lady came out and invited us into the office. Dozens of eyes settled on us. Saliva began drying up from my mouth. My legs were moving forward, but they seemed wobbly.

We took the two available seats. I sat down and took a deep breath. Oh, how I yearned for freedom! I was anxious but convinced that I had a good case. I began to scrutinize the judge, who looked fair, beautiful, and sophisticated in her delicate floral-trimmed suit. She seemed to be a kind, considerate person, too. I hoped that she would put herself in my shoes and grant my heart's desire.

She finally lifted her face from the document in front of her and greeted us. Then she asked me, in French, to tell my story first. I looked up to the ceiling and opened fire, one offense after another, in English.

Towards the end, I took off my jacket and pulled up my skirt, revealing scars on my arms and legs. Then, I handed my medical report to the judge. It clearly stated that Mesape's punch on my face caused the black eye. I explained how he had driven me to the hospital, only after I obliged him. I recounted other past incidents of physical violence and mental abuse. I told how his mistress called home, often, and even as late as midnight and beyond.

It was his turn to speak. Firstly, and to my utter surprise, he went down on his knees, as if his brand new, olive green suit was to blame for his woes.

"Your honor, I love my wife," his voice was trembling, as he lifted his hand. "Please, save my marriage. I'm sorry for all the things I've done," he pleaded, clapping his hands gently. "Judge, please, I won't do that again. Please, pity me," he went on with a teary, charming voice.

The judge asked about Zipora. He said that only professional collaboration existed between them. Then, he vowed to toe the line if he had given me a reason for suspecting an affair between them.

The judge turned to me and asked for mercy. I was indignant. How could she turn a blind eye to the enormous risk in my life? I refused vehemently. She persisted, pleading that I give him a second chance. I reminded her that he was dangerous. He would be glad to accomplish what he had failed to do on countless occasions, I added.

"It's unfair of you to make things worse than they are," she retorted, moving her head towards me.

"*Non, non, non,* your honor" (No, no, no, your honor), I said, shaking my head, from side to side, while frowning.

"You have to listen to me, okay?" said the judge, opening her eyes wide as if I was the culprit.

"Yes, your honor," I said. "Give us a separation then, if you wouldn't grant a divorce," I pleaded.

"You are not listening to me," she said with a louder voice. "According to the law, he must be given a second chance, only after which, you can request separation," she said, stressing every word.

My blood pressure started rising.

"This is the first man, ever, in my courtroom, to show such respect, and openly express love for his wife," she said as she turned and looked kindly at Mesape as if they were pals.

I just stared at her with a frown.

"Many men come in and insult their wives, right here," she nodded. "Don't let your friends deceive you," she added, looking at me pitifully.

"Some of them may want him for themselves," she warned.

"Your honor, I don't believe him," I stated, shaking my head in disapproval.

It's true that other women, apart from Zipora, desired him. As for me, right there and then, I was willing to let him off the hook.

"Take it from me, like someone giving you wise counsel," the judge spoke up again. "This is a loving man. I don't think he would hurt you again," she said.

"Your honor, he needs the chance to finish what he started," I insisted, staring at her, straight in the eye. "You see the bruises on my body...?" I kept speaking while pulling up my left sleeve.

She interrupted before I finished the sentence.

"I understand your pain. But please, just give him another chance," she pleaded. "I'm on your side," she added. "If ever he bothers you after you leave this courtroom, let me know, okay? I'm asking that you give him a second chance first. Please," she pleaded while staring at me.

A freezing chill began overtaking me while my exposed arms yielded to invading goose pimples. I couldn't imagine myself living under the same roof with Mesape, never again. Had he spoken to the judge before coming to court? I wondered.

She was still talking, but I was deaf by then. What would become of my life after I left her courtroom? My troubled thoughts were drowning me. I felt alone in the face of impending danger.

Suddenly, I realized that I had come in with one lion pursing me, but now, I had two, attacking from both sides.

No, I wasn't going to offer myself as a lamb for the slaughter.

In one last desperate attempt, I insisted that I preferred separation to return to live with him.

Chapter 35: Sisterly Intervention

The judge reacted immediately, this time sounding impatient. She raised her voice as she spoke, insisting that I had already broken the law by leaving my marital home without permission. On those grounds, she ordered me to return, without any further ado.

I left her office, feeling cheated and lost. How was I going to protect myself? My future was bleaker than before I walked in there.

Mesape left the room, smiling while I grieved.

When we got to the parking lot, he offered to drive me to my destination. I declined and moved on. I had deliberately left my car at Pam's, my temporary home.

The judge's verdict only added confusion to my anxiety. Where was I going to escape, for the two weeks left, before the journey to the US? What if he continued stalking me? He could even start another fight to stop me from traveling. Or he could request a court order to enforce the judge's ruling. Those fears crowded my mind.

Even though my life was at risk, I wanted, above all, to spend those last weeks with my children.

Three days afterward, I visited them at home, in the company of Mangwi. Though I had chosen a working hour, Mesape was home. Unfortunately. He explained that he was not feeling well. Indeed, he looked pale. I sympathized with him, but I did not doubt that he was suffering from the weight of his crimes.

As soon as the greetings were over, he stood up and moved over, close to Mangwi. Then he pulled her, by the hand, to a corner, and started pleading to her.

"Please, help us to get back together. Talk to your sister for me," he urged, looking at Mangwi, with tears in his eyes.

Mangwi glanced at me. I turned away my face, from both of them, and started focusing on what my daughter was showing me.

"Mangwi, please, talk to your sister for me," he added, clapping his hands in desperation.

He soon gave up his plea and moved towards me. Then he pulled my hand towards him.

"Please, come, we need to talk," he said with petitioning eyes.

I yielded but signaled with my eyes to Mangwi, to stand by the door.

We stepped into the room. I shuddered a little. My eyes quickly glanced at the door to ensure that Mesape was not locking it with the key.

He moved towards the window and shifted the shade. After that, he stood back and began scanning me all over. Then, he lifted my blouse and looked at me. With both hands at work, he carefully loosened my belt. My folded skirt started falling to the floor. I must have lost about four pounds in one week. Suddenly, he covered his face with his palms, fell on his knees, and began weeping.

"Oh, Akong, please forgive me," he began pleading. "This is all my fault," he went on. "Please, don't go away. I will make up for all the trouble I've caused you," he cried.

My eyes fixed at him while my heart was growing too heavy for my chest to bear. I didn't want to cry, but I could not hold back the tears. He stood up and started drying my wet face with his right palm.

"Akong, I'm so sorry for all the pain I've caused you," he said and paused to wipe his tears.

"See how much weight you have lost. Oh, Lord, please, forgive me for all this," he kept moaning while throwing his hands in the air.

Finally, the plea session was over. I returned to the living room and sat on the couch. My little girl climbed on my lap while my son tickled me. We all joined our heads together, giggling and laughing. Even then, I still felt clumsy, like a stranger, in my own house. I didn't know what or what not to tell them. So, we just kept hugging.

Just before nightfall, I returned to my hiding place at Pam's house. Fleeting thoughts of emotional torture filled my days and nights. What sense could I make of Mesape's pleas? How I wished, in the depths of my soul, that he could make whatever sacrifice was necessary, to denounce his dangerous lifestyle, once and for all.

More importantly, what was going to become of my children? I had no way of knowing.

Two days before traveling, I mustered courage and moved in to spend time with them. An uneasy peace was better than the total absence of communication between us, I concluded. I hoped there would be no fights, nothing to prevent my departure. So, I handed over the keys of my car to him. It was certainly less expensive for him to complete payment on it than to repair the battered Mitsubishi Gallant. Then he came with me, to my office, and brought back my books and professional tapes. I left the rest of my personal belongings in his care.

As we moved the stuff that Sunday into my car, I recalled that, of all the things I had packed out of the house, the only item which he had confiscated was my 16x20 inch portrait.

"Akong, one day, I will make a life-size portrait of you, for the children to admire. I will tell them of your short nose and your sweetness of your heart." Over the years, he had often repeated that promise.

However, as I listened to him, I began discerning stuff that had never before crossed my mind. Why was he focusing on my portrait rather than on my person, for his desired celebration? Wasn't he directly and openly predicting that he would have custody over the children if ever we were separated? Or was he implying that he would out-live me?

Nevertheless, I accepted his invitation to go for grocery shopping that evening. He filled the baskets with a variety of meats, vegetables, and treats.

We got home and prepared a sumptuous farewell dinner.

His enthusiasm was unmatched. He decorated the table himself, with the lace clothe which we used during special occasions. Apart from the salad which I made, Mesape prepared the three-course meal himself. The table was full. All of us gathered around it like a model family.

Twenty-four hours afterward, Mesape, the children, and my sister, Azuh, accompanied me to the newly constructed Nsimalen Airport. Some of my Tena friends joined the farewell crew. We took souvenir pictures, posing like a healthy family.

The voice on the loudspeaker began alerting passengers. I hugged Mesape, my children, my sister, and my friends.

Then I picked up my hand luggage and followed the dozens of people, rushing towards the endless corridor.

CHAPTER 36

Landing in America

I fastened my seatbelt, adjusted it, and began listening to the air hostess, who was giving safety tips. When she finished, I checked my bag to ensure that I had not left behind any document or items I needed or treasured.

On Monday, September 11, 1993, I arrived at Dulles Airport in Virginia around 2 pm to take part in the Young African Leaders Program, for training in "Pluralism and Democracy." Under the aegis of the International Visitor Program of the United States Information Agency, the objective was to offer an opportunity for learning through interactions with leaders and pioneers in various domains as well as at multiple levels.

A tall, handsome gentleman walked up to me and introduced himself. He was Toney, our escort officer. Within an hour, he guided six of us (of the seventeen participants from other African nations) to the waiting van.

We arrived at the Crowne Plaza Hotel in downtown Washington, DC, by 5 pm, to a rousing welcome. The kaleidoscope of waving banners at the entrance heightened our spirits.

Beginning with Washington, DC, we made a mini-tour of six states, namely, Maryland, Oklahoma, Georgia, California, and Florida. We met state and local authorities, who presented community projects and lectured on the American system of government. Other speakers and experts showcased initiatives with substantial impact within the community and the country as a whole. The variety of people and structures portrayed the diversity of the country.

Besides, we visited touristic sites in each of the states, including Niagara Falls on the border of New York and Canada. What a time to learn, discover, share, and relax! The newness of everything, including my fellow African counterparts, soothed my emotional aches and weary body, with a therapeutic freshness.

Every night, I retired to my room and prayed, sometimes with my first roommate, Gladys, from Ghana. What a shelter from the physical abuse! I rejoiced. Nonetheless, the separation from my children remained a gnawing sore in my heart. Azuh's loving care of Quydee and Sweetie reassured me as I longed to reunite with my children as soon as the course was over. Our freedom would depend on finding the truth eventually. I hoped to have a clearer vision for our future before returning.

Also, I kept up open communication with Mesape. Each of my letters bore a friendly tone.

My six-week stay soon expired, with the thorny issues between us still unresolved. I waved a teary goodbye to Pius of Namibia as we both stepped out of the Sheraton Biscayne Bay, Miami, Florida. Our flights were the last on that departure day.

There was no place for me to return home to, I thought to myself, as I struggled with the multiple pieces of my luggage. My case was just as bad as that of Laurent from Burundi, who couldn't return home either. There had been a coup d'état in his country the day before.

It was going to be a solo destination. My heart was sore as I missed the company of my new friends. Even the weather was unfriendly. The sauna-like heat of Miami and the yellow taxicab reminded me of the streets in Yaounde, on a humid day, in the dry season. I struggled with the profuse sweating, as if wrestling with the harsh reality of my life, lashing out directly at my face. The sweat drops felt like blood flowing from my soul.

Thank goodness, immediate family support was readily available. Apart from my nephew, two brothers were living in Ohio. One of my brothers and his family welcomed me to their home. I was going to spend some time with them before my visa expired. Three months seemed like enough time to work out a solution with Mesape, howbeit, from 8,000 miles away.

Incidentally, Awah was just an hour away in college in Wilberforce, Ohio. Meanwhile, Mangwi and her family were in New York. Three of us, sisters, had arrived in the US for separate and unrelated missions, within a space of six weeks. How grateful I was for my in-house team of therapists! Their support was undoubtedly going to help me recover from emotional damage.

The following day, I picked up the telephone directory and looked up the address of the nearest Seventh-day Adventist church. On Saturday, my brother, Munga, drove me to the church in Worthington.

The ushers welcomed me with warm smiles and open arms. Indeed, after Sabbath School, the coordinators invited me upfront for a unique introduction to the whole church. I felt honored. The hostess interviewed me for up to ten minutes. She asked about the church in my country, the culture of the people, the political situation, and the historical background. As a journalist, it was easy to answer. I could tell that the congregation of a hundred or so was delighted.

The potluck after the divine service was terrific. Beyond the delicious meals, I began making friends as we chatted freely. Little did I know that there was something extraordinary in store for me. Before the church program was over, on that first day, three women, called me to the side.

"We know that you just arrived," one of them said. "So, tell us, how did you get here?"

"My brother drove me."

"Is he a Seventh-day Adventist?"

"No."

> *Little did I know that there was something extraordinary in store for me.*

"Okay, we have already arranged with three families in the church that are willing to pick you up each time you need to come to church, okay?"

I was so pleasantly surprised that I lacked words to express my gratitude. In addition to the telephone numbers of the three families, others exchanged their home numbers with mine. That evening, before I called my brother to pick me up, the ushers, who had welcomed me, informed me that Sister Mercedes would pick me up on Wednesday for the prayer meeting.

Each Sabbath, the deaconesses promptly updated the list of the families whose turn was next to drive me to and from church on Wednesday, Friday, and Saturday. My biological family would sit back and watch a car arrive in on time to give me a ride to church. On my return trip, the same or another of the three assigned families brought me back home.

Countdown to my return to my Cameroon home began. Yet, there was no positive change in the quagmire of my family life. Nevertheless, I was dying to reunite with my children. I was in a quandary. So, my brother had a long talk with me. He demonstrated, with examples, the unfortunate cases of battered women, who returned to their marital home after escaping, and their husbands killed them. He even shared existing statistics with me. He explained that I was in the mindset of the victim. Thus, third parties had to intervene to help me consider other options that would safeguard my welfare. I resisted. Yet, each morning, my brother woke up with appeals to reason. Afraid for my life, he encouraged me to apply to the State of Ohio to request the extension of my stay.

For days, I pined over what was going to be the most painful decision of my life. When it became clear that it was better to seek asylum than to return, I plunged into despair. How could I go on without my children? During the day, I managed to smile and carry on with domestic duties with my usual zest. However, in the night, I cried myself into sleep after the final prayer for the day. It was to become a bitter pill that I swallowed each night for years, a sort of sleeping tablet that caused my eyes to swell.

Finally, I applied to the state authorities to extend my stay in the territory. To my greatest surprise, it was granted, along with a renewable work permit.

"Akongshee, in six months, you have many more friends than I have in four years," my sister-in-law remarked. Indeed, up to six of every ten telephone calls to her house were for me. My church family was offering the extra help I needed. It was Carmen from the church who drove me to the driving test appointment. At that critical moment, my brother was unable to help because his work schedule did not permit him. Other church members stepped in to support me in other areas. They invited me to picnics and a variety of fun places.

> *When it became clear that it was better to seek asylum than to return, I plunged into despair. How could I go on without my children?*

With the onset of winter, some members of the church gave me gifts of appropriate clothing for the season. Michelle invited me to come along for shopping. She asked me to choose a sweater, dress, or coat, including other accessories, for which she paid. I returned home with a bloated shopping bag. My brother and his wife clapped their hands in amazement.

Meanwhile, the willing families kept providing transportation until when I got my driver's license. What a relief to my brother and his wife, especially to the latter, who was then not willing to drive! They gladly offered me the other car, which I used for church, for work, and the running of family errands.

Barbara, one of my new friends at the Worthington church, who had rushed for tissue when she first heard my tragic story, was full of admiration. "You have a knack for making friends instantly," said Barbara.

"I'm sure it's because she is always bubbling with joy," added Ramona. "No one would suspect that she has been through heartbreaking moments in her life."

Frankly, I never posed an act purposefully to attract attention to myself. Instead, I often immersed myself in any activity of the moment. Spontaneously, joy accompanied my active involvement, obliging the appreciation of others while providing healing power. That may explain why some Cameroonian friends often wondered, "How is she coping with repeated aggression in her marriage?" That, too, for me, served as an alarm.

On Saturday, while I was accompanying Barbara home, she began relating how she had given up on driving, having failed the test four times.

"Experts say that some normal people can't drive," she explained.

I didn't know what exactly she was alluding to, but I just burst out laughing. It sounded outlandish.

"A child of the king of the universe, giving up, just like that?" I asked. "In America, where anything is possible?" I pressed on.

"What else can I do?" she peered into my face, somewhat embarrassed.

Soon, her face began glowing with renewed interest, when I revealed that I had also failed the test two times, though I was an experienced driver in Cameroon, where driving on jammed streets and bad roads rendered the task more challenging.

Despite my promptings, she interjected with a rehearsal of her anxieties and fears of the road.

"So, who oversees all the steering wheels, cruising the highways?" I asked, my eyes fluctuating between her and the maroon car in front of us.

Her hands brushed her face. She shifted in her seat and took a deep breath. There was a soul-searching silence that seemed to propel the wheels of the high-performance sky-blue Honda under my command.

"Do you have a driving illness?" I caught myself asking.

Barbara started laughing, with her right hand over her mouth. She looked more abashed than relieved.

Suddenly, Barbara began naming jobs she could have as well as things she would do if only she could drive. She also mentioned her friends—Millie, Ramona, and Michelle—who were all excellent drivers. Before we separated that afternoon, Barbara decided to go back to driving school.

Within months, she had her license. What's more, a couple of years afterward, the retiring mother of three adult children married a wonderful guy at her local church. Indeed, she and her son had their weddings just months apart from each other.

When I returned to Ohio, Barbara was looking forty in her fifties. The pimples on her face were gone. Her lips were pink while her cheeks glowed with joy and fulfillment. Since then, Barbara, who was born in St Kitts, and I are bonded together like sisters. "You will make a good counselor," Barbara often said.

If I could claim to myself any such expertise, I would say that it was thanks to the constant study of the Bible, as well as the perusing of hundreds of Ellen G. White books, that I could connect some vital dots in life. Upon becoming a Seventh-day Adventist, I began reading the "Spirit of Prophecy" books. Immediately, I lost the taste for the numerous novels, which I used to devour like delicious meals.

A Cameroonian friend soon tested my spotted skill. I happened to have written to my Italian friends, who were living in Washington, DC. In their reply, they mentioned Vera, whose telephone number they freely shared with me.

I called first, and she promptly returned my call on the same day. Our dialogue soon took on a life of its own. Barely a few days after, Vera, who was equally a victim of spousal abuse, began disclosing stuff to me on her marriage. Her bruised heart pleaded for solace while I struggled to hide my shock and embarrassment.

"Are you sure you want to tell me all this?" I stopped her in the middle of a sentence.

"You don't know what a favor you are doing me, Akongshee," she said, breathing in relief.

"But how?" I asked.

"Just by listening," she stated confidently.

She would pause, breathe deeply, cry, and blow her nose while I wondered what to do concretely to help.

One night she took advantage of her husband's absence and called me. She related the graphic details for five straight hours. I only took permission to use the bathroom. Finally, we stopped at 3:00 am. My ears were hurting.

The following morning, when I reminisced over her desperate need to just let it out, I wondered why me? Why not her friends in her state or throughout the US? Granted, she was a former college mate; we had not seen each other for almost a decade. Besides, it was the first time that she confided in me. School mates, including her, used to describe me as friendly, but quiet, and inexperienced in matters of the heart.

"Why do men begin with romance, but gradually become sulky, impatient, and sour?" she asked.

I explained that natural human love was like a branch, cut off from the tree. It dries up gradually, turning his heart into a desert, from where only drops of "the milk of human kindness" come out after it rains. If drops of milk cannot add color to a cup of chocolate, how much less egocentric love can "irrigate" a union of two hearts? She laughed because of the Shakespearean quote that we studied in literature in college. As for me, the imagery of the cut branch was from the Bible, in the book of John, chapter 15.

After several conversations, she dropped the idea of separating from her husband. Since her husband was not violent, she had a better chance than me to groom her children to become noble citizens.

Barely a week after I got installed in my brother's house, he had taken me on a tour of Ohio State University, during which he introduced me to some of his former professors. A few days after our visit, a professor of the African Studies Department contacted him and asked if I could give a lecture to students who were taking a course in International Studies. What an opportunity! The professor asked me to talk on the role and contribution of women to the national economy of the Cameroons. I focused on rural women: While their husbands were working on plantations of export crops, like coffee and cocoa, these women had a dual role—the duty to cater to all the needs of their families as well as feed the nation. Their contribution cut across the value chain of the food industry, from seed selection to soil preparation, planting, weeding, harvesting, and processing to marketing.

Rural women rarely went to bed before 10 pm, to wake up as early as 4 am. Armed with their handheld hoes, they marched to their farms, descending and climbing hills through footpaths, whether it was raining or not. Often, they strapped their babies on their backs or placed them in cushioned basins while working all day. Most of them returned home close to sunset. Then they began catering to the immediate needs of their families. Such duties included cleaning, laundry, cooking, serving meals, and hosting unannounced relatives. A lot of them sacrificed time or treasures to ensure harmony within the clan by mentoring or taking up the responsibilities of negligent parents. Besides, each of them belonged to the village as well as church groups to provide synergy in shared initiatives.

During the weekends and traditional holidays, rural women carried out major food preparation tasks, namely peeling, shredding, grinding, winnowing, pounding, tying, wrapping—all manually done.

Thanks to the retail trading, these women sponsored great leaders, diplomats, engineers, computer experts, doctors, architects, some of whom became presidents. "Some of your professors and fellow students are studying here thanks to their mothers," I stressed. Sadly, those hardworking women neither took vacations, went on sick leave, nor had any time to play.

At the end of my presentation, the class of about forty students asked me lots of questions. The authorities of the department handed me an envelope.

Rapturous applause accompanied me to the door. I was grateful for the token of appreciation I received. Wasn't it an irony that the acclaimed speaker was on the verge of losing her place as an agent of development in her country?

Of course, I was breathing the air of freedom in America. While longing to remain meaningfully occupied, an unexpected opportunity came my way. My brother and his wife threw a party at home. Among the guests was Dr. Ifeanyi, a professor at Ohio State University. He had created a program, "Focus on Africa," which he was hosting on Columbus Cable Television. The moment my brother introduced me to him, he relinquished his duties, insisting that I was more qualified to be the hostess.

The following week, he received me as a guest on his talk show. In the end, he informed the audience that, henceforth, I would be the hostess. Meanwhile, he was in charge of looking for guests. Before long, viewers began giving us positive feedback and words of encouragement.

Though it was a volunteer job, it was a marvelous combination of my newly acquired title as a Young African Leader and my training and experience as a media personality. I frequented the Columbus public library and the OSU libraries, more so, for works on the African continent. Also, as a nightly show, it was easy to continue hosting while doing a day job.

Soon after, I had my first paid job. It was quite a surprise to my family and other Africans since it was in my field. They had advised me to take a short training course for tasks like housekeeping, babysitting, and nursing aide. My duty was videotaping the training sessions of a two-week professional course. In the end, we produced a collection of videos.

A second surprise came in when the State of Ohio recruited me. The authorities hired me alongside a dozen young people to assist in overhauling their archival system by installing a new one. The intensive work took several months to complete.

By then, I began reading books and watching television shows on violence in marriage. Gradually, it dawned on me that if I ventured back home, the threat to my life could be worse. Mesape's intransigence confirmed the new perspective I had on our situation. My heart remained sore like a gaping wound without a cure.

How could he claim to be seeking reconciliation and yet unwilling to face the truth? I decided that his refusal to focus on the mysterious occurrences in my office was an indication that he had a hidden agenda.

> *By then, I began reading books and watching television shows on violence in marriage. Gradually, it dawned on me that if I ventured back home, the threat to my life could be worse.*

Unfortunately, I returned home on Thursday to another reminder that I was homeless, even in the US. My sister-in-law would no longer host me. It was normal in my country for a family to host a needy relative for an indefinite period, until when they become economically viable. Thus, it was strange that my sister-in-law was throwing me out. Yet, wasn't one year enough, despite living in a spacious house with unoccupied rooms?

Unable to communicate an unfavorable message calmly, she resorted to the only means she had. She created a crisis scene of screaming out false accusations, with tears rushing down her eyes. Her terrified husband couldn't stand the sight of his pregnant wife in such a desperate condition. He calmed her down and took over, yelling at me while pointing fingers of accusations. "How can you be so ungrateful, so wicked to maltreat her at this time when her body is fragile?"

I was shocked. Yet, I should have known better. What did I expect of a woman who fumes at the dinner table and rebukes her husband for complimenting his sister for cooking a delicious meal? Besides, she lied to Mesape on the phone that I had gone to the nightclub while I was away for the weekend attending a retreat organized by the local conference of the Seventh-day Adventist Church?

Sadly, my brother refused to listen to me, much less accept any word I uttered in my defense. They issued an order—I had to leave. The following day I went to work, and upon return, my sister-in-law refused to open the door. I stood out in the yard and waited until my brother came back late in the evening. I mustered courage and stepped in through the tense atmosphere. To my dismay, there was a seal on my door.

Desperate, I called Sarah, a Seventh-day Adventist woman, and friend, who was living downtown. Without hesitation, she accepted to host me.

Sarah, a woman with rich life experience, was hospitable. Over time, she taught me the history of the Seventh-day Adventist Church in the Cameroons. Sarah had been instrumental in bringing in more converts to the church through her courageous stance on the Bible. She cited some authorities of the church that were her former Bible students. She mastered the organization and structure of the local church.

"Knowing Jesus Christ is a matter of life and death," she would say to friends and acquaintances alike, often cutting into conversations that had nothing to do with the gospel. I thought she was rude; I would cringe and ask her later, "Why don't you wait until they ask you or until they are ready?"

Then, she would quickly quote Matthew 11:12, while insisting, "If you wait, they may never ask, and they would die in their sins."

In the meantime, Sarah kept saying, "Forgive them for they know not what they are doing," each time my sister-in-law's ruse came up. Unfortunately, my mother, from thousands of miles away, rebuked me for "abandoning" my "sister," close to the delicate moment of giving birth. The effect of the stage-managed eviction dragged on because my mother rejected my phone calls after I disobeyed her order to return to my brother's house. Communication between us remained interrupted for up to a year.

Despite the mental torture, I had to remain focused on the challenge at hand—finding a full-time job in communication. I brainstormed with Sarah; Washington, DC, stood out for international positions.

After a month of staying at Sarah's place, I bid her farewell and left for the capital of the United States of America.

CHAPTER 37

Warmth from My Earthly and Godly Families

On Monday, I boarded the Greyhound bus. Instead of going straight to Washington, DC, I stopped over in New York to spend some days with my sister, Mangwi, and her family.

Unexpectedly, she and her husband pleaded that I stay with them. As an international personality, he convinced me effortlessly; I was going to get a job in my domain. Also, they implored me to live with them for as long as I wanted. Their children were excited.

On Thursday, they helped me to locate the Mamaroneck Seventh-day Adventist Church. On Saturday, I attended the Sabbath service. The members welcomed me with the same warmth as in Ohio. I immediately felt a strong spirit of cohesion among us during Sabbath School. The more I contributed to the discussion, the more they got interested in me. In the end, some of them hugged me and asked for my home phone number. "My sister, you are on fire for Christ," commented Henry, the First Elder. "I'm so happy that you chose our unit," added Beverly.

Within weeks of my arrival, Henry asked me to teach his class. All the members agreed although I was the youngest in age and faith. For those "walking through the valley of the shadow of death," the Bible is a life vest, I thought to myself. I recalled gulping down Bible promises as capsules, to maintain my sanity and to sustain my life. O, how I wish my children were there with me, sitting on the same pew! My son was ten and my daughter was six then. During my absence for a year, we had resorted to writing letters. I tried to console them. Their letters were so touching because instead of focusing on their needs, they were eager to know how I was doing—if I was safe. Otherwise, I telephoned them only when I surmised that they could speak freely without the interference of their father.

The crowning mark of the generous spirit of the Mamaroneck church members, on my first visit, was an invitation from sister Marcella. The slim, fair-skinned woman, of average height, in her sixties, looked gentle. She looked like "a daughter, polished after the similitude of a palace," according to Psalm 144 in her elegant clothes.

She and her husband, grandson, and granddaughter treated me to a delicious lunch of vegetable salad, rice and peas, vegetarian meat, and steamed leafy greens. Her attentiveness and a steady smile lit up her beautiful face and warmed my heart.

Almost three hours after, when I was about leaving, Marcella gave me two white paper bags of gifts. Therein were health and inspirational magazines, books, perfume, handkerchiefs, a pair of brand-new designer pantyhose, winter socks, Costa Rican home-made cassava crackers, and a piece of cake.

"What! All of this?" I asked, staring at her.

"Yes, *ma Chérie* (my dear), it's all yours," was to become her characteristic response.

I returned home and presented the gifts to Mangwi and her husband. "This much love, at the very first meeting?" they gaped. Marcella had included handkerchiefs, fragrances, and rare snacks for my sister and her family.

Since that day, each Sabbath, Mrs. Brook had something special for me. Eventually, she offered me her family piano, the same one I toyed with during my first visit.

"*Ma Chérie*, do you have a minute?" she asked most of the time when I picked up the receiver.

"Yes, *Maman Chérie* (Mother dear)," I responded excitedly.

"I have something for you. Just listen, okay?"

Usually, it was an essay, a poem, a verse, a page from a devotional, or a paragraph from a health article.

Otherwise, it was a radio station or TV channel that she wanted me to listen to or to watch. "*Ma Chérie*, turn to…or to channel… Talk to you later, okay?"

The only regret I had in spending time with Marcella was the quick passage of it. Apart from food, she would place bookmarkers between pages, underline paragraphs, and fold magazine pages before I arrived. After diner, we would take our drinks out to the lounge chairs. We would read, discuss, sniff the blending fragrances of flowers, and sing. Within intervals, she would pause and cuddle her sparkling white Maltese dog, Madonna.

The phenomenal Marcella kept and updated a list of things to do for personal self-improvement, including Scuba diving and riding a motorcycle. Indeed, she started learning how to play the soprano saxophone when she was about sixty-eight.

After the talk-show host, Montel Williams, announced his diagnosis with multiple sclerosis, Marcella gave me an exercise therapy booklet to photocopy appropriate pages and dispatch to him.

Another member of the church, who impacted my life tremendously, was Lydia, a Filipino lady. The average height, slightly plump lady, was a nurse. She had left her family back home and come to America in search of a good-paying job to help support them. Lydia's idiosyncratic smiles and simplicity was heartwarming.

Since Lydia and I were living in Port Chester, we began spending a lot of time together. She often invited me to her home on Sabbaths. Her elegant interior of potted plants was a glimpse of the Garden of Eden. In the quiet of her surroundings, we studied the Bible together, sang, prayed, and ate.

Soon, we started going out together jogging. Lydia would come over at 5:30 am, three days a week. It was a moment when we also shared testimonies and did prayer walks, part of the distance.

I benefitted from Lydia's kindness when the Women's Department of the General Conference of the Seventh-day Adventist Church scheduled a week-long women's conference. It brought together hundreds of women, who lodged at a hotel to study, learn new skills, and pray together. Dozens of presentations and workshops were on the schedule. Lydia, who had attended more than one of those conferences in the past, said, "Akongshee, you cannot afford to miss such a life-changing encounter." From then on, I started longing to attend the once-in-a-lifetime opportunity, though I could not afford it. By the next conference in five years, I would have returned home already. I prayed earnestly every day with Lydia while we wondered how and where to find a sponsor.

On Tuesday, three days before the conference, I returned home after our morning exercise. I was drowsy, but I read Acts 16—the story of

Lydia—and prayed before going to bed. I began meditating over the zeal and hospitality of Lydia. Then I had a dream, in which someone brought me a fluffy, beige teddy bear. He was downstairs at the door, unable to enter because the bear was humongous. So, I got up and rushed downstairs to help. It was then that the telephone began ringing. I woke up and rushed for the receiver.

"Akongshee, I'm sorry to inform you that I won't be able to attend the conference," said Lydia.

"Why not?"

"My father is dead. I have to book my flight today."

"Oh, I'm so sorry to hear this."

"Listen, I am transferring my hotel booking to you. I have also arranged with a friend to pick you up." I began crying while thanking Lydia. I was happy for the opportunity, yet sorry that she would miss it.

"Don't worry about me, Akong. It's a privilege for me."

Meanwhile, my friendship with sister Marcella was growing steadily. To her, I was the daughter with whom she shared some of the best things in life. Her two daughters were living in another city. Besides, they were no longer active members of the church.

Thanks to Marcella, I didn't quit the Mamaroneck church when I became the subject of conflict. The Sabbath School Superintendent, Pauline, disagreed with the First Elder for letting me teach his class; she even took the matter to the board. The elder refused to comply with her demand. So, Pauline confiscated the teacher's manual.

I was disappointed because Pauline once invited me to her home for lunch. I cried and felt personally attacked. The members of the class wanted that I continue to teach, but Pauline made an issue of it. I did not want to be the cause of division in the church. So, I decided to leave the church and continue studying at home.

Incidentally, Marcella invited me to the Co-op City Church the following Sabbath. They were celebrating International Cultures. On her instructions, I came along with some artifacts. The organizers gave me the honor to present Cameroonian art, food, dress, including some unique family traditions. I played a small drum. Then, I explained that, apart from being a musical instrument, it was a communication tool. Village councilors use the drum to convey messages from the chief as well as rally the population. The church members were enthralled.

As for me, it was the guest speaker's sermon that inspired me. Mike focused on the process of spiritual growth by making a compelling analogy with the process of learning a new language.

Coincidentally, I was sitting next to Mike during potluck lunch. I seized the opportunity to ask him some questions concerning his sermon.

While we were still talking, Marcella and Rita informed me that they had just received some news; they would not be able to give me a ride back home. They were rushing to respond to an emergency. So, the head deaconess made an announcement. Mike raised his hand; he was the only one going towards my direction. Indeed, he lived in Port Chester, like me.

After lunch, I was sitting in the passenger seat of Mike's car. Our forty-minute ride became a moment of celebration. The excellent spring weather, with colorful trees along the way, provided a conducive atmosphere for chatting. I began sharing my testimonies. Mike seemed to be absorbing every word since he kept switching his eyes between the road and me. I was speaking and admiring nature. The trees formed a canopy while leaves waved at us. I couldn't help thinking of the Garden of Eden. The blend of orange, red, yellow, green leaves on the approaching and endless rows of trees heightened my joy.

Then Mike wanted to know what had brought me to the US. I shared some highlights of my six-state tour, thanks to the Young African Leader's program. "You just barely arrived, and you have seen more of my country than myself," said Mike. There and then, he promised himself that the next vacation, he would visit Washington state.

I went on to share my experiences. "I have never met anyone like you," Mike confessed.

When we pulled up the driveway, he opened the passenger door of his navy-blue car and closed it with such gallantry that Mangwi and her husband raised their eyebrows until he drove off. What an honor! I looked at him and wondered if he was an angel.

Unknown to Mike and myself, our first meeting was the commencement of an ordained friendship. Mike's sermon had demonstrated the extent to which he mastered the Bible. I had a lot of unanswered questions about my life. Two days after, he called me. I seized the opportunity to ask him how one can determine God's will in their life.

"That is a whole study," said Mike. He gave me a few answers on the spot. Then, we planned a short Bible study on Sundays. It was exciting;

I began jotting down references. We closed each session with prayers. Those Bible studies were providing direct healing to my battered soul.

Three weeks after our first meeting, Mike invited me to his church in Hartsdale. He arrived on time and picked me up. I truly appreciated the rides, especially his readiness and ability to relate my deepest personal concerns with passages and characters in the Bible.

The crowing effect was Sabbath School at Mike's church. It was more profound than I had ever had since baptism. His church was smaller than the Mamaroneck church. So, it was a single class. The pastor and the elders were responsible for leading out. They never limited themselves to the quarterly. The teacher of the day came along with Ellen G. White's passages beyond the text proposed for further reading. The teachers often consulted the encyclopedia in the public library during the week. Besides, Pastor Corno, who had studied Judaism, was a resource person, both for translations and providing the context in Jewish tradition. Sometimes, he turned down the answers of the elders to a common question, dismissing it as a cliché that distorts reality.

"Who told you that?" asked Pastor Corno. "Where did you get that from?"

The elders will become silent, while the rest of the members would be shocked at his straightforward demonstrations. The revelation was gripping; we were stunned as if staring at a precious piece of fabric with hidden strands.

Thus, Pastor Corno and his team rendered Sabbath School the spot where everyone found a comfortable place at the foot of Jesus, staring in wonder at the delicate splendor of God's glory. Members could be absent for any segment of the church program—not Sabbath School.

"My joy is full" was a collective declaration of participants at the end of each lesson review. I often asked most questions, maybe due to my multiple registers. Later, I probed further with Mike. I began looking forward to our thirty-minute, weekly rides through freeway 287, which always conjured up images of chariots of angels. Passing through the surrounding forests transformed the car into a mobile heavenly home. Besides, our conversation mainly consisted of thanksgiving for multiple daily blessings.

"I've never met anyone like you, my entire life," Mike confessed again. I soon noticed that each time, before we got out of the car into the sanctuary, he would say, "Thank you for sharing your joy with me," with a broad smile.

During the week, I took train rides to Manhattan, especially at the UN office, in search of jobs. On Monday, I began attending a women's conference that was open to the public. The discussions that brought together hundreds of participants were being held in advance of the UN-convened Fourth World Conference on Women on the theme: Action for Equality, Development, and Peace. It was going to take place from the 4th to the 15th of September 1995 in Beijing, China. To achieve global legal balance, governments gave their accord for a comprehensive package called the Beijing Platform for Action, aimed at achieving global legal equality.

In the concluding sessions, the organizers launched a contest to choose representatives. I was selected, thanks to my proficiency in English and French, to head the Communication Center in New York, upon return from Beijing.

Mike and I, in our telephone conversation, began praying about the upcoming conference. That evening we spoke for a more extended period than usual.

"I don't know how to leave you, Akongshee."

"Me, too,"

On Friday, Mike invited me for a lock-in retreat; it was my first ever. Our ride that evening was a prolonged viewing of the gentle rays of setting sun, glowing in the pink, purple, orange, brown, yellow, and green leaves of trees. Waving branches applauded our entrance into the magnificence and warmth of the soothing sun, caressing our surrendered faces in defiance of the windscreen.

For the first time since meeting Mike, I felt an unbroken chain of flutters in my heart for him. So, I stole a glance in the tranquilizing silence. He was steady and contemplative as if in readiness for photographers to capture the moment. My reverie was soon absorbed in the engulfing, graying sky, as Mike pulled up into the parking lot of the church. There was already a crowd of chatting members waiting in the yard.

Within a quarter of an hour, we finished with the preliminaries—unpacking our stuff, and drinking tea. Mike led out in the lesson study. I kept raising my hand to questions as if controlled by an electric current. Members turned around, giggled and laughed. The uplifting message and the sweet fellowship transported me into a heavenly delight.

The following morning, another elder presented the follow-up lesson. Having taken part in the previous one, I answered most of the questions.

During the relaxing moment in the afternoon, Mike, who was a few meters away, began staring at me intensely. He seemed arrested in deep thoughts with his inner man as if he had escaped into a different world, into which he was dying to capture me. Suddenly, two members turned around and looked at us enquiringly, noting our momentary unconsciousness. Yet, Mike kept gazing with more intensity, motionless.

Though I was feeling uneasy, I wanted to remain bound in Mike's hypnotizing stare. In an attempt to measure the degree of his attachment, I moved to the other row of pews. His eyes followed me. He was a gardener who had discovered an exhilarating herb. He remained steady like bright beams of light, flashing through a frosted window, dispersing opaque darkness. So, I examined myself to discern the appealing locale for his piercing eyes. Absent. So, I had to absolve myself from Mike's trance, but saliva was dried up. More people began glancing at us. It was time to take a recess from the burning heat of his regard to assess its object for readiness.

Not yet, Mike seemed unable or unwilling to bounce back until George announced: "break time over." He took a deep breath and turned around. Meanwhile, his sudden departure left the sensation of a wave of cold air, brushing over my forehead. I shivered like a child whose finger is pierced by the thorn of a rose flower.

On Wednesday evening, I arrived late for Prayer Meeting. From the street, I spotted Mike, standing by the door.

"What are you doing here by yourself?" I asked in a muffled voice.

"Do you know how many times I've stepped out to look for you?"

Undoubtedly, love was knitting our hearts together.

Thursday was an enchanting summer evening. Mike invited me for tea. After that, we set out for the longest ride so far, without any set destination. Mike often said he wanted to follow the freeway, until when he got tired. I was having fun.

We drove for more than an hour. Then, Mike took me to unfamiliar parts of the city, where he grew up. We slowed down and scrutinized the browning entrances, the stained walls of apartment complexes, imposing landmarks, while glancing at children playing in the park.

On our way back, the little girl in me wanted to play with the young boy in him. The gigantic walls lingering in my mind, and the approaching overhead train tracks, were crushing whatever flimsy barriers still separated us. The little boy, with his gripping "show-and-tell," got the little girl excited. How I wished we were in the field, playing a game, throwing balls, or something! How about running wild in the mud, bathing in the dust, and making laughable figurines with organic Play-Doh® and comparing them! I fidgeted in my seat and peeped at Mike, who was consumed by an unwarranted silence. I was dying to transform the overflowing inspiration into something more palpable than the kiss we had never had.

Too bad for me, Mike preferred video games, and cruising cars, manipulated by his steady arms. He was bent on flying. I felt lonely in a good company. I had to admit that a man could be impervious before a challenge, while a woman fantasizes about an elusive dream. Mike was pensive while I chatted excitedly about imaginary floating balloons, greeting his transition from boyhood into manhood.

Finally, Mike spoke his mind in a formal tone after he parked his car in front of my home. We strolled down the street, that evening in the twilight, amidst the fragrance of blooming flowers. What surprised me was how far he was ready to go. I applied brakes here and there, but he dispelled my reticence. We looked into each other's eyes and took deep breaths repeatedly—a feeling of indescribable joy wrapped us.

"Let's pray about this," Mike said.

I nodded. So, we prayed. Mike said good night and drove away.

Sadly, we did not have the chance to chart the course of the river of our love. Some church members began questioning our friendship, while others threatened to end it.

"Why Akongshee?" asked three young women, angrily. Mike refused to listen to them; me neither. So, they ganged up and confronted him. Didn't he know that she was married before? Why should he choose an African woman? How about the other white and Caribbean women who loved him? Mike ignored them.

Soon, the opposers formed a matchmakers' club. They took Mike through several scenarios—suggesting names and creating encounters with "more suitable" and "accomplished" women. Mike dismissed each and backed out.

Nevertheless, the gossips carried on. A distraught Mike sought the advice of the pastor, who knew firsthand about our friendship. The pastor was aware that Mike and I were taking our time to allow God to have His way. We had decided to wait for up to two years. Despite our surrender and straightforward approach, the clamoring for our separation got louder.

"Not everyone has surrendered to Christ," said Pastor Corno. "Even some of the converted are still immature."

Mike left the pastor's office in tears. As soon as I saw him, I burst out crying. It felt like someone had stabbed me. It hurt so much; my heart was bursting. All those in the corridor began sighing and complaining while others threw their arms around me, some cried along. Mike's friend, Phil, an elder, whisked him away to the back of the building.

Neither Mike nor I were able to take part in the evening's meeting. Phil's wife, Violeta, gave me a ride home. "Dear God, please, help me understand how we have sinned against you," was to become my prayer for weeks.

The following Sabbath, I took refuge in a new church in the area, the White Plains church, at Juniper Hills.

Unable to deal with the pain by myself, since I couldn't speak with Mike, I sought help. Two weeks after, on a Saturday afternoon, Phil and I took a long walk while chatting.

"Do you think Mike prefers that I transfer to another church?" I asked.

"Akongshee, you don't know what Mike thinks of you," he said, looking at me and pausing for a while. "He has the utmost respect for you."

"Really? You think so?" I insisted, eager for an explanation.

"Do you know that it's thanks to you that Mike finally fell in love?" Phil said, looking at me with renewed admiration.

"What?" I shouted.

"Yes, indeed," he nodded with tight lips. "Even my wife and I have benefitted enormously from your friendship. It has healed our marriage," he explained.

I jumped up, shouted with joy; my lingering pain disappeared instantly.

"I don't remember ever seeing Mike happier," he went on.

I smiled heartily, for the first time since the brutal break-up. We had not wasted our time, after all.

No wonder some members used to whisper among themselves that Mike had an emotional block. Indeed, they had concluded that he was either incapable of falling in love or unable to commit to a woman.

I saw it differently, having spent precious moments with Mike. "Many people think that once you accept Christ, all of your problems disappear instantly," I recalled Mike saying, one day, at the park while we were talking about psychological disorders.

"But isn't that the case?" I asked naively.

If only those who try to control love know that it is free, they would admit that each flower blooms at its own time.

Mike was a prudent, God-fearing man eager to practice what he taught. He held both the Sabbath and marriage in the highest regard. Thus, he handled his relationships with women with caution and finesse.

CHAPTER 38

Conquering My New World

Regrettably, I didn't travel to Beijing because I wasn't yet a permanent lawful resident of the US.

However, I got an opportunity to edit some editions of the newsletter of UNICEF, coming from their New York office. Though it was only an occasional source of income, I was honored and grateful for it.

It was a sunny Monday morning in the summer. I tucked a multicolor tee-shirt into my favorite pair of brown jeans pants and armed my feet with white sneakers. I was going to my first fulltime job in New York.

In barely ten minutes, the taxicab slowed down and entered into the nearest shopping center, in Port Chester. There were dozens of stores. I spotted Odd Job Trading, the dollar store, where I had shopped several times with my sister. I walked through the empty parking lot and stopped in front of the wide double door. I glanced at my wristwatch. Other workers were waiting in a queue. A guy in a fading blue denim suit and a blue hat pointed to the adjoining wall. I pulled out my time card from the rack. Next, I took my turn in the line, waiting behind five workers to punch it in.

Store manager, Dale, introduced me first to the five cashiers, whose registers were next to his office. From that vantage point, I took an initial view, my eyes panning from cosmetics, perfumes, calculators, watches, cookies, kitchen utensils, to flowers, and more.

Then I held my breath and tried to make the mental exit from professional personality to an unskilled worker. Was that possible? Except that I had died, then resurrected and returned to planet earth to take a new plunge at life. The unsettling thought lingered in my mind. As unbelievable as it would seem, especially to my former colleagues at CRTV,

In Manhattan, New York, USA

I was excited about it. If I had to survive by sweating in the basement of America, so be it.

I followed Dale. He walked me around the store as well as to the storage room at the back. We returned and stopped at the clothing department. Behind us were towels, stacked on four shelves. In front were stockings for adults and children as well as underpants. A pile of about ten bedsheet samples was to my left. There was a large table in front of us, with a variety of tablecloths. Strewn on the floor were a variety of items. Still, others were partially out of their original packages.

He pointed to the step stool at the corner. Then he showed me how to replace a roll of paper into the price tag machine.

My initiation as head and responsible associate of the department was thorough.

"Go to work, Akongshee," Dale said with a smile. "Don't hesitate to call me if you have any questions."

The need for dollars was spurring me on to press forward though my self-esteem was desperate for boosting. My hands began tagging prices on items and arranging clothes on shelves. At the same time, my mind was straying into the newsroom and studio, where I used to edit stories, anchor the news, interview foreign dignitaries, as well as reporting live to millions on national radio and television from the National Assembly.

SOS! Call emergency, please. Liberate my tormented mind from an indefinite fallow period, and let it soar to novel heights from the bottom of the rugged mountain of my life. Ouf, I survived Day One!

By the time I got home in the evening, tired and looking disheveled, I had an idea, which I promptly executed in readiness for my second day. Between the click-click of my price tag machine, I began memorizing Bible verses as well as the lyrics of favorite songs. Each day I brought printed copies of texts and hymns to commit to memory.

If becoming a blue-collar worker was my hell, I was determined to surrender completely to allow my desire for heaven to prevail. I recalled that way back in secondary school some senior students praised my singing voice. It was time to stop moaning for millions of invisible audiences, 8,000 miles away, to cater to the needs of face-to-face customers.

On Monday evening, Mike came to my job and gave me a ride home. It was a pleasant surprise. Is this not the ideal friendship between a man and a woman? I celebrated the purity and warmth of it all. Mike and I were indeed eating what the Bible calls "the fruit of the spirit" in Galatians 5:22.

By the second week at work, my fellow associates started straining their ears and watching the manager's response to my unauthorized renditions. My singing was becoming, indeed, a news-making event on the store floor. Customers drew closer and sang along.

"Oh, I love that song," said one customer after another.

I saw my manager's frowns, dwindling and changing into a smile. I could only imagine him, turning his prepared sanctions into admiration.

Customers enjoyed my music, to the extent that, if I wasn't singing, they began asking what was wrong.

"Just taking a break," I responded with a smile to one of them.

"Please, sing something before I leave, okay?" they pleaded.

Most of them confessed that even if they found nothing new or particularly useful in the store, for the day, my music warmed their hearts.

Before I realized that, indeed, I had a new set of fans—individuals, as well as couples, came to my corner, requesting a specific song. They nodded, rubbed their hands, or swung from side to side, to the rhythm.

On Monday morning, a lady walked up to me, smiling.

"I just came to say thank you," she said.

"For what?" I asked.

"Your music healed me."

"Really. How did that happen?" I asked, staring at her in total amazement.

"I came here last Friday while suffering from depression," she began but stopped and held her lips tightly to hold back the tears. "As soon as I stepped into the store, I heard your voice. Immediately, I followed the music and came right here," she said, pointing to the shelf behind me.

"I stood there fumbling with the tablecloths. Anyone watching would have suspected that there was something wrong with me," Beverly went on. "I just got stuck there, picking them up, one after the other, while listening to you."

She paused and took in a deep breath.

"As you kept singing, I felt an immediate release and instant relief. I kept praying that you would not be interrupted. And while you were singing, I was being healed," Beverly added.

She stopped and smiled, lifted her hands, and head lifted towards the ceiling.

"I tell you," she went on. "That night, when I returned home, I slept well, for the first time in a week."

Beverly's eyes were wet with tears. Mine, too. I looked at her and blinked.

"What song was it?" I asked.

"How Great Thou Art," she said, lifting her right folded fist, in celebration.

Beverly and I gave each other a high five.

The next day, in the afternoon, Frances, who visited the store practically every day, stopped by my corner to chat with me. She said that she loved my accent. Often, Frances would touch my arms and rub her hands over mine. "Black skin has a wonderful elastic," she said. "Look at that," she went on while rubbing her palm on my arm. "Your skin will never wrinkle like mine, Akongshee."

"You are a wonderful person," I responded, smiling.

Sixty-year-old Frances was a sweet spirit and a warm heart. I looked forward to seeing her each day. Sometimes, when there was a unique item in the food department, she would buy an extra one for me.

The following Monday, Frances brought two large, brown paper bags of winter clothing and handbags for me. Some of the new quality items, including turtle necks, were gifts from her daughter. Her eighty-year-old sister also sent a green cane handbag, which I reserved for special occasions.

My circle of new friends kept widening.

In November, an associate pastor of a Baptist church, Chris, was temporarily recruited at the store for the Christmas season. He was first attracted to me because of Revelation 12:17, which I was fond of reciting.

"Say that again, sister," Chris shouted back from the other end of the store.

Sometimes, he dropped his price tag machine on the heap of merchandise and came over.

"Please, just one more time," he pleaded.

I smiled.

"The dragon was wroth with the woman," I began. Then he skipped a few times excitedly, raising his hand in the air and shouting, "Hallelujah!" while the other guys whistled and giggled.

Before long, Chris and I started taking our lunch breaks at the same time. The other colleagues watched us suspiciously, referring to Chris as "the handsome and smart one."

Eventually, Chris joined our women's prayer group, which met at sunset on Fridays, at Pipi's apartment. We were a group of four women, including Charmaine and Cynthia. After the first two weeks, we decided to take light supper at our meeting place. Soon our half-hour prayers increased automatically to two hours. We began sharing our testimonies on answered prayers; the news reached our friends and acquaintances. Gradually others joined us, making up to twenty per gathering. We had to move to Cynthia's place, where participants reached up to fifty.

I kept working at the store. One of the couples that stopped by often to enjoy my music was thrilled to learn that I also spoke French. Eventually, the man, Bruno, a French American physicist and computer screen manufacturer, offered me a new job. I did bookkeeping for him, among other duties. My benefits included free transportation from home to work.

At the end of each day, I closed my ledger and smiled.

Bruno's wife and I soon became friends. On Friday, she gave me a beautiful pink embroidered nightgown, made by her relative in Vietnam. It was a great souvenir. I completed my assignment after months of working with Bruno.

Destiny or need based, I wound up working with children in my next job—babysitting. Ten-year-old Aaron looked very much like my son, despite his pale skin. Instinctively, I often observed him closely, endeavoring to understand what my son was going through, at that same age.

Coincidentally, his five-year-old brother, David, was just about my daughter's age. His innocence and compassion enabled me to relate to my children.

"Akong, I love you so much," David would often say while hugging me and staring right into my face.

Ours was like falling in love at first sight. I recalled how he fell into my arms upon seeing me for the first time. From then on, he quickly built trust in me.

"What will David do without you, Akong?" one of his teachers commented. "It's thanks to you that he stays in class," she said. She often joked that David's parents needed to give me a special certificate in recognition of my outstanding ability to reassure him. Five-year-old David approached his class each day with the wariness of the first day.

Back home, his two older brothers repeatedly complained that he was too slow while I stood by, nodding and encouraging him. Whenever I granted one of his prized requests or convinced him otherwise, he would just throw himself on me. "Akong, you are the best, the very best," he would often say.

Barely a couple of months after meeting David, he began unconsciously interchanging his mother's title and my name. It was so frustrating to him. "Akong, can I just call you Mom, please?" he asked, pleading with his eyes.

I watched David grow up, from depending on his parents to choosing for himself and defending his own choices.

He was full of wisdom, too. On Thursday, while I was driving him to school, he asked me a question about creation and God.

"God created everything," he said. "Right, Akong?" he went on. I turned back and glanced at him; he was looking at me seriously. I nodded and said, yes.

"And God knows everything, right?"

"Yes, that's right," I affirmed with a nod. I stole another glance; David was smiling.

"But the only thing that God doesn't know is how He made himself, right?" he pressed on, laughing.

That sent me laughing wildly.

The months rolled away. News of my soon departure was not good news, at all, to David. He would stop suddenly in the middle of dinner or his game, from time to time, and sigh. Then he would move closer and cling onto my neck.

"What are we going to do, Akong?" his mother asked, one morning. "This child is hurting," she pined in sympathy. "Ever since I told him that you would soon leave, he has not been sleeping well in the night."

I was at a loss too, sometimes with tears in my eyes. David would fall on my lap and ask if I couldn't, possibly, stay.

However, with time, he started adjusting to the reality of it all. Then, he began showering me with souvenir gifts, drawn from his vast pool of toys. Sometimes we struggled over the best or newest, which he insisted I keep while I persuaded him to keep it for himself. Eventually, my package of gifts included a lion, two twin dogs, and a puzzle box with Jewish symbols. The most unexpected of all was his white karate belt, which he expressly asked me to keep.

"Why?" I asked.

"So that you always remember me."

David's love generated tremendous emotional healing for me. Ours was a refreshing friendship. While he developed self-confidence as the months went by, enough to venture into the bigger world ahead of him, I felt more energetic and healthy enough to revive my profession. Indeed, the idea of writing my story popped up at that time. That was also when I bought my first computer.

Another significant benefit of caring for the three boys was gaining time for myself. Whenever they were at school, I had free time after running the errands that their mother assigned me for the day. Also, whenever they were on sleepovers, I was free. I had time to think, ponder over my life, pray, and write. Also, being a Jewish family, all Saturdays were off-days, too.

It was while I was working with Barabra, David's mother, that I resumed my visits to public places of interest. During my visits to the White Plains Public Library, I stumbled on two opportunities. One of them led me to become a member of the Westchester Toastmaster Club. From my first attendance, I realized that their program goals were in sync with my profession as a communicator. The training that I got from the club during the early stages empowered me to take on the second task—literacy volunteering. It is still gratifying that my student, Ignatia, from Brazil, started speaking English after three months of interaction between us. On the first day that we met at the library, we were communicating with signs. How thrilling to listen to Ignatia tell stories about her personal life!

"I don't know how you did it," remarked the administrators.

"I don't think that it is due to my aptitude as a teacher," I said. "I simply helped her to become self-confident. Then, she brought out all the English from her subconscious." That was an outstanding lever that propelled Ignatia to self-assurance. The glow on her face was exquisite while she related stories about her ten-year experience in the US. Instead of clinging to the community of Portuguese speakers, Ignatia visited big shopping centers and attended public events.

> *"I don't think that it is due to my aptitude as a teacher," I said. "I simply helped her to become self-confident."*

The administrators of Literacy Volunteers gave us an exclusive ticket to attend a horse-racing event at an elite club in Westchester. Later, I invited Ignatia to Barnes and Noble downtown, where, on behalf of the club, I wrapped up packages for hundreds of shoppers during the-end-of-year festivities. Ignatia had a chance to socialize with a totally new and wider community while paying keen attention to the sounds of the English language.

On Wednesday, Batuo, who was then a research student at the university in New York, called and asked if I would be interested in translating some documents into French. The professor had asked for her help, but she said that my proficiency in French was higher than hers.

I agreed to give it a try. That is how I met Dr. Andrée-Nicola McLaughlin, Professor of Languages, Literature, and Philosophy, and Professor of Interdisciplinary Studies at the Medgar Evers College of the City University of New York. She was equally the First Distinguished Chair of the Dr. Betty Shabazz Distinguished Chair in Social Justice, as well as the world Coordinator of the International, Cross-Cultural Black

Women's Studies Institute. I became one of the translators for the series of her global conferences on women's issues.

Later on, in October 2002, Dr. McLaughlin offered me a unique opportunity. I interviewed U.S community activist and presidential candidate, Al Sharpton, alongside the award-winning international journalist, Robert Knight. The televised forum, with an introduction by Dr. Andrée Nicola McLaughlin, took place within the context of "The Tradition of Black Liberation Theology and Social Justice."

The following year, Dr. McLaughlin invited me to the public ceremony, known as the Rites of Ancestral Return. Members of various institutions and organizations jointly paid formal tribute to the African ancestors of colonial America. In October 2003, the US government officially reinterred the remains of all slaves, exhumed from Washington DC, back to their original burial site in New York at The African Burial Ground in Lower Manhattan.

However, one unanswered question remained—when would I finally reunite with my children?

I was grateful for the multiple chances to be meaningfully busy.

However, one unanswered question remained—when would I finally reunite with my children?

CHAPTER 39

A Battle Between Heaven and Earth

While I was still waiting for a radical change that would reunite me with my children, a new element popped up to balance the equation; it seemed to be the answer. It was an urgent letter, an ultimatum, from Mesape's mother, demanding that I return immediately. She stressed that she would put an end to her son's marital infidelity.

Finally! I took a deep breath and clapped my hands, astonished. What happened? I asked myself. What prompted her? Her sudden shift of position raised more questions than answers. She had rejected my distress call to intervene when Zipora came on the scene. "You think I don't know about it? That's not my business."

Now, two years after, she was suddenly ready and confident about ending the attack on my family. However, why was my return a condition for her intervention rather than vice-versa? And why return on her schedule? Had she become remorseful? The questions just kept flowing.

The more I dwelled on returning, the more vividly I recalled four consecutive nightmares, portraying scenes of my return home. In each case, Mesape's mother and her family pursued me with sticks and machetes.

Indeed, in one of the episodes, a ferocious crowd almost overwhelmed me. They blocked all exits. Desperate, I leaped through the roof, vaulting over fences, as high as Mount Cameroon. Whether those nocturnal horrors were warnings or the product of my troubled mind, they had their logic in the rest of the deadly menaces from Mesape and his partners in wickedness.

After two days of pondering over her command, my mind was not at peace. In any case, I couldn't return home immediately, period.

Barely two months after her mail, I woke up one morning from a frightening dream. In it, *I was sharing the same room with Mangwi. Our sleep was interrupted by dozens of rats, as big as monkeys, which invaded our room. We fought them back with machetes, butchering one after the other. There was hardly standing space. So, we carried them in large basins out of the room while the slaughtering went on. Yet, their numbers kept growing, and we went on butchering until my limbs were hurting. So, I abandoned the rest of the few rats charging at us. I was so weary that all I wanted was to retire to bed for a little more sleep. But Mangwi woke me up, pleading that we must finish the job, else, we'd be in trouble.*

Indeed, I was still dreaming when the ringing telephone woke me up. As soon as I said hello, I heard a crying voice. It was Mesape's.

"Ak, my mom is dead. Ak, she is dead ...." he cried.

A cold immobilizing wave rushed down my whole body. Then I started crying along with Mesape. Mangwi's husband rushed in and seized the receiver. I fell on the couch behind me.

The unfortunate loss scared me rather than prompted my return home.

More troublesome and enigmatic events were unfolding. It was just a month since the death of my mother-in-law. I went to sleep that night and had another weird dream. In it, *I was with Mesape's father on the green, undulating hills in Santa, overlooking my parent's home, where I grew up.*

I remember as a kid, how I used to contemplate that expansive greenery, shaped like a gigantic frog, from our yard. It always marveled me.

However, in the dream, *my father-in-law and I were together in the tranquil hills. He was trying to seduce me. I resisted his every move. But he kept on trying, harder and harder. When he finally lost his patience, he grabbed me and tore off my clothes. Scared, I ran away, leaving behind everything. I descended the hills and escaped into the valleys, crossing the river and climbing the opposite hills, onto the long, rugged trail leading to our house.*

When I finally reached the residential area, I covered my breasts with my left hand and palm, and my private parts with my right hand. About three blocks before our house, I saw my former school mate and equally Mesape's former classmate, Lucy. She was standing in front of their family house, mocking my nakedness. I was so angry that I rebuked her.

"Why are you suddenly concerned about my well-being?" I said, staring into her face. "Where were you when I was desperate for help?" I asked and moved on.

I got up in the morning and left for work without recalling the nightmare. On my way home, the scene came back to my mind. I arrived at the house and had dinner with Mangwi and her family.

As soon as we finished, a long-distance call came in for me. I picked up the receiver and said hello. All I heard was Mesape, who was wailing and calling my name.

"What is the matter, Mes? What's going on? Tell me, what?" I pressed on.

"Akong, Akong, how can I tell you? My father…" he said.

"What? What?" I asked.

"My father is dead," he wailed.

Instantly, a flash of lightning went through my head and down through my spine, totally overpowering me. I started screaming. Mangwi and her husband rushed for the telephone.

I deeply regretted the sudden loss of my father-in-law. The shock lingered on for weeks. Uncertainty loomed after I recovered from bereavement. Would the absence of both of my parents-in-law render our family situation better or worse? What move should I make? Mesape was complaining, threatening never to forgive me for not attending his mother's funeral.

Some months after, I received an unexpected guest, Batuo, the same young research student who had referred me to Dr. McLaughlin. She had just returned from home at the end of her vacation, during which she took time off to try to mediate between Mesape and me. I doffed my hat to her, primarily because a few years back, a matchmaker had introduced her to Mesape. Initially, she was interested but gave up when she found out that Mesape and I were married.

Here was Batuo, married, and a genuine family friend, trying to reunite us. During their discussions that dragged late into the night, Mesape blamed me for rejecting reconciliation.

"You are the one blocking the chances to reconcile." Batuo was merely repeating what Mesape had told her. She described his sullen state, the tears flowing freely from his eyes, and his readiness to welcome me back with open arms. Though I could neither rely on Mesape's confessions by proxy, nor was sure of my safety upon return home, I kept an open mind.

"How come you won't forgive me when you are a Christian?" Mesape teased me in his letters.

"Forgiveness cannot happen in a vacuum," I retorted.

"It was all your fault. How come you were so afraid of that little thing?" He was referring to Zipora. "Why abandon your home because of her? What can she do to you?" He went on to ridicule me.

Wasn't this the same Mesape who used to plead with me to extricate him from Zipora's bewitching grip? "Akong, to be honest with you, I don't want to have anything to do with this woman," he confessed innocently in a phone conversation. "But I don't know how to quit."

Or was his mind so messed up?

"Why not just walk away?" I urged him naively.

How else could I help a man who had never shown any interest in the Bible? How else can a captive, trapped in a spiritual revolving door, regain his freedom? After my baptism, I offered him a luxury edition, a limited edition of the Bible with explanatory notes, a concordance, and illustrations, as a birthday gift.

He unwrapped the package and sighed. "Is this what you give me for a gift?"

> *Though I was grateful for the disclosure, I wanted more; he was still holding back a lot of stuff.*

Of course, I had no intention of annoying Mesape. However, had we not reached an age when reason should prevail over vanity, especially given the dangerous situation of our family?

Wouldn't it be foolhardy to walk back into the den of an unrepentant man? He had first to reveal who had orchestrated the scenes of horror in my office, wherein a rat attacked me head-on.

"Zipora waited for you to leave, in vain. So, she became frustrated and tried to get you out of the picture," he disclosed at the opening of our conversation two days afterward. His disclosure confirmed the outlandish story I had heard, while in Yaounde—that Zipora had already bought a wedding dress.

Though I was grateful for the disclosure, I wanted more; he was still holding back a lot of stuff.

As soon as he said goodbye and hung up, my brain was reeling. Sweat was already overcrowding my forehead. I ran upstairs to my room and ran back downstairs. I had to do something, but what? The nagging question was, how could I help myself after he dropped the blazing coal into my palms? Who else, but myself, to begin the fight for my freedom?

The following day, I was still consumed in my thoughts, paying little attention to food. What should I do to move the mountain in my life? I picked up my Bible and read the passage where God was sending Moses to go ask Pharaoh to set His people free. Immediately, an idea clicked in my brain—Moses had an impediment, so did I. So, God asked him to use what he had—his rod.

What was in my hand, that was equivalent to Moses' rod? I walked back and forth in the room, racking my brain.

"*What about your pen?*" a voice from within seemed to ask, suddenly.

"My pen?" I responded.

Immediately, I seized my black pen, and a thought seemed to take root in my mind immediately. I yelled, "victory," while skipping up and down.

By midnight, I had sketched the outline of my story for a newspaper article. Within three days, it was ready. I contacted a print media colleague; I dispatched the narrative. The following week, it appeared in one of the local private newspapers in Yaounde.

Feedback revealed how the piece had survived heated arguments, provoked by its so-called "unsettling contents, as well as its unusualness," among editors. However, in the end, they all agreed that it had a double "out-of-the-ordinary nature," namely, its author and her readiness to share her private life with the public. How unusual! That instantly qualified it as a news-worthy story.

Mangwi lifted the newspaper and began reading the headline news on the front page.

Another feedback, based on eye-witness accounts, reported that the edition sold faster than the latest brand of beer in Cameroon. Commuters stopped, in open traffic, to arrest vendors for their copies, thereby causing traffic jams. Other readers scanned the story and shared it with friends abroad.

The "Love War" account topped the charts as the favorite topic for discussion. Students and workers alike took off break time to analyze it. It became the subject of conversation at meetings and *ndjanguis*. Some people started their scrap book with that article.

Indeed, a national debate got into motion. "The newspaper is the last resort for a woman whose life is threatened" was pitted against, "The newspaper is no place for anyone to discuss family matters." "Is she the first victim of infidelity and physical violence?" against, "It was high time someone mentioned the silent plight of women," and so on. "I'm impressed by your ability to dissociate yourself from your own story and analyze it with a cool head," stated Julius, my former colleague.

Meanwhile, my media contemporaries elsewhere upheld the writer of the interesting article, describing her as the queen of hearts.

A few months after, a university professor in Pennsylvania, USA, sought the permission of the author to use her article for his class lecture, particularly to debunk the common supposition that African women are docile and submissive. "They don't defend their rights" was banished to the past in that class.

Mesape, the central figure, responded to the article: "Akongshee, I see you've tried to kill me," he howled. "Shame on you. You think that's the best way to expose and destroy me?" he went on, on the telephone.

His lack of remorse upset me, causing the thoughts of reconciliation to evaporate. Soon after, I re-opened the divorce file. I dispatched an express mail, stuffed with required documents to the judge, who had presided over our case.

Unfortunately, she said that she was working in another city. So, I used my contacts to hire a lawyer. My absence complicated the case. Also, Mesape declined all summons to appear in court. Instead, he started making attempts to reconcile with me. He even proposed coming to New York "to take me home."

"If you come, I will make sure that you are put in jail, right here," I wrote matter-of-factly in response. I was irate when Mesape stated that he was making the reconciliation to please others.

Whatever Mesape's reasons, I couldn't share the same private room with Mesape, in the absence of a bodyguard. Eventually, he dropped the proposal to come to New York to accompany me on my homecoming. I relaxed.

Since he didn't follow through with reconciling with me, I pursued the costly case, albeit 8,000 miles away from the scene of action. Two years afterward, the presiding judge granted the divorce. A breath of fresh air flushed my lungs. I took a deep breath and lifted my arms like wings.

For the first time, in my long struggle, I started planning my return home. Mesape no longer had any legal right over me. I was going to live as a free person and a single mother.

Sadly, divorce came with unexpected complications. Mesape curtailed communication between the children and me. Indeed, on Sunday, he seized the receiver from my son while we were still speaking. Then, he began yelling at me. I was sad for my son; I wallowed in tears of self-pity, managing to pause only to pray. I pined all through the night until a miracle happened in the morning. Elizabeth, a prominent woman in society, called me by 7 am with a special offer: "Akongshee, your children are right here in my house. Call me back," she announced.

I quickly scribbled her number and hung up. The next minute, I was talking with my Quydee and Sweetie, the best conversation we'd had in weeks.

Elizabeth had brought them over for a play date with her son. How thoughtful of her! It was her first call ever since I was in the US.

We ended the conversation joyfully. I couldn't thank Elizabeth enough for her kindness.

When I reprimanded Mesape for punishing the children, he snapped back, accusing me of abandoning them.

> *My greatest challenge was how to keep in touch with my children until we reunited. As for the divorce, I began wondering if I was going to be happier for it.*

My greatest challenge was how to keep in touch with my children until we reunited. As for the divorce, I began wondering if I was going to be happier for it.

CHAPTER 40

Embattled Motherhood

My meeting with the Morgans, a model couple, was timely. Though I was an employee, a live-in coach for their teenage children, they treated me like part of their family. The soothing words, tender touch, and cheerful looks that Jacques and Melanie reserved for each other were beautiful to behold. "It's odd to make a bed and heap the pillows in the middle," said Jacques. "But that's what Melanie likes, so I do just that to keep her happy."

Melanie's soft angelic voice soothed my aches, even over the telephone. "Akongshee, if you are able, could you…" is how she often started her request for a particular task.

Meanwhile, Jacques was fond of cracking jokes. "I know you've never thought of eating snakes," said Jacques to me. "My policy is to eat it before it eats me up."

Also, the couple maintained a spirit of camaraderie with their two girls. "Julie, darling, do share some piano tips with me," said Melanie. "You have a special touch."

The perfect harmony in their interactions touched areas of my heart that I hadn't realized were sore, let alone reachable. Before I knew, I became more expressive. No longer was I embarrassed to share my story.

On the flip side, I still suffered guilt from the divorce, two years after, and six years since separation from my children. Sometimes, a sense of loss saturated my nights and days. I concluded that it was due mostly to the separation from my children; I sighed repeatedly. My bones froze even during some hot, sunny days.

Likewise, some nights, I woke up suddenly at 2 am, feeling as if my daughter was standing by my bedside. I would jerk up from bed suddenly, go down on my knees, groan, and pray before going back to sleep.

On Tuesday afternoon, I called Mesape to transfer some cash for our children.

"I'm not after your money if that's what you think," he yelled from the other end.

I listened and kept my calm. Then suddenly, Mesape hung up on me. Surprisingly I wasn't upset. Instead, I pitied him.

"I'm sorry about yesterday," he said when I called the next day." He even described me as unique, whatever he meant.

A short silence ensued, after which he asked an unexpected question.

"Do you want us to start again?" he asked, sounding as tender as when we first met each other.

"Yes," I answered without any misgivings.

Exactly ten days afterward, I received an eight-page love letter from Mesape, in his exquisite penmanship. He apologized for hurting me, promising to repair the damage. Instantly, it produced an emotional high like fireworks charging my dying love batteries. I wrote back promptly. I realized that I had become more expressive about love. Soon, we started exchanging letters without waiting for a reply to the previous one. Each week I received a letter, some delivered by express service.

"*Akong, between us, you are the one who has paid the higher price. It's all my fault. I will do whatever I need to do to set things right again. I have learned the most bitter lesson of my life. But it will never happen again. I believe it's God's will for us to be together.*" Love and compassion flew from his pen.

He was singing my song, and I was all ears. I began dreaming of a better future than the beautiful years of the past. I sent him a gift, a pair of boxer shorts with "Unchain My Heart" embroidered on it.

"*Akong, how come you often said you didn't know what I liked? Is this not a perfect gift?*" he wrote in gratitude.

Our mutual effort towards reconciliation was taking on a life of its own. Next, we started seeking visas for our children to visit me.

I agreed to return. We started planning to reunite officially. Mesape encouraged me to come back quickly so that we could "praise God together."

Before long, we were talking about a church ceremony, the lack of which jealous women often used as a pretext to attack our relationship.

They insisted that marriage without the wearing of a veil by the bride was null and void.

Mesape and I even chose a theme for our nuptial blessing—"Reconciliation and Thanksgiving." We exchanged notes and chose our preferred colors; we began selecting bridesmaids.

However, amid those plans, I kept wondering whether Mesape was still having an affair with Zipora. Did his confession in the letter mean he had repented? He had never mentioned anything about the mysterious occurrences in my office except when I pressured him. Was he innocent? He was quoting the scriptures in all his letters. Had he or was he willing to accept Jesus Christ as his personal Lord and Savior? I had no way of knowing with certainty.

However, I marveled at his newly-acquired ability in biblical romance. He supported his statements with fitting scriptural verses. Could there be a better love story than the one unfolding before me?

Another unclear area was the choice of denomination. Would the wedding be Adventist or Roman Catholic? I needed answers before allowing excitement to overtake me.

Within weeks, the details started coming in writing: "You know I'm not yet a Seventh-day Adventist." He sounded encouraging. "I know your church will take precedence in all."

What was he implying? That I was doggedly committed to my faith, leaving him no choice? Or that he was planning on becoming Adventist? After all, he had earlier mentioned that he had read, practically, all my notes. I had the unbroken habit of scribbling notes, in which I state the speaker's name, the church, and the date.

Love is not just a collection of apt words that quicken the heartbeat for momentary romance. Beyond Mesape's endearing declarations, he had to fulfill one critical condition—proving that he had denounced his past links with Zipora.

Alas, while I was looking forward to higher commitment, Mesape blasted out in anger, in the next letter. "Don't drag us into your Adventism, your vegetarianism. You were not supposed to have divorced in the first place; the Bible does not allow it."

My stomach churned while I was reading his chilling harangue. Were those his gut feelings, or was he relaying the opinion of his detractor-mentors? I wondered.

"I've gone ahead and arranged for a wedding with the priests, whom you know just too well," he went on.

Why dictate when we started out sharing views? Why attempt to control when love esteems the other's opinion better? A wrenching pain got hold of me; it was splitting my heart. I fumbled about in search of instant healing.

The doorbell rang, momentarily arresting my confusion. It was the mailman with an express letter. My hands trembled while I opened the big brown envelope. It was a closely-written, four-page document from Mesape; it was replete with apologies. He stated that he had just been teasing me in the previous letter.

Just how could I believe him without further probing? Either he was pretending or trying to conceal his real feelings.

"I cannot package four years into four months of sudden plans," he went on. "You should return." Instantly, I remembered having suffered five long years of trauma from violence. Each knock on the door set my heart beating faster. I would have a strong urge to run and hide somewhere in the room rather than rushing to open the door.

Incidentally, my former boss, Ebongue, who used to be the mediator between Mesape and Zipora, told me worse than I had surmised.

"Yes, on and off, as usual," he responded from Chicago in our telephone conversation, when I asked if they still saw each other.

"Are Mesape and Zipora still having an affair?" I pressed the question.

"Yes," he answered. He was firm and stopped at that.

My heart was palpitating, even while I was speaking. Words vanished from me as I held the receiver with a gaping mouth.

No wonder Mesape did not send a message or parcel through Ebongue, to consolidate our plans. And how revealing when Ebongue himself disclosed that Mesape was the person who accompanied him to the airport!

"What?" I screamed in shock.

How could he be planning a wedding amid an affair? My whole body began shaking; a cold wave ran through my body. It was worse than mental torture. What was going on? I imagined the worst. Was Mesape a member of the secret male cult, in which all signatories have lost their first wife, under mysterious circumstances? Maybe that explains why he wanted me back immediately. I could be wrong, but I bet on it fifty, fifty.

The refusal of visas to our children hurt me even more. I cried all night long. Why didn't God grant us a miracle? I had no consolation; much less could I understand God.

Weeks went by, and my heart remained sore. Gradually, each new day came with more clarity on the matter. Finally, I started tagging the pieces together, forming a quilt of the strings of my life wrapped around each other. I spread it out and began interpreting it. Diagonally: If my children come, I won't let them return home without me. Triangularly: The man I was going to wed in a church, the father of my children, was still roaming with a murderous woman, in an enticing witchcraft-driven affair. Circularly: If Akongshee steps foot on the territory, the plan to "take her out of the picture" will go operational quickly.

My hypothesis was convincing. So, I went down on my knees and prayed; I gave thanks to God for the ability to discern. It was consoling.

From then onwards, I began focusing all my attention on my children. Did they still recall or understand the gravity of the circumstances which separated us? Did they have an idea that I was struggling relentlessly to reunite with them?

I took a journey down memory lane. Credit goes to them, at ages 9 and 5, respectively, for letting me escape for life in the first place. What's more, my sister, Mafor, gave an impressive report about them. She said she had never seen children more concerned about the well-being of their mother. After spending a weekend with them, she remarked how I was the subject of their frequent prayers.

"Please, God, provide food for our mommy, too," was their dinner request.

"Please, Heavenly Father, give our mother a bed and sound sleep tonight," was their bedtime prayer.

One year after a second visa refusal, my mother traveled to the US. Mesape's commission to her was to bring me back. She, like two of my sisters, was convinced that if I returned, everything would be normal again. Mesape had taken the time and traveled to the village. During their discussion, he swore to them that he would never marry someone else. Indeed, he repeatedly told them that he had severed all ties with Zipora. Ever since then, they began holding me responsible for my family falling apart. "I will remain single without Akongshee until I go gray," he vowed in front of my mother, my sisters, and brother-in-law, during that meeting.

Of course, they believed him, and after that, they started persuading me to return home. My mother kept harping on Mesape's sincerity. Indeed, if she had her way, she would have put me on the next plane homeward bound.

On Sunday afternoon, I called to speak with my son, who had just arrived home for vacation. Also, I needed the telephone number of the family home where Sweetie was spending her vacation; it was the first time that she decided to spend up to a month at a friend's house. For a whole week, their father refused to give me the number.

Mesape reached home when Quydee and I were still exchanging the preliminaries. He stepped in through the door and seized the receiver from Quydee. That was the second incidence of abuse within two months. He had earlier confiscated the letter my son wrote to me on the promise of posting it. Unfortunately, the first artwork, dedicated to his mother, was in that envelope. Regrettably, it never reached me.

Was he finally admitting that he had been trying to kill me? Just the inkling startled me to the point of choking me. It was like a bombshell tearing me apart.

Instead of giving me the telephone number and returning the phone to Quydee, he began complaining that I was no longer "writing nice letters to him." When I insisted on talking to my son, he said I did not have the money to cater to the needs of our children. Where was the link between the two? Besides, he threatened to take me to court, for what I did not know.

"You've been trying to kill me," I yelled at him spontaneously and repeatedly.

"That has become a song," he replied.

Without warning, he hung up on me without a further word. Had I put him on the spot by naming his plot? Was he finally admitting that he had been trying to kill me? Just the inkling startled me to the point of choking me. It was like a bombshell tearing me apart. Or was it a panic attack? I started reeling around, uncontrollably, in excruciating pain. Who was going to call the ambulance for me? I feared that the end for me had come.

At the very instance, there was a knock on the door. My sister, Mangwi, had brought along my mother. She walked through my door like an emergency doctor. I fell into her arms and started crying.

"Help, help me, Mother!" I clung onto her until my convulsing body, disjointed from the mind and the spirit, reunited.

My mother's direct witness of my discomposure from a long-distance call left her gaping.

"So, what will happen if you find yourself face to face with him?"

I just stared into her face, lost.

From that day onwards, she stopped blaming me for the ruined marriage.

Yet, the puzzle remained unsolved. Who was Mesape? Or what had he become? Was he born with the art of manipulation? Was this the man with whom I was in a relationship that was once the talk of the town? Was this the man whose friends used to say that from the moment they found their life partner, they would come to him for training in the art of romance? Was this the man, because of whom Dr. Eyoh, our former professor in the faculty, often described our relationship as a model? Was this the man of whom colleagues would say, "Haven't you realized that each time the two of you enter this building, everyone goes silent?"

Whatever the case, I had to find closure. The chain of acts of deception, physical and mental abuse, was well-crafted to render me insane or to lure me into an early grave. Hadn't I received a personal warning before my baptism? "For you, it is a choice between life and death," the divine voice had said repeatedly.

"I am happy that my mother is alive because one day, I will have the chance of seeing her again," wrote Quydee, at ten, in a letter to my sister, Mangwi.

I began taking better care of myself for my children.

CHAPTER 41

Defending My Worth

My son, Quydee, sent me his report booklet after the promotion exam. His performance was below average; he failed in his hitherto best subject, math. I pined for him. The consequences of my absence were staring right into my face.

How best could I help my children? I prayed and thought about it for a long time; two ideas came up. Firstly, I registered at Westchester Community College, where I had taken courses in psychology the previous years. This time around, I chose mathematics. Secondly, I began making audio cassette messages. Then, I bought a select number of general knowledge books for reading during the vacation, both of which I despatched home for my children.

Winter classes at the college started; three days a week, I had an early morning class in mathematics. It was a tough challenge. Firstly, in secondary school, I bid farewell to math, after writing the GCE "O" Level exams. Though only ten of forty-something students used to bluff about the subject, it was hard for everyone.

Secondly, it was the first class in the morning. For three months, I braved the cold and the pressure of time to arrive in class on time.

After each lesson, I got a letter writing pad, on which I exposed the topic, wrote out the formulae, and provided worked examples. Every other day, I mailed a letter to my son. Whether the problem or theorem, on any given day, matched the curricular emphasis of Quydee's class or not, whether my sample solutions were useful to him or not, I was confident that somehow my action would inspire him.

Finally, my efforts paid off marvelously. At the end of the next term, Quydee passed in mathematics with an A grade. After that, he maintained excellent scores in mathematics and overall good grades in other subjects.

He performed so well in his graduation exams, that, in addition to math, he included further maths in his select subjects for GCE.

Meanwhile, I became a full-fledged member of the White Plains Seventh-day Adventist Church. It was the biggest of all the previous ones—about four hundred members. I had noticed something spectacular from the first day of attendance. Members arrived earlier to pray before the opening time. An outstanding case was that of First Elder Roy McDonald. Though he and his family lived out of state, in Connecticut, they were often among the first to arrive. Even after they relocated to New Jersey, more than an hours' drive away, they arrived at the premises much earlier, up to an hour before church services began.

On Sabbath morning, at its unique location on a hill, with one end bordered by a forest, members would be praying, hand in hand. A men's and boys' group at the vast parking lot; A women's group in the sanctuary; a girls' group in one of the classrooms, and so forth.

Juniper Hill was as busy as a beehive during the week. Apart from regular meetings, on one Thursday per month, needy people in the neighborhood gathered there to receive gift packages, offered by supermarkets in the locality. On Mondays, the Women's Ministries coordinated the reading of a book or led a discussion of a biblical theme.

The church was also a place to nurture youths. Indeed, non-Adventist parents dropped off their children in the morning and only picked them up after sunset. The Sabbath afternoon programs, patterned after the life-application format, and mainly run by youths, were the talk of the town. They sketched out targeted scenes at home, in school, the workplace, in the courtroom, et cetera. Otherwise, they organized musical concerts, open to the public.

Then, on Sundays, while the health department was sponsoring healthy lifestyle demonstrations, the Pathfinders counselors, notably Neville Francis and Marva Seawright, dedicated the day to the training of youths in life skills.

Every member was actively involved, even in games. Eventually, I joined the communication department.

On Saturday, one of my new friends, Charmaine, invited me home, in Elmsford, for lunch, in the company of two other friends. Her grandmother welcomed us to her home with open arms. A few days after that meeting, Charmaine disclosed that Grandma Ivy had not stopped talking about me.

"Akongshee, I've never seen anything like that," said Charmaine, popping her eyes and exclaiming, while steering her black Honda.

"What do you mean?" I asked.

"Grandma has been going through a lot," she disclosed. "Then you walk through the door, and she falls in love with you," she said, raising her voice at the end.

"You'd smile even in your death bed," my dormitory mates in college often said. Joy has opened the hearts of total strangers to me.

Grandma Ivy bonded almost instantly. She cherished me like the biological daughter she missed having, while I looked up to her as my adoptive mother. She was full of wisdom and mastered the Bible.

"How come you can recite a whole Psalm?" I asked.

"That's how we grew up in Jamaica."

There and then, I decided to start to memorize Bible texts.

At age 80, Grandma Ivy was vibrant like a forty-year-old. She steered the wheel of her brown station wagon like an actress in cowboy movies. Thanks to her, I drove the outlandish size Ford Country Squire. As a retired nurse, she was a volunteer at the local county office. Meanwhile, she was taking computer lessons.

Clad in her designer skirt suits, the average height woman, with glowing brown skin, maintained the gait of a military officer, on guard. At church, she stood up, alongside younger and highly educated men and women, to teach one of the ten adult Sabbath School classes.

During our dialogue, Grandma Ivy counseled me on the intricacies of my life. She reiterated that despite God's might, solutions do not always come overnight. She would rub my legs gently and console me with fitting Bible verses whenever I was agonizing over my children.

Similarly, each time I set a date of my return home, she would warn me against risking my life.

"Akongshee, the devil never gives up."

"But isn't God more powerful?"

"Of course. But our Lord doesn't work according to human logic. Please, wait until the winds of evil have passed. The Lord will signal you when the coast clears up."

Chapter 41: Defending My Worth

I would concur, falling back on Quydee's words as a buttress—"There is someone in this world, with an open heart, ready to receive me!" At the age of ten, he healed me with his words. Then, I would get lost in past thoughts. The games we played together, daily homework, poems and songs we wrote, the music we made, recipes we tried together, in our very own kitchen, and the Sabbaths we spent, worshipping God.

Then, as if touching the strings of a guitar, a song of victory would come to mind, and Ivy and I would begin singing.

Reminiscing over those exhilarating moments always provided healing energy. My children's letters were pieces of treasure. My daughter's vocabulary was growing. Thanks to her, I learned of a color known as terra-cotta.

"Akongshee, how come you are so happy, despite your problems?" asked Pearl of the Juniper Hill church.

Pearl was a new friend in my neighborhood. We met while she was wrestling with loneliness. Her abusive marriage had lasted a barely year. She left with a child.

Yet, ten years after leaving, she still shuddered over the vivid accounts of physical violence. She said she felt betrayed, more so, because her former husband was an evangelist.

On Sunday, Pearl invited me to accompany her on an hour-long drive to her psychologist, an appointment that she kept once every month. She enjoyed chatting with me, maybe because of my silly responses, which always lit up her face. She would laugh and drop her forehead on the steering wheel.

However, on our way back, she complained so much that I began comforting her with Bible promises.

Despite my efforts, the gaping emotional vacuum in her seemed to be widening. Maybe that's why she couldn't understand how on earth I could live with my crisis.

"Why don't you consult my psychologist, Akongshee?" she asked after I accompanied her the second time. She insisted, along with several attempts to persuade me, also to seek professional counseling elsewhere.

"Me, for what?" I asked, frowning.

"My psychologist is excellent. You should try him," she insisted.

"Oh yeah? And who would I consult after the session, to comfort me?" I teased.

Pearl smiled mechanically and blinked. She hoped I would soon come to realize that there might be underlying issues I needed to confront.

I didn't think that I had issues to confront. Instead, I had a past misfortune to bury, deep into the soil, walk away from, and soar to greater heights. That was my method of letting new opportunities begin to germinate in my soul.

Despite her proposal, Pearl began treating me like a live-in therapist. She often invited me over for weekends. However, instead of enjoying relaxing moments, my hostess would engage me in a repeated analysis of her case. It was recycling of mental trash, the painful moments of her life, which she kept exhuming. She would drag the hurt into our delayed sleep at night. In the morning, she would dig them up again, and sprinkle them into her breakfast, while reserving a chunk for lunch.

Later in the day, while jogging in the park, she would carry it like a heavy load on her head. In the end, she would become depleted of energy, by stretching out and tumbling up the worn-out details of what might have caused this or that boyfriend to walk out. Otherwise, she would dwell on how to win back a recent one, who quit without an apparent reason.

After the first weekend, I returned to my own home. It was smaller and couldn't conveniently accommodate Pearl. So, she began pleading with me to return. The first time, I did.

On workdays, she would bombard me with haunting self-pity calls from her job, two to five times a day. The next, after the first, was a repeat of horrible sketches that we had already rehearsed a thousand times.

Our friendship was gradually turning into a doctor-patient relationship. Pearl pleaded, referring to me as the only genuine person she had met in our immediate community.

"Akongshee, but how do you do it?" she often asked me.

"Do what?"

"You sit so calmly as if nothing is bothering you."

"Mine is too big to carry on a human head," I tried to explain. The solution belongs to the only One who is invincible," I went on.

"That's true; I know that," she agreed. "But I've tried that for a long time, and it doesn't seem to work," she insisted.

"Be still," I advised, "for longer than you've ever allowed yourself to be," I proposed, for lack of what else to say.

"But how does that help?" she asked innocently.

"If an elephant is still enough, a fly can move it," I said, hardly knowing how I came about that. "Do you believe?" I asked.

"Yes," she said.

"Watch until the elephant starts kicking its hind leg because of the fly in its ear," I said.

"You are so silly, Akongshee," she said.

We burst out laughing like two wild animals.

Pain, frustration, and daunting challenges in America, land of opportunity, have, in some distinct ways, brought out the best in me. Even my Toastmaster friends began noticing my progress. I became more composed, projecting my voice while articulating better.

Also, years of teaching as a literacy volunteer, have helped me to realize that I have much more to offer than to pine over.

Overall, I am a lot more motivated about life in general. My resolve has always prompted me: Whatever the challenge; I'll keep excelling, and by God's grace, with proper communication, rise to the occasion.

On Thursday, I saw a notice at the White Plains Public Library. A visiting professor was coming to lecture on poetry writing. On Monday, I was among the first to arrive. She shared some tips and read select poems. In the end, she gave us twenty minutes to write a poem. To my greatest surprise, mine, entitled, "My Grandma's Underskirt," was selected as classic.

Whatever the challenge; I'll keep excelling, and by God's grace, with proper communication, rise to the occasion.

In the meantime, dialogue remained minimal between Mesape and me. Strangely, he would drop a riveting phrase in a dull telephone conversation or a boring letter.

"Akong, I want you to remember that I will love you until I die," he writes. "You are simply the best I've come across."

"I love you, too," I responded.

Yet, the clash between the tenderness of our first love, and the spate of acts violence was always evident. By depriving me of the pleasure of raising my children, he reduced me to a dreaming mother. Each day I stepped out, I would stop to observe the behavior of children. To keep hope alive, my friends would refer me to Bible verses.

Indeed, on Sabbath, Grace, from Nigeria, rushed to me and exclaimed, "I found it!" It was Isaiah 43, an apt Bible chapter. That same Sabbath, in the middle of the pastor's sermon, I began hurting so badly that I started weeping. I tried to muffle the sound of my sobbing soul. A lady from the next pew, a deaconess, approached and offered to accompany me outside.

"I want to be where the presence of God is most evident," I managed to mumble amidst the chocking pain and flowing tears.

Another lady, who was sitting behind me, patted my shoulder and said, "Cry, if you want to. It's okay." Immediately, the river gave way. In the end, I was relieved.

On Sunday, I decided to celebrate indestructible love. I took my Bible and sermon notes and began writing inspirational poetry. The number was growing. So, I contacted three of the friends with whom I had participated in the poetry writing workshop. We began meeting at the library, two to three times a week, to read and to edit each other's writing.

Finally, I wrote enough for a book; my first published collection was entitled, *Earth, Breath & Touch*.

Barely weeks after my book was published, Patricia Tomlinson, one of my close friends at church, invited me to the Martin Luther King national commemoration day at Mount Vernon, the city where she lived.

We got to the event center long before the start time. Pat introduced me to one of the organizers, who was excited to meet an African from the continent. Pat told her that I had just published my first collection of poems.

"How I wish I met you before," said the lady. "We would have included you in the program."

"Meeting you is the start of the collaboration," I said. I took out a copy of my book from my bag and gave it to the lady.

Pat, her children, and I went and took our seats. Her husband was away at work. Ten minutes before the evening's program started, a gentleman came rushing for Pat. He whispered in her ear. Pat lifted her hands, chanted a joyful tune, and turned towards me.

"Please, follow him," she said.

The members of the organizing committee told me something that got me jumping up and down. They had decided to include me in the presentations for the night. So, I will open the program with the reading of two poems of my choice.

The oval theatre was silent, though full of hundreds of people. I was standing in front, on an oval stage, a little lower down. Guests were seated in ascending order. I had to lift my head to see all of them. The lights went off. Countdown began. Then, suddenly, but gently, the lights came over me, while the rest of the theatre was dark.

Someone gave the signal. I flipped open the page my finger was on. "When I reminisce over creation morning," I began reading, the poem entitled, "Creation Morning."

The sustained applause was thunderous. That gave me time to catch my breath and open the next one, "Black or White God?"

As I moved through the aisle to my seat, all I could hear from both directions was, "Akong, please, give me one copy … two copies … three, please." That evening, I autographed books until my hand hurt. Most surprising of all was that, while I was selling a copy for USD10, some paid USD100, others USD50, and yet others USD20. They were so impressed; they wanted to compensate me for my efforts.

"We were born here. We have been trying for decades to publish our work unsuccessfully," said some participants at the end of the event. "Now, you come so far away from the continent, and you show us how."

"She got the ISBN," one lady spoke up and nodded in admiration.

They bought all the two cartons of books I had brought along. I was busy pressing money into my handbag while giving out my phone number. I got home and counted my money. It was just a couple of dollars short of a thousand dollars.

After that, I began receiving calls requesting guidelines for publishing. Some budding writers, not only from New York but from other states, sent me their manuscripts for editing.

"You have gotten back your joy," said my mother, one sunny Sunday, when she came calling, in the company of my sister, Mangwi. "So, why don't you get married to someone else?" urged my grieving mother. "He has married and moved on with his life."

Indeed, Mesape officially got married to Zipora several months ago. My family had been shocked by the news while I remained numb and speechless. Some had suggested that I either send someone or return home to stop it from happening, but not me.

I saw it differently. I would never again place myself in a situation where Mesape would oblige me to choose between life and marriage. It was better to be free, enjoying peace of mind. My sole worry was for my children.

I made one more effort to request visas for them. Their father refused to cooperate with me. His tone was sterner than before. An analyst explained that it was unlikely for Zipora to carry a pregnancy to term due to her small size. Nonetheless, she conceived a few months later. Our local community was astonished while I was relieved. Her desire for my children would disappear.

"You would be miserable if you don't get married again," my mother urged me repeatedly.

"A seed has to get rotten to yield a new crop," I tried to console my grieving mother.

"Not exactly, my dear—the new crop shoots up before the old gets rotten," she corrected me. As a farmer, my mother knew better.

"Really?" I asked. I remained still for a long while, trying to reassess my journey through life so far. Has it been a success or a failure? Or what is the better way to evaluate it?

Interviewed by Bernard Ngwa and Motto Young; Jean-Pierre Olinga & Sissako Tamko, at PM's Office Medal Award ceremony, for CRTV.

CHAPTER 42

Forgiveness and Healing

My papers expired, and it was time for me to leave the American territory. It was time to return home. My children were in their adolescent years. I could not let that period slip out of my hands.

Surprisingly, the US government announced its intention to regularize the status of all aliens with irregularities. Finally, I would be able to invite my children to join me, to visit my country of refuge, and then we would return home together.

On Monday, I woke up early and drove for four hours to Albany. I was among hundreds of others who showed up at the office. In the early afternoon, the authorities invited us into the reception office. They screened our documents. Then, they requested that we move to the next room.

It turned out to be a mini court session. A prosecutor, who was ready and waiting for me, stood up and accused me of having violated the laws of the land.

Shocked, I tried to explain my case, brandishing the letter that I had received from the Immigration Service. No one was interested in it, neither in what I was saying in self-defense. Within minutes, another officer approached me with handcuffs. Shock waves went down my spine; I began explaining that there was a mistake, with tears rolling down my cheeks. No one was interested. I barely had time to call my family members before they drove me away. That evening, I became the latest inmate at the Erie County Holding Center, Buffalo, New York.

At the reception, my clothes changed. My body went numb. Was I having a nightmare? No.

For the next forty-nine days of my life, I lived underground.

Several years after, I found out that I should never have gone to jail. The petition (Form I-130) for an alien relative, filed by my brother, on my behalf, had been approved on the 15th of June 2002. That was almost a year and a half before my incarceration. The notification from the U.S. Citizenship and Immigration Services never reached me.

During my detention, two notable things comforted me. All the sermons that I had heard since my baptism were playing back in my mind, one after the other. Otherwise, the pages of my sermon notebooks were flipping over, one at a time. A more recent memory that came repeatedly was the sermon of Evangelist Emilio Knechtle. He was the guest speaker at an Adventist church in the Bronx, New York. I had come with friends of mine. He recounted a gripping paralled of the story of Jesus, depicting a man who went on a long and unsafe journey, during which he met face to face with the woman that was the love of his life. They got married, and he returned to build their future family home, promising to come back soon to take her with him to live happily forever. Emilio's story captivated me.

More surprisingly, he invited me upfront during the afternoon session. He was troubled after hearing my story. So, he requested the congregation to pray for me.

From my cell, that scene, along with the love story, became a source of comfort. Though I was locked up in a small space, deprived of sunlight, making do with monotonous and dull days, and denied the choice of what to eat, I knew that the bridegroom would come back for me.

My second source of consolation was the poems that I wrote each day. Then, in the evenings, the only time that the authorities allowed us to come out and socialize, I read them to other inmates.

After forty days in jail, the prison authorities released me. However, when we got to the airport, the runway was packed full of snow. The airport security canceled the scheduled flight. The guards brought me back to prison, where I spent nine more days.

Finally, I was free. On my return trip, two security officers, Mr. Scot and Ms. Wendy, one on each side, watched each move I made. They escorted me out of the US territory on Thursday, the 5th of February. Though under restraint, I felt like a VIP. On Friday, the 6th of February 2004, my plane landed at the Douala International Airport.

My sudden arrival was a surprise to everyone, but for my sister, Mafor, who welcomed me. The following day, she and I traveled to Victoria to visit Sweetie, who was a boarding student at Saker Baptist College. The timing was perfect because it was Parent's Day.

Chapter 42: Forgiveness and Healing **291**

Lake Awing, Cameroon

Mafor and I stood in the open field, outside the dormitories, since visiting hours were over. Her school mates rushed to look for her. During those ten or so minutes of waiting, I experienced the tensest moment of my life—what if I don't recognize my daughter, amidst dozens of girls in the same uniform?

Meanwhile, the students, who informed her that she had guests, did not know that I was her mother. They simply said your aunties. The minutes were passing while I was struggling to push back the avalanche of tears. There were groups of girls moving, up and down, and crisscrossing the campus.

Soon, three other girls began walking towards us. One of them had a perfectly round face. I quickly recalled that my friends always described me as having a round face, something I kept refuting.

At that instance, she and I recognized each other. I opened my arms, and she planted her head into my shoulder. At fifteen, she was slightly taller than I. All we did was cry. Maybe we cried for up to ten minutes. One of her teachers, Mrs. Ngalla, who had been observing, approached us.

"Why don't you leave it like that?" she asked. "Has someone died?"

"Please, leave them for a while," said Mafor. "Let them cry out the deep-seated pain from their hearts."

Then, without warning, Sweetie paused, pushed herself backward, and looked into my eyes.

"Are you going back?"

"No."

With full strength, she grabbed me tightly and shook me, excitedly.

My sister handed her the two goody bags. While waiting for her to go empty the totes and return, Mrs. Ngalla, who had been watching us, came and asked who we were to Sweetie.

"Now, this child will have peace of mind," said the teacher. "I always knew that there was something wrong with her, despite her excellent grades."

The meeting with Quydee, the following day, did not have the element of surprise. I had called him already. My sister, Mafor, graciously accompanied me to Yaounde. Mesape himself picked us up from the Garanti bus station and drove us home, where we met Quydee. We held onto each other for a long while. Then, we sat opposite each other, staring endlessly, as if to fast-forward the lost years of our lives. He had declared, some years ago, that our reunion would become "one of the eight wonders of the world."

A few weeks after I settled in Yaounde, I requested a formal meeting with Mesape. He accepted. He brought along Quydee and Sweetie, explaining that he hadn't the courage to face me alone. So, it turned out to be a family healing session.

We divided the talk into two parts: the first was just between the two of us, and the latter with our children. As parents, we revisited some of the issues that they needed to know. They listened, absorbing everything as we spoke. We each took turns to ask them to forgive us for having turned their lives into a living hell.

At one point, Mesape burst out crying profusely, taking the blame for exposing our family to a painful disaster. In response, Quydee and Sweetie expressed their gratitude for our honesty; they forgave us.

In the end, we reconciled and hugged each other. Mesape offered me a ride. I accepted. He dropped me off at my friend, Josephine's house.

A few months after, I returned to the Ministry of Communication, after giving up my place at the Corporation, CRTV. It was preferable to earn less and have peace of mind than throw myself into a potentially worse fire of demonic destruction.

Eventually, the Minister of Communication, Fame Ndongo, appointed me as Head of the Technical Unit for Professional Performance at the first-ever Press Center, downtown Yaounde.

On Wednesday, after a press conference, a handful of regular visitors stayed back to share a drink with us. Some of those journalists were seeing me for the first time in years. The issue of my marriage came up. I expressed regret over personal loss.

"Do you honestly think that your marriage would have survived?" asked Gilbert.

"Why not?" I asked. "There was a strong bond between us."

"Hahaha," they laughed out.

"What are you insinuating?"

"It's not an insinuation. You guys were holding each other's hands and parading the streets. Do you think that that could go on for long, in this society?"

"Why not?"

"Okay, you tell us. Who else does that here?"

"What a waste!" a friend sighed after hearing my story.

A success or a failure? Looking back, I have realized that marriage, a piece of heaven on earth, could also become hell. Unfortunately, mine turned out to be the latter.

Nevertheless, I survived, despite several threats on my life; Mesape now has concrete evidence of God's power to protect those who have surrendered their lives to Him. Besides, I have peace of mind, the type that only Jesus Himself gives, found in John 14:27, which Paul also describes in Philippians 4:7 as "beyond understanding." May I continue to live my life to praise God!

What can I render to those who provided a motherly shoulder for my children? I equally thank them for sharing their mother with many other boys and girls in the world.

Though Quydee and Sweetie excelled in school, they still need help to heal their deep bruises. Far from becoming emotional wrecks, by God's grace, they will recover fully and become models for their peers.

Writing and reading this story has been therapeutic for me. I must stop here and shout out joyfully, "Let everything that has breath praise the Lord!" Psalm 150:6.

TEACH Services, Inc.
PUBLISHING
www.TEACHServices.com • (800) 367-1844

We invite you to view the complete
selection of titles we publish at:
www.TEACHServices.com

We encourage you to write us
with your thoughts about this,
or any other book we publish at:
info@TEACHServices.com

TEACH Services' titles may be purchased in
bulk quantities for educational, fund-raising,
business, or promotional use.
bulksales@TEACHServices.com

Finally, if you are interested in seeing
your own book in print, please contact us at:
publishing@TEACHServices.com
We are happy to review your manuscript at no charge.

www.ingramcontent.com/pod-product-compliance
Lightning Source LLC
Chambersburg PA
CBHW071143160426
43196CB00011B/1996